PLAYS OF THE YEAR
Volume 43
1972–3

'I do not claim that they are the best plays of their period. I submit merely that all are good of their kind, and that they share qualities for which a true playgoer looks.'

Preface to *Plays of the Year*, Volume One, 1949.

PLAYS OF THE YEAR

EDITED BY
J. C. TREWIN

CROWN MATRIMONIAL
Royce Ryton

THE DAY AFTER THE FAIR
Frank Harvey, based on a story by
Thomas Hardy

WILLIE ROUGH
Bill Bryden

VOLUME 43
1972–3

PAUL ELEK LTD
LONDON

© PLAYS OF THE YEAR COMPANY
AND PAUL ELEK BOOKS LTD. 1974

Published by
PAUL ELEK BOOKS LIMITED
54–58 Caledonian Road, N.1

CROWN MATRIMONIAL
© *Royce Ryton*

THE DAY AFTER THE FAIR
© *Frank Harvey, based on a story by Thomas Hardy*

WILLIE ROUGH
© *Bill Bryden*

*Printed in Great Britain by
Clarke, Doble & Brendon Ltd.,
Plymouth*

FOR WENDY
Unexampled

CONTENTS

INTRODUCTION
page 7

CROWN MATRIMONIAL
page 11

THE DAY AFTER THE FAIR
page 93

WILLIE ROUGH
page 203

*I doubt whether a new generation can under-
stand what the tale of King Edward VIII and Mrs
Wallis Simpson meant to the British people—for
that matter, to the world at large—during the
midwinter of 1936. Few could speak of the matter,
or the ensuing abdication, impartially; for a few
days, often longer, many families and friendships
were rent. Since then, of course, the abdication has
become one of the legends of history; the realities
of the time have been blurred by innumerable published recollections, prejudiced on one side or the
other.*

*At this period I was on the staff of a great High
Tory newspaper, the oldest London daily. (Within
another twelve months it had died; it was 'merged',
which in Fleet Street means the same thing.) On
the night of the abdication it fell to me to write
about the ex-King's farewell broadcast, as 'Prince
Edward'; and I still remember looking up after the
last words and seeing round me the senior members
of the staff, most of them unfeignedly in tears.*

*CROWN MATRIMONIAL, Royce Ryton's
play, is about this extraordinary period, the end of
a reign, the loss of a king who, when Prince of
Wales, had probably been the world's most-
regarded royal personage. Though it surprises*

7

many who lived through those times to realize that the story can now be brought to the theatre, the manner of its telling absorbs them. Certainly it has been fascinating younger playgoers for whom any event on the far side of the gulf of war can seem almost primeval.

The play—Mrs Simpson does not appear in it—is a dramatist's idea of what could have happened at Marlborough House in the winter of 1936 (and, as epilogue, on an afternoon in 1945). Mr Ryton has not misused the new freedom of our stage. His chronicle is sober and dignified; in performance, only one scene—for the then Duchess of York—failed to persuade me. It is always an entirely honest speculative reconstruction of what passed in Queen Mary's room in Marlborough House at the height of the debate. On the Haymarket stage Wendy Hiller (Queen Mary) and Peter Barkworth (King Edward) were, in aspect, astonishingly like their originals. At this remove, CROWN MATRI-MONIAL reminds me, after early experience of the genre—of a restrained and superior Ruritanian love-of-duty drama without the uniforms and the overcharged romantic swell.

In some quarters a silly piece of inverted snob-bery is to dismiss 'West End' or 'Shaftesbury Avenue' plays as if the very label were damning; it is a label conveniently forgotten when a produc-tion from the outer world is duly transferred to Central London. I found THE DAY AFTER THE FAIR, which opened and ran at the Lyric, much more valuable than most of the publicized plays bred on a modish 'fringe'. This is a technician's version of a short story by Thomas Hardy (who knew what a loveless marriage could be) and it is beside the point to compare too closely the hand-ling of story and script. Naturally, there must be an expansion in stage terms; Frank Harvey has

8

managed it uncommonly well. Certainly the audience at the première was moved to the kind of ovation that need not (another legend) go automatically with a first night.

The scene is Salisbury and the dramatist's chosen date is 1900. An illiterate village girl, in the service of a wealthy brewer's wife, is infatuated with the young man she has met at and after the fair. When he writes to her, she persuades her mistress to answer the letters. The mistress, herself caught up in a loveless marriage, writes with so much fervour that the young man (an aspiring barrister) is overcome. Inevitably, the deception must be discovered; the final scene, on the wedding day, should be experienced in the theatre where the dramatist has followed Hardy with uncompromising truth. The play calls for a sequel: it sends the mind probing forward, with horrified curiosity, to the Bloomsbury years ahead and it goes on stinging in the imagination long after the night is over. Deborah Kerr, Julia Foster and Paul Hastings were particularly good in the Lyric production.

Our third play, WILLIE ROUGH, set in and around Greenock during 1914–16, had a season, with its Scottish company, at the Shaw Theatre. It should have stayed longer, but length of run is by no means an index to the quality of a play. Turning on the Clydeside shipyard workers' strike during the first world war, this is a document, closely written, in which the author, Bill Bryden, has kept a firm resolve not to be facile and to reject any 'big' scene (strike meetings, trial, and so on) that could have been theatrically effective but obvious. His people are true, not a dramatist's pawns; he reveals clearly two forms of strike leader, the man who is sincere and obstinate and the brassy careerist.

In the theatre the play (splendidly done in

9

London by its Scottish cast) needs an ear for Clyde-side speech. In the text nothing gets between us and dialogue that is profoundly felt. We do not forget Willie's final words: 'Ah've got taw show folk what it's like tae live by somethin' ye believe in. Mebbe ah can change them by showin' them that. Mebbe ah canny. But ah want tae, ah want tae show folk me haudin' ma heid up so that they can haud their heids up in the air an' stick up fur themselves an' no be feart tae demand whit's theirs by rights. . .'

J. C. TREWIN

Hampstead, 1973

I am, as ever, deeply grateful to my colleague, Mrs Judith Rayner, for her unfaltering collaboration and her patience.

CROWN MATRIMONIAL

A Play in Two Acts
by
ROYCE RYTON

Michael Codron presented *Crown Matrimonial* at the Theatre Royal, Haymarket, London, on 19 October, 1972, with the following cast:

MABELL, COUNTESS OF AIRLIE
Joan Haythorne

QUEEN MARY   *Wendy Hiller*

THE HON MARGARET WYNDHAM
Barbara Atkinson

QUEEN'S PAGE (John)   *Leonard Cracknell*

KING EDWARD VIII (David) *Peter Barkworth*

THE PRINCESS ROYAL (Mary) *Jane Wenham*

THE DUCHESS OF GLOUCESTER (Alice)
Heather Kyd

WALTER MONCKTON, K.C.   *Noel Johnson*

THE DUCHESS OF YORK (Elizabeth)
Amanda Reiss

THE DUKE OF YORK (Bertie)   *Andrew Ray*

Directed by Peter Dews

Designed by Finlay James

Lighting by Mick Hughes

CHARACTERS

MABELL, COUNTESS OF AIRLIE, *Lady-in-Waiting to the Queen.*

QUEEN MARY, *aged 69, mother of Edward VIII and George VI.*

THE HON MARGARET WYNDHAM, *Lady-in-Waiting to the Queen.*

PAGE

KING EDWARD VIII (David), *aged 42, later Duke of Windsor.*

PRINCESS ROYAL (Mary), *aged 39, sister of Edward VIII.*

DUCHESS OF GLOUCESTER (Alice), *aged 34, sister-in-law of Edward VIII.*

MR MONCKTON, K.C., *aged about 40, legal adviser and friend of Edward VIII, later Sir Walter Monckton.*

DUKE OF YORK (Bertie), *aged 41, younger brother and heir to Edward VIII, later George VI.*

DUCHESS OF YORK (Elizabeth), *aged 36, sister-in-law to Edward VIII.*

The action takes place in late summer, autumn and winter of 1936 except for the last scene which takes place in 1945.

The setting is Queen Mary's private sitting-room on the first floor of Marlborough House, London.

PROLOGUE

As the houselights go down the Proclamation is heard over the front of house speakers.

Whereas it hath pleased Almighty God to call to his mercy our late Sovereign Lord King George V of blessed and glorious memory that the High and Mighty Prince, Edward Albert Christian George Andrew Patrick David (*Guns boom.*) is now by the death of our late Sovereign of happy memory become our only (*Guns.*) Lawful and rightful Liege Lord Edward VIII (*Guns.*) by the grace of God; of Great Britain, Ireland, and the British Dominions beyond the seas (*Guns.*) King, Defender of the Faith, Emperor of India. God Save the King.

The curtain rises.

ACT ONE

Scene 1

*The Queen's drawing-room is on the first floor.
The Queen is sixty-nine years old in 1936, recently
widowed and the mother of Edward VIII and the
future George VI. She is too well known in appearance—certainly by audiences who were in their
teens in 1953 when she died—to have to be
described in detail. Not tall, she held herself so
erect and with such dignity that she seemed so.
She invented more or less her own style in dressing,
which defied fashion. The emphasis was again on
dignity. Her hair is grey, beautifully dressed. She
has at all times many jewels, not from vanity but
because she is a queen. The throne with its occupant and its preservation is her unquestioning
creed. She has a deep voice.*

*The room being her private drawing-room reflects
her own taste absolutely. This is good. She has a
tendency for having only Bibelots which are in
some way connected with the family. For her the
family—the Royal Family—is all-important. It
would be too much to say that her life has been
sacrificed in its service. Her life has been full, rich
and satisfying. But there can be no doubt that she
would have, if necessary, sacrificed her life and
indeed very nearly did so. Only fate saved her
from an act of self-sacrifice in the name of duty
to the family. Her marriage to George V was ideally
happy. An excellent constitutional monarch, an
admirable husband, he was a difficult man and a
far from easy father. Queen Mary considered it
her duty to support him in all things. It is late
morning in early September 1936. She was widowed
in January of that year. She is still Britain's only*

17

queen for her eldest son, the new King, has as yet no wife.

There are big doors back centre, a second door right, a big window left, a sofa left, armchairs downstage right and left, a desk upstage left and a table against the wall downstage right. Right centre is the Queen's armchair with a small table right of it.

Lady Airlie (Mabell), a life-long friend and lady-in-waiting, is found on stage. She is elderly, dignified and sensible, dressed in travelling clothes. The Page opens the door and the Queen comes in. Mabell rises and curtseys.

QUEEN : Mabell dear. How good of you to come here so quickly.

(*Mabell and Queen kiss.*)

MABELL : Your Majesty.

QUEEN : I'm afraid we have very little time. The King has proposed himself for luncheon. I see him so rarely nowadays that I jumped at the opportunity.

MABELL : Quite.

QUEEN : Do sit down, dear.

(*The Queen sits and so does Mabell.*)

You must be exhausted after your journey. Did you have a good crossing?

MABELL : The weather was glorious. It was a mercy when we got out to sea. New York was like an oven. My son very kindly met me at Waterloo. He tells me you've seen Baldwin.

18

QUEEN : I never stop seeing him.

MABELL : Ma'am dear, have you spoken to the King yourself?

QUEEN : No, no. Yes, I know I should, but I can't. You have no conception how extraordinarily difficult and evasive he can be. He's like Queen Alexandra when he wants to be. Charming, vague, elusive. I never have been able to talk to him. Dear Mabell, we can't put off the dreadful moment any longer. Is the American Press as bad as they say?

MABELL : Oh, it's worse. She is being openly spoken of as the next queen. One paper has even given the actual date of when she will take up residence in Buckingham Palace.

QUEEN : Are they mad?

MABELL : Far from it. Another paper says that she is being consulted on the redecoration of both Buckingham Palace and Windsor Castle. According to them she's already done over Sandringham and Balmoral. One headline in a Chicago paper referred to her as 'Queen Wally'.

QUEEN : Wally.

MABELL : W.A.L.L.Y. Her Christian name is Wallis.

(*Queen Mary braces herself. The shock to her should not be underestimated. Throughout her life the throne and its occupants have been objects of respect. To have a king, and that king her son, the object not of respect but of cheap newspaper gossip, disturbs her tremendously. Lady Airlie is aware of this. She rises and crosses to the window.*)

Then this cruise in the Balkans. They have been photographed everywhere together, ma'am. 'The King rumbas with Queen Wally'.

QUEEN : Rumbas?

MABELL : It's a dance. He's been photographed swimming with her, rowing a boat with her, shopping. The King seems to be almost deliberately drawing attention to her. There are endless stories of her family background, her past life, her husbands.

QUEEN : Dear God !

MABELL : Her first husband, who's still alive, was given to drink, I think. As far as I can gather, her own upbringing was actually perfectly respectable, but all the American press are convinced of one thing. The King, they say, intends to marry her.

QUEEN : But there can be no question of marriage. Apart from every other consideration, she's still the wife of Mr Simpson.

MABELL : She's divorced one husband. Why not a second?

(*Queen Mary rises in her agitation and moves about.*)

QUEEN : He's—he's head of the church, Defender of the Faith. It's out of the question.

MABELL : The American press is convinced there's going to be a divorce. Mr Simpson now resides permanently at the Guards' Club. My son confirms this. Furthermore, the Americans believe the divorce will go through and be made absolute even before the coronation.

QUEEN : What?

MABELL : My solicitor says it's perfectly possible, provided the case is undefended. It's September now, if the case is heard in October she will be free in April. The coronation is still planned for May.

QUEEN : It's nonsense. Sheer nonsense ! It must be nonsense. Mustn't it?

MABELL : Everything points to its not being. The King was received in Istanbul by Ataturk. Mrs Simpson was beside him the entire time. In an official drive through the streets they sat side by side, for all the world as if they were man and wife. Her friends in London already treat her as if she were queen. They do everything but curtsey to her. Ma'am, so far you have seen the crisis as one of the King being—how shall I put it?—possibly having an open liaison with a married woman. I believe we are going to have a much graver problem than that to face.

(There is a pause. The Queen, after her instinctive reaction of amazed disbelief, is now in perfect control of herself.)

QUEEN : It'll be the end of monarchy. I feel ill with shame. There's nothing to stop him, you know, Mabell. The Royal Marriages Act applies to a monarch's relations, not to the monarch himself. He is restrained only by the Law of the Protestant Succession and of course she's not Roman Catholic.
MABELL : No. I'm afraid not.

(Margaret Wyndham, another lady-in-waiting, comes in. She is devoted to the Queen but not in the same intimate terms as Lady Airlie.)

MARGARET : Do forgive me, ma'am, but the King's car has just driven into the courtyard.
QUEEN : Thank you, Margaret. Mabell, dear, I cannot thank you enough. I wish I could ask you to stay to lunch.
MARGARET : I've arranged for Lady Airlie to have lunch with me, ma'am.

MABELL : That's very kind of you, but I'm meeting Bruce. Will I see you, ma'am, before I go to Scotland?

QUEEN : Oh, I hope so, dear. And if not, the moment you return. Evelyn is making out a fresh rota for my dear ladies, so you will be hearing from her soon.

(*Page enters.*)

PAGE : His Majesty.

(*David (King Edward VIII) comes in. He is forty-two and has been King for only a few months. He is small with devastating charm and devastating youthfulness. He looks twenty-five to thirty at the most. He has proved a superbly successful Prince of Wales. The youthful charm is well to the fore. His smile is dazzling.*)

DAVID : Mamma.

(*All three women curtsey and he kisses the Queen's hand.*)

Please, Mamma. Lady Airlie. Miss Wyndham.

(*Lady Airlie and Miss Wyndham murmur 'Your Majesty'.*)

QUEEN : David, my dear, you look so brown.
DAVID : Well, it was very hot in the Mediterranean. I sunbathed a great deal.
QUEEN : So I gathered. Lady Airlie is just back from America.

22

DAVID : Really. (*He is quite at his ease. The reference to America leaves him quite unperturbed.*) I'm dying to go there again. I hope to make one of my first state visits to Washington. Do sit down, Lady Airlie.

MABELL : I was just about to go, sir, when you came in.

DAVID : What a shame! I hoped you were staying to lunch.

QUEEN : She's lunching with Bruce.

DAVID : I'm sure my mother would be delighted to see him, too.

MABELL : It's very kind of your Majesty, but we're having quite a family luncheon. The Queen can hardly be expected to feed the entire Ogilvie clan at a moment's notice.

QUEEN : You are quite a tribe.

(*They laugh.*)

DAVID : Give Bruce my love. If he's in Scotland next week, tell him to ring me up at Balmoral. Where were you in America?

MABELL : New York mostly.

DAVID : Ah, yes. Have you ever been to America, Miss Wyndham?

MARGARET : No, sir.

DAVID : You should go. You'd like it.

MARGARET : Do you think so?

DAVID : I'm sure of it. It's such a wonderful country. Vital and full of pep. (*Laughs.*)

MARGARET : Too full of pep if the films are anything to go by. I'm sure I should be completely bewildered the entire time. I'm not modern like you, sir.

(David, if aware of an underlying criticism, shows no sign of it.)

DAVID : Well, we need progress. We must move with the times.

MARGARET : Only if the times are moving in the right direction. I often wonder if they are.

QUEEN : Mabell, dear, we mustn't keep you from your family gathering.

MABELL : Ma'am. Sir.

(She curtseys twice, as does Margaret, and they both withdraw.)

DAVID : Well . . .

QUEEN : Help yourself, dear. George and Marina tell me you've acquired a taste for the cocktail. But in this house you'll have to make do with a glass of sherry.

DAVID : A glass of sherry will be delicious. *(He smiles at her.)* But cocktails aren't terrible at all. If you could only bring yourself to take the plunge, I'm sure you'd like them.

QUEEN : They have such peculiar names. A Side Lady—a White Car.

DAVID : It's the other way round. It's a Sidecar and a White Lady.

(They laugh. There is something just a little forced about this exchange of pleasantries.)

QUEEN : Tell me all your news.

(David is pouring out his glass of sherry. He waves the bottle in her direction.)

24

Well, perhaps just this once. A very small glass.

(*She is trying to be friendly. That is the trouble. He knows she is trying to be friendly.*)

Did you see Paul of Yugoslavia?

DAVID : Yes.

QUEEN : Does he like being Regent?

DAVID : No.

QUEEN : That's what Marina says.

DAVID : He's worried about Hitler.

QUEEN : We all are.

DAVID : I don't know. It depends what happens, I suppose. Paul's even more worried, and quite rightly, about Stalin.

QUEEN : Stalin? You do surprise me. How was George of Greece?

DAVID : He'd rather be back at Brown's Hotel.

QUEEN : Naturally being an exile would give him more freedom, but when Greece voted for a monarchy he had to go back. He had to obey the call of duty.

(*The meaning behind her words is not lost on the King. He laughs.*)

DAVID : Well, George is consoled by one thing. He had his fortune told the other day and he was told he'd die of a heart attack.

QUEEN : And he found that consoling?

DAVID : Well, yes. Until he was told that he was convinced he'd be assassinated.

QUEEN : You didn't go to Venice?

DAVID : Eden thought I shouldn't.

QUEEN : Mussolini is very tiresome.

DAVID : I agree absolutely. But it's idiotic, to push

25

him straight into Hitler's arms. It would have been far more useful seeing Mussolini and charming the pants off him than seeing Paul or George or Boris or even Ataturk.

QUEEN : Charming the what?

DAVID : Pants. Trousers. It's an Americanism.

QUEEN : So I gathered. (*She smiles.*) You're very fond of American expressions.

(*She looks at him. He smiles back at her. They both know what is on her mind, what she cannot say.*)

Tell me, is it true that Paul of Greece is going to marry Frederica?

DAVID : No. She is going to marry him.

QUEEN : She's very young.

DAVID : And very determined.

QUEEN (*pause*) : David—

DAVID : Weren't you at her parents' wedding in Berlin?

QUEEN : Yes, that was the last time I saw the poor old Kaiser and the Tsar. The Tsarina wasn't there. She was ill. As usual. You know she was the greatest single cause of the revolution. By her obsession for Rasputin she made the throne an object for common gossip, and once anyone does that, they are lost. If Carol of Romania goes on behaving as he is doing much longer he won't last. I'm so glad you decided not to visit him.

DAVID : I'm glad you're pleased, but I wanted to go. My government advised against it and both of you are wrong. All you're concerned about is Carol's morals.

QUEEN : He's treated Hélène abominably.

DAVID : What's that got to do with it? Do you

26

know what is going to destroy us? Classical education and Puritan morals. Put a classical education and Puritan morals together and you get a dodo. We're governed by dodos. The only politician who's any good is Churchill and he was useless at Harrow and not even his best friends could call him a Puritan.

QUEEN: And he's never been more unpopular.

DAVID: He's never been more right. It is perfectly obvious what is going to happen. They are terrified in the Balkans and I don't blame them. You see both the Germans and the Russians want the Danube basin. They're both after the granaries of Hungary, they both want a way into the Mediterranean and once they have that they both want Persian oil, which means they both want to threaten Turkey, Egypt, Suez, India and us. It's as clear as daylight. Now, to meet this threat we need friends and we need military strength. As it is, we have no army, no airforce and an enormous navy composed of obsolete ships without ammunition. Consequently nobody dares to be our friends.

QUEEN: We are rearming.

DAVID: We're manufacturing one rather small gun a year. The dictators are radiant. (*He picks up the ashtray from the table beside the Queen's chair.*) May I? (*Taking the ashtray.*) I was questioned most carefully about our rearmament programme by Ataturk. I said what I could, of course, and he won't be an enemy, but with an army worth mentioning he'd be our friend.

QUEEN: Why don't you tell Baldwin all this. He's so steady and sensible.

DAVID: He looks solid and sensible. That's why he gets away with it all. Actually he's lazy and narrow-minded. Anyway, at the moment he's on holiday.

QUEEN: Exactly. He's gone abroad. He must see and hear things.

DAVID: How can he when he's asleep in a deck-chair the entire time? On the rare occasions when he wakes up, he reads a detective story set in cosy old England, talks to his wife who resembles nothing so much as a cosy old teapot, then they go into the residents' lounge filled with cosy old colonels—all British—and drink a cosy old cup of tea. The one thing you can be certain he never does is talk to well-informed foreigners.

QUEEN: And what about Eden? He shares your point of view, doesn't he?

DAVID: Only partially. Anthony is busy conducting his little duel with Mussolini which is sheer waste of valuable time. All he's done is to make him Hitler's ally. If you can see any sense in that course of action, you're cleverer than I am. Sometimes, Mamma, I'd like to impeach the entire Cabinet. I'd dismiss them if I thought it would do any good.

QUEEN (*profoundly shocked*): David!

DAVID: Don't worry. I won't. Apart from anything else, his Majesty's loyal opposition is almost as idiotic as his Majesty's government. All they can talk about is goodwill among the world's workers, no rearmament whatsoever and hark back to the General Strike and where that policy would get us I shudder to think. So I shall continue my own holiday. I'm going to Balmoral.

QUEEN: Oh, good. I am glad. The rest will do you good. From all accounts your Balkan adventure was far from restful. Though interesting, I'm sure.

DAVID (*carefully*): I suppose you read a good deal about it in the papers.

QUEEN: A certain amount. The foreign press was, I gather, rather a nuisance.

DAVID : I asked everywhere to be received with the minimum of fuss. Actually Ataturk was the only one who gave an official reception.

QUEEN : He would. But then he's not a monarch.

DAVID : No. He received us very formally.

QUEEN (*after a deliberate pause*) : Us?

DAVID (*after a tiny hesitation*) : Me and my party.

QUEEN : Oh, yes. Bertie and Elizabeth are already up at Birkhall.

DAVID : Oh, good.

QUEEN : They hope you won't mind but they've asked Archbishop Lang to stay.

DAVID : They can ask whom they like and why should I mind?

QUEEN : They know you don't care for him.

DAVID : I'm indifferent to him.

QUEEN : I think he was hurt not to be asked by you.

DAVID : He wouldn't have fitted in. George and Marina will be staying with me.

QUEEN : They'll like that. George's so much less wild now he's married.

DAVID : When's her baby due?

QUEEN : December some time. I've been very lucky with all my daughters-in-law so far.

DAVID : Yes. Mamma?

QUEEN : Yes?

DAVID : Would you like some more sherry?

QUEEN : Not for me. Do help yourself to more, though.

(*Pause.*)

Who else have you invited to Balmoral?

DAVID : The Buccleuchs, the Roseberys. One or two others. Some American friends of mine.

29

QUEEN : On the whole I don't care for Americans. They're so loud.

DAVID : I rather like them, Mamma. In fact I like one or two Americans very much indeed.

(*The all-important subject is nearly embarked upon. They look at each other warily. Footman enters.*)

FOOTMAN : Luncheon is served.

(*The chance is lost.*)

QUEEN : Shall we go in? It's just ourselves.

Curtain.

Scene 2

It is two months later, before dinner. Princess Mary, the Princess Royal, comes in, followed by Lady Airlie.

The Princess Royal, Countess of Harewood, supports her mother dutifully in all things. She is in her late thirties.

MARY : I wanted a word with you before I saw the Queen.

MABELL : Ma'am.

MARY : How is she?

MABELL : Exhausted, I should imagine. Five extra audiences today on top of her usual commitments. She won't put off a single appointment.

MARY : Has anything else happened?

MABELL : I think so. But what exactly I don't know.
The telephone has never stopped ringing. The
Palace is in absolute turmoil.

MARY : Where is Mamma now?

MABELL : She's dressing for dinner.

MARY : But she's usually dressed long before this.

MABELL : Mr Baldwin has been on the telephone
for over half an hour.

MARY : Good heavens!

MABELL : It must have been important. You know
how her Majesty hates the telephone. For all I
know the Queen may still be talking to him.

MARY : Oh, dear.

MABELL : The whole country is rife with rumours.
I'm sure this press silence is unwise.

MARY : Unwise? It's the one thing we're grateful
for.

MABELL : In my view open discussion is preferable
to all this speculation. Every MP knows and they
all have relatives and friends. The household all
know. We are none of us without families. Every
person who goes abroad knows and comes back
spreading further stories. The moment anyone
realizes I've recently been to America, they ask
me about her. What are they saying in America?
How many times has she been married? Is she a
millionairess several times over? They then go to
the other extreme and rush round telling everyone
her family were nearly destitute. The truth is the
last thing they want to know.

MARY : What is the truth?

MABELL : She comes from a reasonably well-off
American family. Her second husband is English
and rather well-to-do.

MARY : I've heard she was a debutante before the
war.

MABELL : Not over here.

MARY : No, no. In Baltimore.

MABELL : Oh, that's quite different, ma'am, that doesn't count.

MARY : Have you met her?

MABELL : Once.

MARY : Where?

MABELL : Last month at Balmoral.

MARY : Did you like her?

MABELL : Yes, I did. She was exceptionally well-dressed. She was very witty. I would think her a most sensible woman as a rule. At the moment I suspect that after your mother she is the most bewildered woman in Britain. I don't think she knows what is happening to her. The King has put her into the most terrible predicament.

MARY : He's put us all into a predicament. As a family we have to be loyal to the crown, that is to say the King. But not only the King. To the whole idea of monarchy as well. So what do we do now? Be loyal to him personally or to the crown as an institution?

MABELL : That is a question we are all facing, the Queen most of all.

MARY : Have you ever been with the King when he's been unexpectedly recognized?

MABELL : No.

MARY : I was once. I took him shopping in York. It was my own fault. I can shop there as a rule quite privately and peacefully. When I was with the King, suddenly he was recognized. A woman shouted, 'It's the Prince of Wales'. A crowd gathered and it took over half an hour for us to get to the manager's office. Police had to be called and we drove away in state with a motorcycle escort. It must be dreadful to be the object of such adulation all your life. You lose all privacy. All peace. The rest of us, my brothers, me, even my mother, can go about our business in peace. He can't. He never can. I sometimes wonder if he is breaking under the strain—if his lack of wisdom, his impatience, aren't all symptoms of—well—an incipient nervous breakdown? Perhaps I'm talking nonsense.

MABELL : No. I've heard this theory before. Forgive me, ma'am, but I'm not certain I agree with it. After all, what has he done since he's been King? We've had six months court mourning when public appearances are kept to a minimum. The moment summer came, he was off on the Balkan cruise. True, he made some official visits but he had whole days at sea in between. There are no cheering crowds in the middle of the Mediterranean. No, ma'am, if I may say so, the King hasn't begun to feel the strain of monarchy yet.

(*The Queen comes in quickly.*)

QUEEN : Ah, my dear, thank goodness you are here before David.

(*Mary curtseys to her mother, then kisses her.*)

QUEEN : He's seen Baldwin. But I can find out nothing.
MABELL : I thought you were speaking to Number Ten just now, ma'am.
QUEEN : Only to the secretary.
MARY : Harry, my husband—
QUEEN : Yes, dear, yes.
MARY : Well, Mamma, it is confusing having a husband and a brother called Harry. I had to make

clear which Harry I meant—anyway, he was at the House of Lords and he heard nothing.

QUEEN : No one knows anything. The family least of all. Did Mabell tell you about Balmoral?

MARY : Only that Mrs Simpson had visited there.

QUEEN : You know nothing about Aberdeen, then?

MARY : No.

QUEEN : For six months at least he had agreed to open a hospital in Aberdeen. At the last moment he cancelled.

MARY : Why?

QUEEN : Mourning for Papa, he said. And then on the very day that he should have opened the hospital he drives into Aberdeen in his shooting brake to meet her at the station. Of course he was recognized and within minutes Aberdeen was in an uproar. If they had sat and thought about it for months they couldn't have conceived a more foolish course of action.

MARY : Not possibly.

(Margaret Wyndham enters.)

MARGARET : I telephoned Fort Belvedere as you asked, ma'am. His Majesty left some time ago and so he shouldn't be long.

QUEEN : Thank you.

MARGARET : How are you, ma'am?

QUEEN : Splendid, splendid.

MARGARET : Tired, no doubt.

QUEEN : It's been a trying day.

MARGARET : Yes, of course. I do hope this evening won't be too difficult.

QUEEN *(brightly)* : I hope so, too.

MARGARET : It's always darkest before the dawn.

QUEEN : Always.

MABELL : Margaret, dear, are you ready?

MARGARET : Oh, yes.

MABELL : Margaret's dining with me, ma'am. The King will be here soon and we cannot scuttle away like a couple of kitchen-maids the moment he arrives. Your Majesty. Your Royal Highness.

(*They curtsey and start to go.*)

Oh, ma'am.

QUEEN : Yes?

MABELL : Shall I telephone the Duchess of Gloucester again?

QUEEN : No, no, it's too late. Besides, I couldn't possibly put her off at the last moment.

MABELL : Ma'am

(*The two ladies-in-waiting go out.*)

QUEEN : I like Margaret. I really do. I just wish she wouldn't relish the crisis so much. She talks to me as if I was a hopeless case in a hospital for incurables.

MARY : Anyway, Lady Airlie saved you.

QUEEN : Mabell is wonderful. A tower of strength. And so are you. I couldn't manage without you. Dinner this evening is not going to be much fun.

(*At this unaccustomed display of emotion, Mary moves away. She is devoted to her mother but like her, dislikes emotional scenes. The Queen is in no way rebuffed. She would have done the same.*)

MARY : What's all this about Alice?

QUEEN : Oh, it's too awful. I've done the most dreadful thing. Well, it isn't dreadful, really—it's

35

dreadful of me to say it's dreadful, as I like her so much. Oh, dear, I'm becoming incoherent. It's like living on the edge of Vesuvius. Every morning my hands tremble, literally tremble, as I open my paper. I shall never forgive David for what he's done to us. Never. Even when it's all over I shall never feel quite the same towards him.

MARY: Mamma—

QUEEN: I mean it. Oh, I shall always love him. Always. But to expose us to this ordeal is unforgiveable.

MARY: He couldn't help falling in love.

QUEEN: He could help this crisis. Did he imagine his choice would be welcomed with open arms?

MARY: He's so in love, I believe he did.

(*The Queen takes a cigarette from box beside her and tries to light it with table lighter.*)

QUEEN: As long as she was married to this— (*Holds lighter out to Mary.*) Please—

(*Mary lights her cigarette.*)

Poor Mr Simpson—thank you—he wasn't able to marry her, so there could be no actual constitutional crisis. He could say with impunity that he would brook no interference in his private life. The moment she embarked on these divorce proceedings the situation changed. But he doesn't understand that.

MARY: You've seen him?

QUEEN: No, no. Baldwin's seen him. I've seen Baldwin. The family doesn't exist as far as David's concerned. But about today. First of all, Baldwin

telephoned me to say he was going to Fort Belvedere to see David. And why is he out there, quite
inaccessible? He's absolutely no consideration. He
should be at the Palace—anyway, then David
telephoned me, 'Could he come to dinner?' I said,
'Of course'. Would we be alone? I said, did he
mind your being there? He said your being there
suited him admirably. It would help.

MARY: It would help?

QUEEN: Those were his words. So it was all
arranged and he rang off. Then, and only then,
I remembered that Alice was coming to dinner.

MARY: Couldn't you put her off? She won't mind.

QUEEN: I can't find her. Your brother Harry is at
some army camp and Alice has been on an official
visit to Worthing. It might just as well be Mars. I
simply could not contact her. Admittedly I tried
for only half an hour, because then I had Baldwin's
secretary on the telephone asking me to receive
the Editor of *The Times* as soon as I could. Naturally I agreed. Mr (*trying to remember the name*)
Dawson?

MARY: Yes.

QUEEN: Dawson came round at once and told me
The Times was being inundated with letters about
Mrs Simpson, all hostile to David.

MARY: Is he going to publish any?

QUEEN: He is not only planning to publish them,
he intends to support them with a bitter editorial
attack on David. And once that happens, all other
papers will join in the fray, the floodgates will be
opened and we—the monarchy—will be bang in
the middle of a political crisis. The country will be
split in two. I implored Dawson to stay his hand
and for the moment he will. He won't publish the
letters yet. But that's all he'll say.

(Page enters.)

PAGE : Her Royal Highness the Duchess of Gloucester.

(The Duchess of Gloucester enters. Known as Alice, she is attractive, dark and very shy. She curtseys.)

QUEEN : Alice, dear.

(They embrace.)

ALICE : Mamma. *(She kisses Mary. To Queen.)* How are you?

QUEEN : I am a little distrait, I fear. I've had a trying day. You must forgive me.

ALICE : Of course. Is there any news?

MARY : Not yet. Have some sherry, Alice?

ALICE : That would be lovely.

MARY : Mamma?

QUEEN : Not for me. Alice, dear, David is coming to dinner.

ALICE : I see.

QUEEN : He asked if he might come and I think wants to talk about business matters. Oh, dear, this is so awkward.

ALICE : It isn't a bit. Obviously it would be far simpler if you and Mary were alone with David.

QUEEN : You're so nice and sensible. I knew you would be. If only David would marry someone like you!

ALICE : I feel so sorry for you over all this.

QUEEN : If you could just make some excuse after dinner, say you're tired and slip away—

ALICE : Wouldn't it be simpler if I escaped now?

QUEEN : No, no. I won't hear of it. I asked you to

dinner and dinner you must have. I refuse to be inhospitable.

(*Page enters.*)

PAGE : His Majesty.

(*David enters wearing tails as he is dining with his mother. They all curtsey. He kisses the Queen's hand. Page withdraws.*)

DAVID : Mamma.

QUEEN : I've asked for dinner to be served as soon as you arrived. I know how busy you are, David, you won't have long to wait.

DAVID : Thank you, Mamma. (*He glances at Alice.*)

QUEEN : Poor Alice! She's exhausted. She's been at Worthing all day and she's asked if you wouldn't mind if she went straight home after dinner.

DAVID (*with almost audible relief*) : Of course not. Hullo, Mary. How good of you to come. How are you?

MARY : Lovely to see you. Sherry, David?

DAVID : I am too tired. Is there any whisky?

MARY : Yes.

DAVID : If I could have some?

QUEEN : Of course.

(*There is a pause.*)

DAVID : Worthing?

ALICE : Yes.

DAVID : That's near Brighton, isn't it?

ALICE : Yes.

MARY : By the sea.

DAVID : It's got a new Town Hall. Did I open it?
QUEEN : No. Georgie did.
DAVID : Why did I think I did?
QUEEN : It was before he was married. He lived in York House with you then. Perhaps that's why.

(*There is a pause.*)

MARY : It's so awkward having a brother and a husband called Harry. Don't you find it so, Alice? I find myself saying things like 'my husband Harry' or 'my brother Harry'—
ALICE : It is awkward. I have a brother called George and a brother-in-law called George also.

(*Another pause.*)

QUEEN : Of course in Queen Victoria's day every branch of the family had to have a daughter called Victoria. It was most confusing.
MARY ⎱
ALICE ⎰ (*together*): Mm—
DAVID : To say nothing of all the Alberts.

(*Pause.*)

QUEEN : I'm glad to hear that the outside of Buckingham Palace is to be repainted. It's not before time.
DAVID : Yes. It's for the coronation.

(*Dreadful pause.*)

I must congratulate you, Mamma. I saw in *The Times* that your favourite charity, the London Needlework Guild, has had a record number of contributions.

40

QUEEN : Yes. I'm very pleased.
ALICE : You must be.
QUEEN : Dinner, I'm sure, will be very soon.

Slow Curtain.

Scene 3

After dinner. David on stage alone. He looks at his watch, goes to window.

Mary enters, shown in by Page.

DAVID : Oh.

MARY : That was, I think, the most agonizing meal I've ever sat through.

DAVID : I feel so sorry for Alice. I seem to do nothing else but have strained meals with Mamma.

MARY : I don't know what you are planning to say to her now, but do be gentle. She's terribly upset.

DAVID : Yes, I know.

MARY : You know how self-controlled she always is. Well, just before you arrived she almost broke down.

DAVID : Have you ever thought that things would have been far happier for us all if Mamma—just once in her life—had actually broken down? When Papa nearly died in 1928 I know and you know that she was distraught. All she ever said was 'Dear me. It's all very worrying'. This spectacular self-control and poise, admirable as it is for public life, is perhaps not quite admirable in private. She loves us. All of us. Even me. But I never really understood that until I was grown up.

41

MARY : She felt—still feels—that everything has to be sacrificed to the crown.

DAVID : To Papa.

MARY : And now to you.

DAVID : Not necessarily. Papa never stepped out of line. It seems I do. Papa married when he should have done, fathered several sons and served in the Navy. He was conventional in every conceivable way. I am not. It was much easier for her to sacrifice everything for him than to do so for me.

MARY : She didn't do it alone. He did it, too. He wanted a naval career. He had to give that up when he became Prince of Wales.

DAVID : Yes, but he had a private life to turn to. He was happy with Mamma. He was middle-aged when he became Prince of Wales. I was sixteen. Throughout my life Papa always told me to remember who I was. Well, who am I? One day I sat down and worked it out. It's as if I was the last goldfish in the world. The rest of my breed has become extinct. I was never just a prince. I was an heir and now I'm a monarch. No other large empire remains, so no other royalty has my celebrity value. Since 1918 I've been a freak.

MARY : I think that's putting it a little strongly.

DAVID : And then I looked at Mamma and Papa. They've been so busy being parent figures to the nation they've never had time for us.

MARY : And I think that is putting it far too brutally. David—you are fond of Mamma?

DAVID : Yes. Yes, I am. If I didn't like her, which I do really, this evening would be easy. Instead of which it's going to be hell.

MARY : What is going to happen?

DAVID : I don't know for sure. (*Suddenly he smiles gaily, confidently.*) But I shall win.

MARY (*taken aback*): Win?

DAVID: You'll see.

MARY: What do you mean?

(*Page opens door and the Queen enters.*)

QUEEN: I've told them we won't be having coffee, so we won't be disturbed. Brandy is over there.

DAVID: Thank you. Mamma? Mary?

QUEEN: No, thank you.

MARY: No, thank you.

(*David pours out his brandy.*)

DAVID: That was a delicious dinner.

QUEEN: I thought you'd like it, so I sent for Mrs Grant and complimented her.

DAVID: Oh, good. I sent a message to her myself by the page. I can never remember his name.

QUEEN: John.

DAVID: Oh, well. It's a very usual name.

(*There is a silence. It is not a hostile silence. It is just that no one knows what to say. His mother and sister are already seated.*)

Well. This isn't easy and the trouble is that not only have I so much to tell you that I don't know where to begin. I am uncertain as to how much you already know.

(*David has never seemed more touchingly youthful than he does now.*)

This is sounding like a prepared speech and I suppose that's what it is. I have rehearsed again

and again how to tell you. How much in fact do
you know?

QUEEN : Nothing for certain.

MARY : We have heard rumours, of course.

(*David sits.*)

QUEEN : I wish I could help you to tell me. I wish
I could convince you that I am not unsympathetic
to your difficulties. My parents, were both very
excitable people, their emotions were always on the
surface. They frequently embarrassed me. Perhaps
that has made me reticent about my own feelings.
I wish only to help you. You're my son. You're my
king.

DAVID : That's the trouble. I cannot be one without the other. I'm in love.

(*There is a silence.*)

I'm in love with an American woman called Wallis
Simpson. She is married to a Mr Ernest Simpson.
They are divorcing. As soon as she is free, I will
marry her.

MARY : Marry her, David?

DAVID : Yes, of course. What else can I do? I love
her. I must therefore marry her.

QUEEN (*speaking carefully*) : I understand perfectly
that having fallen deeply in love, you would wish
to marry the object of your affection. But in this
instance there are certain difficulties.

DAVID : They can be overcome.

QUEEN : First and foremost you are Head of the
Church.

DAVID : A meaningless title.

QUEEN : Not to the general public.

MARY : It may be a meaningless title in Mayfair.
It's not where I live in Yorkshire. Or anywhere
else in the country. David, as Mrs Simpson will
be divorced—has already been divorced, I understand, from a previous husband—how can you
marry her?

QUEEN : Mary has put the position perfectly. It is
impossible for you to marry her. Surely you understand that?

DAVID : Unfortunately I do not.

QUEEN : But, David—

DAVID : It is impossible for me, with the church
ruling on divorce as it now stands and in my present
position, to marry a divorced woman.

QUEEN : Well then?

DAVID : But rulings—even church rulings—can be
changed if necessary and my position altered. One
or the other will have to be done.

QUEEN : Both are impossible and what's more—

DAVID : Let me finish, Mamma. I know you will
find this difficult to believe and Archbishop Lang
would be amazed, but I am not without religious
scruples. If I were there would be no problem.

QUEEN : Dearest boy, I accept that absolutely.
What I am unable to accept is the form your religion takes when it allows you even to contemplate
marriage to a divorced woman.

DAVID : You do realize, Mamma, that there is
nothing to stop me marrying Wallis tomorrow in
a civil ceremony the moment she is free, and if I
had no respect for religion, nothing to prevent me
from being crowned before she was my wife.

QUEEN : I realize that only too well.

DAVID : Very well, then. So you must understand
that if there is a crisis, it is not because I am lack-
ing in serious principles, but because—*because* my

religion means a great deal to me. Lang and everyone else in authority equate religion with solemnity.
I do not. Surely it is possible to enjoy life and even
seem frivolous and still feel deeply about religion.
QUEEN : No one doubts the depth of your feelings.
DAVID : But you do. You all do.
MARY : Whom do you mean by all?
DAVID : Lang, Baldwin, everyone. I find the Church
of England, like the present government, increasingly out of touch. And just as they underestimate
my religious feelings, so they underestimate my
desire for marriage. It is essential for me to marry
the woman I love. Not just in a civil ceremony,
but in church.
MARY : But how can you expect the church to bless
your marriage?
DAVID : It must change its laws or else my position
must be changed.
QUEEN : David, David, David! Please believe me
when I say I sympathize with you. I really do. But
we must be realistic. Now I am the first to agree
that you never had a chance to settle down. There
was the war. Then those long Empire tours, following one after the other. I said at the time they were
a mistake. I said as much to your father.
DAVID (*surprised*) : Did you?
QUEEN : Oh, yes. And to Mr Baldwin, too. Oh, I
know you did a splendid job. Many people think
you held the Empire together but it gave you no
chance to build a life to settle down.
DAVID : No.
QUEEN (*with warm sympathy—she feels she is getting through to him*) : I really do understand how
much you want to marry and I'm sure Mrs Simpson is charming. I know George and Marina like
her very much, so do the Mountbattens.

DAVID : Oh, Mamma, I love her so much.

QUEEN : I'm sure you do.

(*They are closer than perhaps they have ever been, the Queen continues.*)

But however much you love her and however charming she is, as your wife, as your queen, she is out of the question.

(*The Queen had thought the King was weakening and he had thought she was. He stares at her aghast whilst she continues gently, calmly but relentlessly.*)

You have your duty to do as King. You must give her up.

DAVID : Why?

(*For the first time his voice betrays his inner agitation. His disappointment is echoed by her. Their voices start to rise.*)

QUEEN : She's been divorced.

DAVID : There's no other reason?

QUEEN : What other reason could there be?

DAVID : You know nothing against her?

QUEEN : Other than the divorce, no.

DAVID : She's not a criminal, for example? An alcoholic, perhaps?

QUEEN : David.

DAVID : I can marry with the church's approval a criminal alcoholic, but the church will not allow me to marry a divorced woman.

QUEEN : David, there is nothing to be gained by getting excited and talking wildly. The church would have no reason to oppose your marriage to

47

a criminal alcoholic. The government would inter-
vene. To the vast majority of us a marriage is for
a lifetime. Now I understand that this is a fact you
find unpalatable. Nevertheless it exists and you
must face it.

DAVID : Wallis's first husband drank, their marriage
became a mockery.

QUEEN : I don't know the American form of marriage service, but presumably she took him for
better or worse.

DAVID : She left him for a time, then went back to
him and tried again. Having failed with him twice,
she finally decided on a divorce. She was the
innocent party.

QUEEN : I'm sure that's all true. I understand that
with her second divorce she's again the innocent
party. But divorce itself is what is wrong.

DAVID : Not in my view.

QUEEN : The church's teaching is quite clear.

DAVID : The church's teaching was laid down by
men specially dedicated to a spiritual life, on top
of which not one of its present leaders has the
remotest understanding of the twentieth century.

QUEEN : Be that as it may—

DAVID : Furthermore, do you realize that the marriage vow is the only unbreakable contract? You
can cease to be a clergyman, the Roman Catholic
church will release nuns and monks from their
vows. Only a husband and wife are to be tied
together in permanent misery.

QUEEN : David, as a constitutional monarch you
can act only within the government's wishes and
in this instance the government supports the church.

DAVID : Only where I'm concerned. Civil re-
marriage for everyone else is perfectly legal and
respectable.

QUEEN : You are in a unique position. You have to pay a unique price for it. You cannot have the privileges of your position without its responsibilities. Mr Baldwin has explained this to you. You seem to understand no one's point of view but your own. As head of the church—

DAVID : The church is wrong and in my view uncharitable and unchristian on this issue of divorce and remarriage.

QUEEN : Nevertheless, the government—

DAVID : Nevertheless, the government, incapable of a coherent foreign policy or of a constructive home policy for that matter, is prepared to be firm only on a matter of hypocritical virtue.

MARY : David! You are quite right when you say the Royal Marriages Act does not apply to you as monarch. The moment Mrs Simpson is free you can certainly legally marry her. The Press—despite all the gossip, the Press in Britain is still silent—

QUEEN : —for the time being—

MARY : —but once they know you plan to marry her, how can they continue to be silent about her then? The King's bride will be an object of legitimate interest. Her past will become public property.

DAVID (*icily*) : What do you mean, her past?

MARY : We all have a past. When George married Marina, the entire Greek family history was in all the papers. When any of us marries this happens, it's a fact we have to live with.

QUEEN : Exactly.

MARY : The Press cannot fail to mention her former marriages, her divorces. The public will want to know when and how you met her. They will see that she divorced Mr Simpson in 1936 and married you in 1937. They will realize that you knew her, fell in love with her when she was still married to another man. The people of this country are fundamentally moral and they will disapprove most strongly of such a marriage. Consequently, they will disapprove of you and your wife and, however nice she is, however much you love her, such a state of affairs can only do the throne damage.

DAVID: Temporarily.

QUEEN: We cannot be sure of that. It could be lasting damage.

MARY: David, Mamma and I are concerned for your happiness. But we are royal. We are also concerned for the throne.

QUEEN: It is impossible—impossible, David—for any king of England, any son of mine, brought up as he has been in the tradition of service to his country, to put the throne in danger.

DAVID: There is absolutely no question of that. The throne has been damaged temporarily before, yet it survives. My predecessors—

QUEEN: Your predecessors lived in an age when republicanism was not at all common in other countries. Now it is. We are the only major power still a monarchy.

DAVID: I intend that we shall remain not only a monarchy but also a major power.

QUEEN: Then, David, my dear boy, what are we arguing about? Your duty is clear.

DAVID: We are now coming to the real point. You see if I raised the religious issue of my marriage, it wasn't just from my own selfish viewpoint, but because I believe the Church of England must become more modern.

QUEEN: Modern?

DAVID: Up-to-date. We must all become up-to-date. The whole country. We cannot hope to stay a major power unless we do. I believe in evolution, Mamma, and not revolution. But if we do not evolve, and with some speed, too, we will face revolution.

QUEEN : Have you already forgotten our Silver Jubilee? It was only last year. We were overwhelmed with demonstrations of affection.

DAVID : Towards you and Papa personally but not for the existing system.

QUEEN : The throne has never been stronger.

DAVID : And the country never weaker. The throne is strong because it changes and the country is weak because it won't.

QUEEN : The throne has never changed.

DAVID : Of course it has. You changed it. So did Papa. Victoria changed it. She made it respectable when her uncles had made it scandalous.

QUEEN : That's quite true, but—

DAVID : Grandpapa made it gay, social and continental when his mother's old age had made it provincial.

QUEEN : It was never provincial.

DAVID : She never visited London at all. She spent her life in Balmoral and Osborne and that is all. Papa made it British when before it had seemed German. And I—I must be allowed to change it, too.

QUEEN : May one ask how?

DAVID : People say that I don't want to be king, but I do. Would I have worked so hard as Prince of Wales if I didn't? I want to bring the monarchy into the twentieth century. I want to stay on the throne but on or off the throne I will marry Mrs Simpson.

(*Pause. He has said it. The bomb has exploded.*)

QUEEN : What did you say? On or off the throne?

DAVID : That's what I said, Mamma.

QUEEN : Mary—

MARY : Mamma, dear.

QUEEN : Are you serious?

DAVID : Perfectly.

QUEEN : Oh, no—no. I know you are headstrong and stubborn but not even you could be so silly. Yes. Silly. If you feel so strongly about reform of the church, dealing with unemployment and the international situation, it is your duty to stay on the throne and advise the government accordingly. All your arguments, every single one of them, are arguments for staying on the throne. Not for running away. Cannot you see that? David, you can influence any government but behind the scenes. That is your right. That is your duty. Your duty. You must be patient. It will take time.

DAVID : If I don't fight over this private issue, it will be over a public one and that would be far, far worse. Don't you see that by making it over a personal issue I am avoiding a major conflict between the government and me.

QUEEN : But you must surely understand that you must never come into open conflict with the government at all.

DAVID : I understand that perfectly, that is why I am trying to contain our disagreement. I am a man as well as a king and I must marry Wallis Simpson. I have told Baldwin this.

QUEEN : And?

DAVID : He advises, so far unofficially, against it. So I have two choices. To give her up and stay on the throne or to marry her and abdicate.

QUEEN : Then only one answer is possible. You must give her up. It must be terrible to love someone you cannot marry. But I will help you. The family will help you.

DAVID : I have chosen to abdicate. So you see there will be no open conflict. You see, Mamma, there is something you do not understand in all this. I cannot live without her. Not a day. Not an hour. I've known more beautiful women and more charming women. I must have done, because I know when I first met her I thought her neither the one nor the other. But to me she is the most fascinating woman in the world. Her gaiety, her curiosity about life constantly delights. To me she has also become more beautiful and more charming than anyone else alive. When I'm with her I am rich and fulfilled. When I'm away from her I feel only half alive. She gives my life significance. Without her it is quite pointless. So I didn't hesitate a moment when Baldwin advised me not to marry her. I said at once, 'Very well, I'm prepared to abdicate'.

MARY (*at length*) : What about us?

DAVID : Us?

QUEEN : What about the family?

DAVID : Well, what about it?

QUEEN : What is going to happen to the throne?

DAVID : Bertie will succeed. He'll do it very well really. He's what you all want. He'll do exactly as he's told. After all, he always has.

QUEEN : You are prepared to abdicate—to desert your post?

DAVID (*sharply*) : I cannot be king unless I am married to Wallis.

QUEEN : To desert your post, deny your duty.

DAVID (*with great emphasis*) : I am fully prepared to work and work hard at being king, but I must be allowed the fundamental right of every male in

53

the world. To marry the woman I love. You all wonder if she's good enough for me. I wonder if I am good enough for her. Mamma, you would understand my whole attitude and why I feel as I do if you would meet her. Will you receive her? Will you see her?

QUEEN: You feel strongly about divorce and re-marriage. So do I. My views are the exact opposite to yours. I cannot change now. No. I cannot receive her.

DAVID: Mary?

MARY: I agree with Mamma.

DAVID: Wallis made two mistakes in her life. And a Christian society cannot forgive her for them.

QUEEN: If you stayed on the throne, if you did your duty, you could change that society.

DAVID: But you see, I'd only succeed with her by my side. That is what no one understands. Not even she does. Wallis is your strongest ally, Mamma. She wants me to stay. She wants me to give her up. But I won't. Not now. Not ever. If the only way I can marry her is by abdicating then I shall abdicate with joy.

He turns and walks out of the room as

The curtain falls.

ACT TWO

Scene 1

It is now a fortnight later in early December. It is late morning. The Queen is talking to Mr Monckton, KC, a dark, attractive man of about forty. He is charming, wears glasses, and is very able.

QUEEN : But surely you understand, Mr Monckton, that the present state of affairs cannot go on much longer. The King must reach a decision soon. A fortnight ago he said in this very room that he wanted to abdicate. What is going on?

MONCKTON : You must remember, ma'am, that until very recently his Majesty was the most advised man in the world. Now, in this supreme crisis of his life, apart from Mrs Simpson, he has no one. His government, his court, even his family are all opposed to him. So he has turned to his personal friends for advice, and surely this is reasonable, ma'am?

QUEEN : On the face of it, yes. But who has he turned to? You, Mr Monckton, I know, are a man of great good sense. All of us are fortunate that you have agreed to act as intermediary between the King and his Cabinet. But what about the others? What about Churchill? What about Beaverbrook? They are anxious, not so much to help the King, as to attack Baldwin. You must know that as well as I do.

MONCKTON : Churchill is a born Cavalier. He sees his loyalty to the King in terms of high romance. Beaverbrook may want to attack Baldwin but it doesn't matter if he does, as the King is determined to behave with constitutional correctness.

QUEEN: You mean he doesn't take their advice either.

MONCKTON: That would be one way of putting it.

QUEEN: He never would listen to anyone.

MONCKTON: Ma'am, the King's friends are all urging delay. But the only advice he wants is how to stay on the throne and still marry Mrs Simpson.

QUEEN: But surely his friends all realize the nation will never accept her as queen.

MONCKTON: She needn't become queen.

(*Long pause.*)

QUEEN: Mr Monckton, you're not seriously suggesting a morganatic marriage?

MONCKTON: It's the only loophole open to him. A few days ago Esmond Harmsworth took Mrs Simpson to Claridge's for lunch and put it to her that she could become the King's wife without becoming queen.

(*The Queen looks at Mr Monckton.*)

After all, ma'am, European royal families did it quite often.

QUEEN: And they were always disastrous.

MONCKTON: Franz Ferdinand's was a happy marriage, ma'am.

QUEEN: No doubt. But it was a source of constant embarrassment to everyone and it split the Imperial Family in two. What does the King think of the idea?

MONCKTON: He considers it distasteful but a possible solution.

QUEEN: It's quite impossible. For him to contemplate it at all makes one despair all over again. I called you in to discover what has been going on, Mr Monckton, and you have confirmed my worst fears. His secretary, Alec Hardinge, sent him a perfectly reasonable letter suggesting Mrs Simpson leave the country, warning him of the impending crisis and telling him quite properly that the government might call an election to be fought over his proposed marriage. And what does the King do? He flies into a terrible rage and refuses to see or even speak to Alec Hardinge again.

MONCKTON : I don't think it was a reasonable letter, ma'am. It was far too brutally worded. It put the government's point of view so exactly it might have come from Baldwin's secretary instead of from his own. To suggest that Mrs Simpson leave the country was a fatal mistake and would only make the King furious. His courtiers have been most unwise in their handling of the monarch. They have made the grave mistake of making it plain that they disapprove of him and what employer would like that from his employees? On top of which they have allowed their dislike of Mrs Simpson to reach the point of venom. Do you know that some of his staff and their wives refer to her as 'the kitchen maid'?

QUEEN : No. I didn't know. It is most unfortunate. Most unkind.

MONCKTON : It's worse than that, ma'am. It's disloyal.

QUEEN : Mr Monckton, his court may have been stupid and snobbish. I don't believe any of them are disloyal. You must remember, they are concerned not just for the King himself but also for the throne. The throne is more important than its occupant.

MONCKTON : Those are Mrs Simpson's sentiments, too.

QUEEN : Then why doesn't she give him up?

MONCKTON : She can't. She wants to leave. He won't let her. In his present frame of mind he's capable of following her in a battleship to China.

QUEEN : That I can well believe. Please sit down, Mr Monckton.

MONCKTON : Ma'am. (*He sits.*)

QUEEN : Clearly the love he has for her is no ordinary love. I met her once, you know. At a reception we gave for the Duchess of Kent before her marriage. My son submitted a list of guests, so of course, along with the rest of his list, she had to be invited. I can remember nothing about her. I cannot recall even what she looks like.

MONCKTON : She's an extremely nice woman. I like her very much indeed. She's calm, sensible and discreet. But what woman, in her present position, wouldn't make a few mistakes? She's more than the wonderful society hostess she's always called. She's kind and thoughtful. She's also quite without personal ambition.

QUEEN : Without ambition?

MONCKTON : Personal ambition, yes. The stories about her being an unscrupulous adventuress bear no relationship to fact at all. Of course she'd be very ambitious for her husband. It may sound ironic, but she has a profound respect for marriage.

QUEEN : With two divorces. Really?

MONCKTON : Oh, yes. She expects her marriage to be ideally happy and her husband to be a success and she will work very hard to achieve both those aims. She's constantly described to me as the driving force behind this. She's not at all. The King wanted her to divorce Simpson—when Mr Baldwin asked him to stop the divorce, of course he refused. The King knows they are thought immoral and it infuriates him. He's passionately moral. So is she. It would be easy for them both to be immoral, with a little discretion this immorality would be winked at. *That* is why he's been indiscreet. He has deliberately dragged her round Europe, deliberately given dinner parties for her, so as to make a discreet love affair between them absolutely impossible.

QUEEN: You're a remarkably eloquent advocate, Mr Monckton. I hope the King and Mrs Simpson appreciate you. The fact remains that whatever his motives my son has outraged the church, the government, his court, all of his relations and world opinion. But tell me, Mr Monckton, if Mrs Simpson is a sensible woman, why didn't she stop my son deliberately parading her?

MONCKTON: May I ask, ma'am, have you ever tried to stop the King from doing anything? I've known him since Oxford and I certainly can't. I implored his Majesty to wait a while before he put the morganatic marriage idea to Mr Baldwin, but he absolutely insists on going ahead.

QUEEN: But if he does that, the Prime Minister will be bound to put it to the Cabinet and then this whole business will become official.

MONCKTON: I'm afraid so.

QUEEN: I've tried to help and guide my son. Quite without success. You will stay with him, Mr Monckton?

MONCKTON: Yes, of course, ma'am.

QUEEN: He's going to need your help.

MONCKTON: I think I should warn you, ma'am. The Press will have to break its silence soon.

QUEEN: And then God alone knows what will happen. As I look into the future, Mr Monckton, I am filled with foreboding.

The curtain falls.

Scene 2

It is late in the evening two days later. Margaret is found on stage reading a newspaper. Several others are at her feet. These have enormous banner headlines. Margaret is reading with a certain gusto. Mabell comes in. When she sees what Margaret is doing she is almost openly irritated.

MABELL: Oh, Margaret, do put those papers away. The Yorks have arrived.

MARGARET: It's all simply dreadful. Crowds outside the palace have been shouting 'God save the King from Baldwin'.

MABELL: People should know better.

(Page opens door and the Duchess of York, followed by the Duke, comes in. The Duke, two years younger than his brother, is shy and retiring with a stammer which becomes pronounced in moments of stress. He is however also very tough when he has to be; his shy, quiet manner is deceptive. The Duchess, then thirty-six is pretty and slightly plump. Formerly Lady Elizabeth Bowes-Lyon, she is now quite used to being royalty and normally, from all accounts, quite extraordinarily charming. She is very distressed, upset and even angry, at first she is controlled. Later, for what may have

60

been the only time in her life, her distress causes her anger to break out.)

ELIZABETH : Lady Airlie.
MABELL : Your Royal Highness.

(Mabell and Margaret curtsey. The Duchess and Mabell are old friends, so they kiss as they do so. The Duke talks to Margaret.)

BERTIE : How is Mamma?
MARGARET : Oh, wonderful as ever, sir. Perfectly calm, but of course very worried. I'll tell her you're here.
BERTIE : If you would.

(Margaret goes out.)

ELIZABETH : Is the Queen very distressed?
MABELL : Oh, yes. These dreadful papers were a terrible shock.
ELIZABETH : It's difficult to know which one is worst. I am still very, very upset. We arrived from Scotland this morning totally unprepared for this deluge of publicity. Why were we not warned by the Palace?
BERTIE : They may not have known, darling.
ELIZABETH : Papers come out in the early morning, Bertie. Why wasn't a signal sent to the train? At Euston we were greeted by what seemed to be every cameraman in London and huge newspaper placards shrieking, 'The King and Mrs Simpson'. *(She sits.)* I don't think, Lady Airlie, that I shall ever be able to hear the words 'Mrs Simpson' without a shudder. *(She laughs.)* Actually it was rather funny. We went to some reception and the butler announced, 'The Bishop of Kensington and Mrs

Simpson'. The room absolutely froze. And in walked the bishop and on his arm was his amiable wife.

BERTIE : That was the first indication we had that the secret was no longer a secret. Is the King here yet?

MABELL : No, sir.

ELIZABETH : But he is coming?

MABELL : He said so.

BERTIE : Mamma wanted us here first, darling.

(*The Queen comes in.*)

QUEEN : Thank goodness you're both here. Elizabeth, my dear.

BERTIE : Mamma.

(*He bows, kisses her hand, then embraces her warmly. As he does so, Elizabeth curtseys, then also embraces her.*)

QUEEN : Dear Bertie.

(*Lady Airlie goes tactfully to the door, curtseys and withdraws.*)

BERTIE : Mamma, have you any news?

QUEEN : Only what I read in those dreadful newspapers. I sent David an urgent message and he's coming round after ten, he said.

ELIZABETH : Why so late?

QUEEN : I've no idea. I'm in the dark. I'm never off the telephone, yet nobody knows anything. She has, I gather, at last left the country.

ELIZABETH : Yes, but too late. When Alec Hardinge suggested it three weeks ago, it might have done some good—but not now.

QUEEN : David wouldn't let her go. It was only because he was frightened for her safety that he agreed now to her going. You've both got to understand one thing—he loves her. He loves her with all the passion of a boy in his first youth.

ELIZABETH : Yes, but he's not in his first youth. He's forty-two.

BERTIE : I would be very grateful if someone would explain the situation. We hear vaguely from Number Ten from you, but never from Fort Belvedere. Never from David. Of course we've been in Scotland.

ELIZABETH : There are, I believe, telephones in Fort Belvedere. And please correct me if I'm wrong, but I'm sure it's possible to ring up Scotland from Windsor Great Park.

BERTIE (*soothingly*) : David is under great strain, darling.

ELIZABETH : And so are you. No one seems to understand that, least of all David. You are under great strain. If he deserts his post you would have to take over.

BERTIE : He would never dream of doing a thing like that. B-Baldwin's warnings were merely routine. I'm sure it won't happen. It can't. If that's what's making you so upset, I'm sure you're being upset about nothing. I know David. The government knows him. They know that in him they have a first rate king and they wouldn't let him go. You'll see. No, what distresses me in this is that I am his heir, his brother and I would like to help him—somehow. I just wish he wouldn't ignore me.

ELIZABETH : Darling Bertie.

(*It is clear that this is a love match. For a moment*

*they might have been alone, they are talking quietly
to each other.)*

QUEEN (*suddenly and sharply*): It's not out of the
question.
BERTIE (*surprised*): Hm?
QUEEN: It's not impossible. Your taking over. It's
not at all impossible. The government will let him
go. They are at loggerheads over everything. The
impossible is happening. It shouldn't be. But it is.
That is why I wanted you here before David. To
tell you what you are up against. Mr Baldwin's
warnings were not routine. They were meant.

*(The shock to Bertie and Elizabeth is terrible. They
stare appalled at the Queen. Clearly, whatever
may have been told them before they had refused
to accept. Now they believe it. Bertie is like a
prisoner who, told repeatedly by his lawyer that
he will get a heavy sentence, refuses to believe it
and then nearly dies of shock when he gets it. He
can hardly speak. She holds him. When Bertie
speaks the stammer becomes pronounced.)*

BERTIE: Why do you think David will d-desert?
QUEEN: Because he believes his duty to Mrs Simp-
son is greater than his duty to his country.
ELIZABETH: When is he going?
QUEEN: I've no idea.

(They stare at her horrified.)

You have been in Scotland. A country composed
of relatively sane people. I have been inhabiting
Cloud Cuckoo Land where there are no answers to
any question except another question. You say you
should have been warned. Of course you should

64

have been. But what are we to say to you? And it's all so simple. You either do your duty or you don't.

BERTIE : What am I going to do, Elizabeth? I've not been trained to be k-king.

(*Page enters.*)

PAGE : His Majesty.

(*David enters. Page goes out.*)

(*The Queen's greeting is definitely cool. He kisses her hand. Bertie gets up and bows. Elizabeth curtseys.*)

DAVID : Mamma. Bertie. How was Scotland, Elizabeth?
QUEEN : We are anxious for news, David.
DAVID : Yes, I know.

(*The strain is telling. His charm is less overwhelming, his voice sharper.*)

There is nothing definite to tell you.
QUEEN : You have seen the papers?
DAVID : Naturally.
QUEEN : I find them extremely disturbing.
DAVID : No more than we do, I assure you. Wallis was appalled.
QUEEN : Are you going to abdicate?
DAVID : Nothing is settled. You have urged so strongly. Naturally I am trying to remain.
QUEEN : If you are set on marrying this— then obviously you cannot remain.
DAVID : You may refer to Wallis by her Christian name or by her present surname which is Mrs Simpson.

QUEEN : I do not know the lady, so naturally I cannot refer to her by her Christian name.

DAVID : The fact that you do not know her is not her fault. Nor is it mine.

QUEEN : David, I know how devoted you are to Mrs Simpson.

DAVID : I've had to send her abroad, you know.

QUEEN : Yes, dear, I know. I assure you I do not mean to add to your obvious distress. However, we —the family, your family—are distressed, too.

(*Bertie is visibly distressed.*)

BERTIE : Why are we told nothing?

(*Elizabeth is standing slightly away from the rest of them. Hearing her husband's stammer, she glances at him. She is absolutely still and silent.*)

DAVID : Because I wish to keep you all out of it. This is not a fight between the whole royal family and Parliament, nor is it about the principle of monarchy and Parliament, but between me and the Cabinet, me and Baldwin. If you were any of you to become involved, particularly you, Bertie, you would be an ally of mine and should I fail, then it would not be just my failure, but your failure, too—the whole family's failure.

QUEEN : Fail at what—

DAVID : In my fight with Baldwin. Do you realize he won't take this to Parliament? Parliament has not been consulted. He won't even let me broadcast. And why? Because he knows there's a body of opinion in my favour. He wants to present Parliament with a *fait accompli*, which Churchill says is unconstitutional.

QUEEN : When was Churchill ever right about anything? Look at India and the Dardanelles. His support is of no value to you. And in this instance everybody supports the Prime Minister absolutely. Mr Attlee supports him. Can't you see that by refusing to put it openly to Parliament, the Prime Minister is protecting you. Protecting the crown from becoming a point of political controversy. You should be grateful to him. If the crown becomes a point of controversy it will lose its entire value. We are the centre of affection. We are the heart of the nation. We are a rallying point in national disaster. No president, no prime minister can fill that role and you are destroying us.

DAVID : How can I be when I have removed the argument from any possible political controversy?

QUEEN : But to argue *at all* with your Prime Minister and to have the argument made public is in itself making the crown controversial.

DAVID : No. I am a point of controversy. Not the crown.

QUEEN : You cannot separate the two. Nobody can.

DAVID (*quietly and patiently*) : I am prepared to go. I stated that clearly. Right?

QUEEN : Yes.

DAVID : So if I am prepared to go—should the government wish me to go—then there is no conflict. I have agreed. How can there be conflict?

QUEEN : So you are definitely going?

DAVID : Oh, no.

QUEEN : David, dear. I am growing old. I speak German and French and Italian. Double dutch I never mastered.

DAVID : I said I was PREPARED to go. I did not say I WANTED to go. There was no hint of a desire to go in my choice of words.

QUEEN : Dear David, in uttering them at all, you

abdicated and you never even knew it. I don't think you understand anything.

BERTIE : If you go, David, what is going to happen?

DAVID : You will take over, of course. What else?

ELIZABETH : I was waiting for that.

QUEEN : If you stay and marry Mrs Simpson, what will happen? You won't have a government. Mr Baldwin will resign. His entire Cabinet will resign. Mr Attlee won't take over. The Labour Party disapproves of your proposed marriage quite as bitterly as I do. The working-class woman is a respectable woman. She is used to having one husband and sticking to him.

ELIZABETH : I agree.

QUEEN : You won't have an Archbishop of Canterbury. Not one bishop will attend your coronation. Oh, I daresay you'll be able to persuade some renegade clergyman to crown you and I daresay to marry you, but it will be a public humiliation and a mockery of all the throne stands for. So you will have no government on the one hand and will be at loggerheads with the church on the other. May I ask, do you propose to become a dictator? And a pope?

DAVID : No, Mamma.

QUEEN : Really, we might as well be living in Romania. Let me make one thing clear to you. Even if you should succeed in staying on your own impossible conditions, in no circumstances whatsoever will I receive Mrs Simpson.

DAVID : Not even if I marry her morganatically?

QUEEN : Not even then. Never. Never as long as I live. Monarchy symbolizes the family. It is that which gives us our strength. We are born, we marry, we die as a family. A wife shares in every way her husband's position. A morganatic marriage in which Mrs Simpson is your wife but not your queen, strikes at the whole principle of family life, it'll never work. The Cabinet can only reject the idea.

DAVID : And if she did become queen? What would you do then?

QUEEN : I have lived my life on certain principles which I know you deplore and consider narrow-minded, and I will not abandon them now. I will never receive her nor attend any function which she attends.

DAVID : I am sorry you have ranged yourself with my enemies, but I expected nothing else. Neither you nor Papa could ever miss an opportunity to criticize me.

QUEEN : That is not true.

DAVID : I have a royal memory, too, and can quote examples at length if you so desire. But I'm as dedicated as you are to the monarchial system and I have no wish to abdicate. What I am striving to do is to find a formula by which I can stay *and* at the same time marry Wallis Simpson.

ELIZABETH : You could give her up.

DAVID : Could I? You are happily married, Elizabeth. Could you give up Bertie?

ELIZABETH : We are already married. It's not the same.

DAVID : It's the same to me.

ELIZABETH : And when we married we did not divide the country.

DAVID : You married Bertie because you loved him and I trust you have stayed married for the same reason.

ELIZABETH : I waited some time, months if not years, before I was certain, and being certain I

69

then made vows which to me mean a great deal. I would never have made them if I hadn't meant to keep them. All married people make these vows of their own free will. No one forces us to do so. Wallis Simpson has made them twice and broken them twice.

QUEEN : To do so once may be allowed in the most terrible of circumstances, but to break your marriage vow twice, to divorce twice, is unforgiveable.

ELIZABETH : Naturally I sympathize with your desire to escape, I was myself reluctant to become royal.

DAVID : I have no desire to escape.

ELIZABETH : It's in everything you say and do.

DAVID : You are reading into my words what's not and has never been there.

QUEEN : You are putting your personal wishes before your duty to your country. The throne asks for the supreme sacrifice in time of war, a sacrifice millions of men make. It is inconceivable to me how you can accept such a sacrifice from them, yet refuse a far lesser one in return.

DAVID : I don't mind dying for my country. What I refuse to do is live in misery for my country. No one is asked to do that.

QUEEN : You know I was engaged first of all to your father's elder brother. If he had lived marriage to him would not have been at all easy. It was made clear to me where my duty lay so I agreed to marry him.

DAVID : Oh, yes, I know, but either way you would have had a private life and children. I have none. Nor can you know how such a marriage would have affected you. It might even have made you tolerant.

ELIZABETH : The truth of the matter is that you are

convinced that our sacrifices in the name of duty are always unimportant compared to yours. Bertie's sacrifices have been endless and he makes them cheerfully without complaint. On top of which he's had to fight ill-health and a stammer. None of this interests you in the slightest. The only things which concern you are your own emotions. I've heard all about your plans for bringing us into the twentieth century. They can't mean much to you as without a thought you are prepared to endanger them. The weight of opinion against you is overwhelming. Yet you are so vain—

DAVID (*interrupting*) : Yes—all right—thank you—

ELIZABETH (*continuing without stopping*) : —that not for one moment do you think this opinion could be right and you wrong.

DAVID : O.K., weight of opinion is the correct expression. There's Baldwin about to retire from an inglorious career at the end of which our country is defenceless. Lang, whom you all admire, nauseates me with his unctuous hypocrisy and I wonder if there's a bishop under sixty? The church, if it continues its present lamentable career, will soon be so out of touch it'll become extinct. The Labour Party is led by elderly Trade Unionists and desiccated dons who can read Latin and Greek fluently but have never seen a Hungarian close to and aren't sure where Belgrade is. But there are young people in this country. Young people who will take over, who reject these outmoded codes of behaviour. Must the crown always be a backwater of fossilized opinion?

BERTIE : All this passion is very fine. But what is happening now?

DAVID : Now? I am striving to stay on the throne. It is a private personal difference of opinion

71

between me and Baldwin. That's why I live at the Fort, my private home, all the time.

ELIZABETH : What will happen if you are told to go?

DAVID : I'll go. And naturally Bertie as my heir will take over.

ELIZABETH : Just like that.

DAVID : If I died that's what would happen.

ELIZABETH : Death is not deliberate. This act of yours will be. Bertie is unprepared. You knew for twenty-six years you would be king. You have always taken Bertie for granted and without the slightest consideration you take him for granted now. We have two children whom we hope to bring up in reasonable privacy. Now if you go, we'll have to bring them up in a glare of ghastly publicity. And if you dislike being king, do you imagine Bertie will enjoy it? You are prepared to put a burden you regard as intolerable on to your own brother's shoulders.

DAVID : I regard it as intolerable only because I'm not married. He is.

ELIZABETH : This past year has been a hell on earth for all your court, your relations, your mother and for Bertie and me. We have been through the tortures of the damned in Scotland these past weeks, having to go to endless functions, told nothing by you, rumours, whispers surrounding us—

DAVID : I was keeping you out of it.

ELIZABETH : We have as much at stake as you have. More. We will have to clear up the mess. When did you get the papers this morning?

DAVID : First thing.

ELIZABETH : We were in the train. Why didn't you get a message to us? You knew it would be an appalling shock to Bertie. Yet you could allow us to arrive at Euston to a blaze of publicity with placards screaming your name. Oh, you will career round the country putting on a tremendous show of concern for the poor, but nothing is to be allowed to interfere with your dream of happiness. You can't sit at a desk and read State papers.

DAVID: That's all anybody can think of. State papers. My father read them all and Baldwin did as he liked and we are in a mess.

QUEEN: Your father was a conscientious monarch. How dare you suggest otherwise!

ELIZABETH: As for your plans for the future of this country, they sound like a nightmare. Everybody divorcing everybody. You say you want to reign, but on your terms. You say you wish to be a constitutional king and will act only through the government. But it has to agree with you. You say the church is out of touch, but only now do you say it when you want to break its laws. Everything has to be sacrificed to your vanity, the country, Bertie, the children, your mother, me, the throne, everything and everyone, so that you can be happy in your private life. You are mesmerized by your own legend.

QUEEN: Elizabeth, David is still the king.

DAVID: Don't forget you have a legend, too. The perfect wife and mother. I hope it's not making you smug.

BERTIE: David! You are not to be rude to Elizabeth! Do you hear? I won't have it! I will take over if necessary. But, David, let me put it to you this way—don't you think it's your duty to stay as king? You would do it better than anyone—no, he would, dear—don't you think it's your duty to stay even without Mrs Simpson?

DAVID: It's my duty to try and be a good king . . .

Without her I'd be a bad one. So without her I cannot be king. I know it's unthinkable, but if Elizabeth were to leave you, do you think that you'd be a good king?

BERTIE : I'd try to be.

QUEEN : And you'd succeed, Bertie.

DAVID : Very possibly, Mamma. But you see, I'd fail. That's the difference between your sons. Without the woman I love beside me, I'd fail.

(*They all look at him.*)

So what can I do?

Curtain.

Scene 3

It is early evening two days later. Margaret comes in quickly. Mabell is sitting at a desk.

MARGARET : Mabell!

MABELL : Yes?

MARGARET : Have you heard the news? It's just been on the wireless. It's over.

MABELL : What's over?

MARGARET : The crisis.

MABELL : He's abdicated.

MARGARET : No, no. She has.

MABELL : She can't. She's not queen.

MARGARET : No, no. She's given him up. She's issued a statement from the South of France saying she's withdrawing from an intolerable situation. So it's over, aren't you delighted?

74

MABELL : No. Because it isn't over at all. It can't be. It's far, far too late.

MARGARET : But he hasn't abdicated yet.

MABELL : Morally he has.

MARGARET : Nothing's signed.

MABELL : He's committed to her beyond hope of recall. A month ago—even a week ago—a dignified joint statement renouncing each other and marriage could have worked but now, after everything that's happened, how can he accept her renunciation?

MARGARET : But what if she insists?

MABELL : She can't. It would be pointless. She's his strength. He could only fight it out with her beside him and to force her renunciation she has to be beside him, too. The crisis can only end when he goes.

MARGARET : Goes!

MABELL : I'm sure of it.

MARGARET : You mean—goes—

MABELL : Yes. That's what I mean.

MARGARET : But everyone is begging him to stay.

MABELL : Yes, but none of them mean it, least of all the politicians. He interferes too much. Look at that visit to the Welsh miners. 'Something must be done', he says. Well, *of course*, something must be done, but even Attlee agrees the King can't tell the government in public what to do.

(*Page opens door. The Queen enters.*)

QUEEN : Well! This is a pretty kettle of fish. I've just heard the news from dear Archbishop Lang. What are we going to do now?

MARGARET : I hoped you were going to rest, ma'am.

QUEEN : So did I, Margaret dear, but some idiot

from the Earl Marshal's office sent me fifty pages of foolscap about the forthcoming coronation. Quite apart from anything else, I would like to know whose coronation are they planning. David's or Bertie's? David was to abdicate today. Now he may not, only I don't know if David's king or if Bertie's king or even if we have a king at all. I've had just about as much as I can bear. (*She is very near tears.*)

(*Bertie comes in.*)

BERTIE : Mamma, it's all over. I'm—king.
QUEEN : Oh, my dear boy.

(*Margaret and Mabell hastily withdraw and such is their agitation that for once neither curtseys. The new King and his mother do not even notice that they have left.*)

BERTIE : I'd sooner face a firing squad than be k-king. I never wanted to be k-king. I can't even say the word.
QUEEN : Listen to me, Bertie.
BERTIE : It's the most terrible event in history, my becoming k-
QUEEN : Just listen to me. David was confident of success. Sure of it. Yet he failed.
BERTIE : I know, I know, and—and—
QUEEN : And unlike him, you'll succeed.
BERTIE : M—m—
QUEEN : Don't interrupt me. It was because he lacked your qualities that he failed.
BERTIE : He's clever. He's astute. He can talk to people. He can dominate a crowd. I've seen him. I can barely make a speech—if I have any popu-

larity at all it's because of Elizabeth and the children.

QUEEN : You're like Papa. Very like Papa. He, too, had difficulties to overcome. You mustn't imagine that just because we were so popular at the end of our reign we were as popular at the beginning. Far from it. I hadn't Queen Alexandra's beauty. I hadn't her charm. Elizabeth is popular, but so are you. They know she would never have married a man not worthy of her.

BERTIE : You're saying all this to comfort me. But you're wrong. It'll all blow up in our faces.

QUEEN : What will?

BERTIE : The m-monarchy.

QUEEN : Nonsense.

BERTIE : I've had my first red boxes.

QUEEN : They are rather alarming.

BERTIE : I'd barely been a king a minute when they were there piled up in front of me. They've not been looked at for days. So I had to deal with them at once. (*He looks at his mother.*) I didn't know anything. It was the most terrible moment. T-Tommy Lascelles had to explain the simplest things to me. I've always been devoted to David all my life, supported him as best I could when he quarrelled with Papa. I've never criticized him. Never. All right, he can't live without her. But surely he must have realized he was landing the rest of us in the most dreadful muddle.

QUEEN : I doubt it. And that is the difference between you. You would have thought of everyone else. Prepared them in good time. And that is why you will be a far better king than David would ever have been. Truly.

BERTIE : I c-can't speak. I could hardly get through the Accession address. I live in terror of the

c-c— Oh, God! (*Pause, gets the words out slowly.*)
Of . . . the coronation . . . oath. You feel so bloody
stupid standing there stammering.

(*His panic at his own responsibility, the fact that
his wife is ill, his fear of the future and his fury
with his brother all combine to flood over him in
this his last moment of weakness. The Queens pats
his head gently, breaks from him, walks about in
agitation and then pulls herself together.*)

QUEEN : Yes. Well. The first thing for you to do is
to have some whisky.

(*She pours out a large glass of neat whisky.*)

I'm not quite sure what a double or a treble is, but
I'm convinced this is a quadruple.
BERTIE (*taking it*) : It's enormous, Mamma. I shall
be drunk.
QUEEN : Good.
BERTIE (*smiling*) : There's a crowd outside. I can't
be seen leaving here in a state of intoxication.
QUEEN : I don't suppose after the amazing events
of the past week it would in any way surprise them.
All I do ask of you, Bertie, is not to fall flat on
your face as you get into the car. It would be a
discouraging start to your reign which I feel sure
will be in every way a tremendous success. Now
let us look at all your assets and, yes, your defects.
We'll get rid of the latter first. You are shy. So
was I. So was Queen Victoria. You don't know
anything about the working of the government.
Nor did your grandfather and he came to the throne
older than you. You stammer. That is all but conquered. It's only because you are upset that it is
rather stronger today. Your coronation oath can

be learnt and rehearsed in advance. You feel stupid stammering, but your audience admires your courage. Now your assets. They are so many I hardly know where to begin.

BERTIE : Mamma! Really!

QUEEN : I do not exaggerate. You have courage. Not just physical courage. Moral courage, and that's far more important. You persevere. That's how you conquered your stammer. By perseverance. You're as good a mixer as David. Look at your years in the Navy. Your splendid boys' camps. You know quite as much about industrial affairs or else why did your brothers call you the Foreman? You are patient. David isn't. You're considerate. He's not that either. You have true humility.

BERTIE : I have got Elizabeth. And the girls. And you, Mamma.

QUEEN : And me. And the family. We must all behave as if nothing was wrong, nothing had happened.

BERTIE : Well, we'll do our best.

QUEEN : It's the only thing anyone can ever do. Tell me, is the K-, is David really going to broadcast?

BERTIE : Yes. The g-g-government has decided that now he's no longer king they can't stop him. They don't want to be accused of censoring him.

QUEEN : I think it's a pity.

BERTIE : Hm. Personally I think it a wise decision. He feels very strongly about it and a public statement from him will make it clear he's abdicating by his own choice. The BBC were going to announce him as Mr Edward Windsor.

QUEEN : That's quite wrong.

BERTIE : Don't worry. I told them that. As the son of a king he's a Royal Highness, so he'll be announced as Prince Edward. The Privy Council queried this, but I pointed out that if he's not royal he's a private citizen and as such he could if he wished stand for Parliament. As that's the last thing anyone wants, they agreed with me at once. I shall give him a dukedom.

QUEEN : That would be best.

BERTIE : I'll suggest making him Duke of Windsor.

QUEEN : No—he can't take that title—it's the name of our dynasty.

BERTIE : Exactly. In time it will merge in with the rest of us. He's broadcasting from Windsor Castle after dinner tonight. I'm giving a family dinner for him at Royal Lodge.

QUEEN : I take it Elizabeth won't be there?

BERTIE : Apart from every other consideration she's too ill. Her temperature's 103. But I hope you'll come.

QUEEN : Oh, yes. And after the broadcast?

BERTIE : He'll drive to Portsmouth. I've arranged for an unescorted destroyer to take him to France.

QUEEN : He said something about going to Switzerland.

BERTIE : He's changed his mind. Mrs Simpson has arranged for him to stay with the Rothschilds in Vienna.

QUEEN : Poor David. What will his life be like now? And what's so awful for him is that he won't be able to marry Mrs Simpson or even to see her for six months. He's going to be very lonely.

BERTIE : Yes.

(*There is a tiny silence.*)

QUEEN : You must go back to Elizabeth. Dear Bertie.

(She extends her hands to him. He kisses them and then embraces her warmly. He turns and goes to the door.)

Bertie.

(He turns. She curtseys to him. He bows and goes. A moment later Mabell comes in.)

Order a car for me, dear. I'm dining at Royal Lodge.

MABELL : That's better, ma'am.

QUEEN : What's better, dear?

MABELL : You look cheerful again.

QUEEN : When I first curtseyed to David he protested, looked embarrassed. I've just made my first curtsey to Bertie, to King George VI, and do you know he accepted it as his right. He will make a good king.

Curtain.

With the curtain down the Abdication Broadcast is heard over the front of house speakers.

Broadcast

ANNOUNCER : This is Windsor Castle. His Royal Highness Prince Edward.

DUKE OF WINDSOR : At long last I am able to say a few words of my own. A few hours ago I discharged my last duty as King and Emperor and now that I have been succeeded by my brother the Duke of York, my first words must be to declare my allegiance to him. This I do with all my heart.

81

You all know the reasons which have impelled me to renounce the Throne. But you must believe me when I tell you that I have found it impossible to carry the heavy burden of responsibility and to discharge my duties as King as I would wish to do without the help and support of the woman I love.

This decision has been made less difficult to me by the sure knowledge that my brother, with his long training in the public affairs of this country and with his fine qualities, will be able to take my place forthwith without interruption or injury to the life and progress of the Empire and he has one matchless blessing, enjoyed by so many of you and not bestowed on me—a happy home with his wife and children.

During these hard days I have been comforted by Her Majesty, my mother, and by her—by my family. Ministers of the Crown, and in particular Mr Baldwin, the Prime Minister, have always treated me with full consideration.

I now quit altogether public affairs and I lay down my burden. It may be some time before I return to my native land, but I shall always follow the fortunes of the British race and Empire with profound interest, and if at any time in the future I can be found of service to his Majesty in a private station I shall not fail. And now we all have a new King. I wish him, and you, his people, happiness and prosperity with all my heart.

God bless you all.

God save the King.

Scene 4

It is afternoon nine years later in 1945. David comes in, followed by Margaret.

DAVID: I'm afraid I'm earlier than expected.

MARGARET: Her Majesty will be back in a moment, sir.

DAVID: Thank you.

MARGARET: The King and Queen had to cancel a drive through the East End, so her Majesty went instead. I expect the crowds detained her.

DAVID: I expect so. How have you been keeping, Miss Wyndham?

MARGARET: Very well, thank you, sir. Of course we've all been working so hard for victory, we're all a bit tired, I think.

DAVID: And the Queen?

MARGARET: Very well really. Like the rest of us, thankful the war is over. And you, sir? How are you?

DAVID: I'm quite well, too. (*There is a long pause.*) So is my wife.

MARGARET (*in an expressionless voice*): I'm so glad. The Queen is really taking longer than I thought. The enthusiasm with which the royal family is greeted everywhere is remarkable.

DAVID: I'm sure. My brother and sister-in-law were always very popular.

MARGARET: Would you like tea now?

DAVID: No, no.

MARGARET: I'm sure her Majesty wouldn't want you to wait.

DAVID: I would prefer to, all the same. (*He smiles charmingly.*) I'm so looking forward to seeing my family again. Of course the Gloucesters are in

Australia, but everyone else is here. I shall stay at
Harewood with my sister for a while, too. And then
there are all my old friends. Monckton. Beaverbrook. Churchill.

MARGARET : I was shocked beyond measure when
he lost the election.

DAVID : Were you? I wasn't.

MARGARET : He was so popular.

DAVID : Oh, but you can't rely on popularity.

MARGARET : No.

DAVID : Or on gratitude. Both are very ephemeral
emotions. Don't you agree?

MARGARET : Yes.

DAVID : No one votes out of gratitude. Tell me, is
it true that no one dresses for dinner any more?

MARGARET : Oh, dear me, no, sir. That's quite out.

DAVID : Amazing. Just as well my father wasn't
alive to see that. I remember how cross he was
when I took to wearing a bowler in London instead
of a top hat. And there was very nearly a diplo-
matic incident when an American ambassador
refused to wear knee breeches when he was being
presented to my mother.

MARGARET : Times have changed, sir, as you wanted
them to. No one wears court dress at all.

(*Enter Page.*)

PAGE : I thought you'd like to know, sir, the Queen's
car is driving up.

DAVID : Oh. Thank you. John, isn't it?

PAGE : Yes, sir.

DAVID : That's not bad for nine years, is it?

PAGE : Marvellous, sir.

DAVID : Miss Wyndham, would you make sure my
mother knows I'm here?

(*Margaret withdraws.*)

John, is my mother very changed?
PAGE : No, sir. She uses a stick sometimes now, sir.
DAVID : A stick? I didn't know.
PAGE : That's the only difference really, sir. She liked living at Badminton. She loved going into the village and made great friends with the locals.
DAVID : Really! How splendid. Thank you, John.

(*Page goes to door, sees Queen approaching and opens both doors.*)

(*The Queen comes in. She is older, dressed in a coat and her famous toque, with a stick. Page withdraws.*)

QUEEN : My dear, dear boy.
DAVID : Mamma.

(*They embrace. Pause.*)

QUEEN : How nice to see you. I was so sorry I was out. Bertie has a cold and poor Elizabeth had to receive General de Gaulle, so I went to the East End for them.
DAVID : I was early. You look A1, Mamma.
QUEEN : I'm older—older. Well—well—well. Sit down, David. I'm so delighted to see you again. So much has happened.

(*They sit. There is an awkward pause.*)

DAVID : London doesn't seem so very changed. I thought the damage would be worse.
QUEEN : I've only just moved back here. This room

and my bedroom are all right. There's a great deal to do elsewhere. Everywhere, in fact. Was Paris badly bombed?

DAVID : Not really.

QUEEN (*pause*) : You're very brown, David. It suits you.

DAVID : Five years in the Bahamas.

QUEEN : Yes, of course. There's a great deal of clearing up to do in the world, so we'll all be very busy. All my treasures to be got out of store. They were sent somewhere in Wales. I suppose you had to leave everything behind when you escaped to Spain?

(*David deliberately seizes his chance and firmly mentions his wife.*)

DAVID : Wallis and I have been very lucky and most of our things haven't been damaged or looted.

QUEEN (*avoiding the challenge*) : Didn't you write and say there were landmines in your garden?

DAVID : In the south of France at La Croe. Not in Paris.

QUEEN : Are they cleared away yet?

DAVID : Not yet. We can't live at La Croe until they are. We were wondering what to do. Our lease is up in 1947.

QUEEN : You could renew it, I suppose. It might be wise.

(*The hint is not taken.*)

DAVID : Living in France was only a temporary measure. We're not certain we want to stay there.

(*The 'We' is faintly emphasized.*)

QUEEN (*easily*): I'll ring for tea. We're still rationed.
I'm told we will be for some time. I hope these bells
are working. They weren't, but someone at last
came and put them right. (*She rises.*) You're dining
with Bertie and Elizabeth tonight?

DAVID: Yes.

QUEEN: I must prepare you, I think. He's older.
He's very tired. You'll find he looks it.

DAVID: I'm sure.

QUEEN: He never spared himself throughout the
war. Nor did she. I think they worked harder than
anyone else in the country. I really do. They're
very, very popular.

DAVID: I was sure they would be. I am so glad,
Mamma.

QUEEN: I was reading the Parliamentary reports
yesterday. The Colonial Secretary was very compli-
mentary about your administration in the Bahamas.
I was delighted. I was so proud of you.

(*The Queen is striving to be warm and friendly.*)

DAVID: Wallis worked tremendously hard to help
me. Any success I had is as much hers as mine.

QUEEN: Marina hopes you'll go and see her at
Coppins.

DAVID: How is she?

QUEEN: I think she's recovering at last from
Georgie's death. Her grief was overwhelming. I
miss him.

DAVID: So do I.

QUEEN: Eventually I had to tell her that in the
family we cannot have the luxury of a private
grief. Or of private joys for that matter.

(*Page enters.*)

Oh, good! The bell is working.

PAGE : Yes, ma'am.

QUEEN : Tea, please.

(*Page bows and goes.*)

DAVID : Nothing has changed, Mamma.

QUEEN : Certain values never change, no matter what happens. I believe we're going to have a welfare state. A revolution without the upheaval of one. I don't quite understand it all. Mr Attlee is very persuasive on the subject. I like him.

DAVID : I thought I'd go and look at the Fort.

QUEEN : It must be terribly overgrown. Why distress yourself needlessly?

DAVID : Wallis and I thought—if we weren't going to get another job—another governorship—we might settle there again.

QUEEN (*accepting the challenge this time*) : That would be a mistake.

DAVID : Wallis and I have been happily married for eight years. Does that mean nothing to you?

QUEEN : To know that you are happy means a great deal to me. But it doesn't alter the basic principle. Neither Elizabeth nor I can receive anyone who is divorced. She is the wife of the head of the church and I am his mother. As to the question of a job, what job? You refused Bermuda.

DAVID : Whose macabre idea was that? I cannot agree to being shunted from remote island to remote island. It's a wonder I wasn't offered St Helena.

QUEEN : Bermuda would have accepted you. Nowhere else will. You do not seem to understand at all how very upset the entire Empire was at your abdication. No self-governing dominion will accept you. Bertie cannot force you upon any of the colonies, since it is obvious you will take your wife with you. It means he would be suggesting as the Governor's consort a woman his wife and mother cannot receive.

DAVID: Wallis has done more work as the Governor's wife than any other Governor's wife. Did you know that she ran canteens, organized clinics. Any other woman would have received a decoration. She has received nothing, not even a letter of thanks. As the wife of a retiring Governor she's entitled to be received at Buckingham Palace. Because she's my wife she isn't.

QUEEN: Not because she's your wife. Because she's divorced.

DAVID: It must be lovely for you and Elizabeth to feel that you've never even made two mistakes. You base your views on Christian morals, but what is Christian about them? Christ forgave people. You don't.

QUEEN: Dear David, we are meeting after nearly nine years. Please, please do not let us quarrel now. (*Quickly.*) The reason for our separation grieves me beyond belief, but I couldn't change then and I can't change now. Let us accept the position. With mutual goodwill and tolerance it should be possible for us to meet without these upsets.

DAVID: Mutual goodwill? I've been full of goodwill for you all ever since I abdicated. But there's no return of goodwill to me or to my wife. Why did Bertie deny Wallis her true position as my wife? Why is she not acknowledged a Royal Highness?

QUEEN: The government advised against it.

DAVID: Yes, of course. They all hated me. Very convenient.

QUEEN : The Dominion governments advised against it. You had abdicated.

DAVID : I am a Royal Highness by right of birth. Bertie did not make me one and he knew it. My marriage is legal, consequently according to the laws of this country my wife must take my position. If I'm king she is queen. If I'm a prince she is a princess.

QUEEN : As monarch Bertie has to act within the wishes of the government.

DAVID : Not even a government can act illegally and Bertie's action in barring Wallis from her full position as my wife is illegal. I could fight a lawsuit—I am advised I have an excellent case. I could have refused to sell Bertie Balmoral and Sandringham just as I could settle in England in defiance of your wishes and the British public be subjected to the edifying spectacle of lawsuits within the royal family. Oh, don't worry, I won't. But when you are reflecting, as I'm sure you often do, on the innumerable virtues of your second son and his wife, you might just occasionally remember that your first son and his wife are not without virtue either.

(*Page enters with tea trolley.*)

QUEEN : Is the lift working?

PAGE : It's a bit hesitant still, ma'am.

QUEEN : Put the trolley by me. Thank you, John. David, will you bring up that table?

(*Page goes.*)

There's bread and butter. I don't quite know what this cake is made of.

DAVID : Thank you.

QUEEN : Will you be staying in London long?

DAVID : Only a week or so. We have to get our things in order in Paris. Wallis is very busy. There's a lot to do.

QUEEN : Of course. (*She pauses.*) You must both be busy.

(*David glances at her. She pours tea.*)

DAVID : Like you we've been living out of suitcases in other people's houses. We can't wait to get into our own home. Of course our Paris house, like La Croe, is only rented, but there's a house not far from it we want to buy.

QUEEN (*casually*) : Are Paris houses very expensive?

DAVID : No more so than in London, I should imagine. I haven't gone into it yet. It'll be very convenient living in Paris though. I can pop over and see you from time to time.

QUEEN : I'd like that, David, so much.

(*Page enters.*)

PAGE : A telephone call for his Royal Highness.

DAVID : Who is it?

PAGE : It's from Paris, sir. (*Goes*)

DAVID : That'll be Wallis. If you'll excuse me, Mamma—

QUEEN : Of course. (*He starts to go.*) Oh, David.

DAVID : Mamma?

QUEEN : I send a kind message to your wife.

DAVID : Thank you, Mamma. That's very good of you.

David goes out. The Queen, seated bolt upright
as always, pours herself another cup of tea. She
has unbent as far as she was able. As she calmly
sips her tea:

The curtain falls.

THE DAY
AFTER THE FAIR

A Play in Two Acts
by
FRANK HARVEY

(Based on a short story by Thomas Hardy
entitled *On the Western Circuit*)

On the Western Circuit, by Thomas Hardy, is
published by Macmillan & Co. Ltd., London

Frith Banbury and Jimmy Wax presented *The Day After the Fair*, by arrangement with Arthur Cantor, at the Lyric Theatre, London, on 4 October, 1972, with the following cast :

ARTHUR HARNHAM	*Duncan Lamont*
LETTY	*Avice Landon*
EDITH	*Deborah Kerr*
SARAH	*Jiggy Bhore*
ANNA	*Julia Foster*
CHARLES BRADFORD	*Paul Hastings*

Directed by Frith Banbury
Décor by Reece Pemberton
Lighting by Joe Davis

CHARACTERS

ARTHUR HARNHAM

LETTY

EDITH

SARAH

ANNA

CHARLES BRADFORD

ACT ONE

Scene 1

The play takes place at the turn of the century in the front room of The Brewer's House in a west-country cathedral city.

It is a still handsome room, although now its Georgian proportions have, to a large extent, become overlaid by Victorian drapes and an excess of furniture and bric-a-brac.

Above the study door, heavily curtained sash-windows look out at the market square; in the opposite wall, folding double doors reveal the entrance hall, part of the staircase and a further door leading to the dining-room. Prominently placed, is a portrait of Arthur Harnham's great-grandfather, founder of the brewery and the family fortune. Many of the other paintings in the room are of fine Clydesdale horses, and several silver cups and trophies which record their successes on the showground are displayed in a convenient Georgian niche.

Almost the only feminine note in the room is struck by a small but elegant Sheraton desk which stands between the windows and the study door.

When the curtain rises, it is a little before sunset on a cloudless May evening. In the market square outside, a fair is in full swing and gay, brazen music from a steam-organ is filling the room with sound. Miss Harnham (Letty) stands looking out at the square, a coffee-cup and saucer in her hands. Although nearing sixty, she is still a forceful, attractive woman. For a moment or two, her atten-

*tion is held by some distant activity in the square
and she moves her head from one position to
another to obtain the best view. Suddenly, as someone apparently passes quickly along the pavement
outside, she turns from the windows and crosses to
the coffee tray which stands on a small, occasional
table. On the way, she recovers a second coffee-cup,
returns both to the tray and waits expectantly.*

*Arthur Harnham lets himself in through the front
door and appears in the hallway. In his middle
fifties, red-faced and solidly built, he is the third
of his line to hold the chairmanship of Harnham's
Brewery. Still carrying his hat and a sheaf of papers,
he comes down to Letty excitedly. To be heard
above the racket from the the steam-organ, he is
obliged to raise his voice.*

ARTHUR : Well, we've put in a bid, Letty. We've
made them an offer.
LETTY (*pleased and excited*) : You haven't !
ARTHUR : Yes—and the board's behind it 100 per
cent. There wasn't a voice against me.
LETTY : Oh, Arthur ! How splendid !
ARTHUR : Mind you, it means a lot of—here, half-a-
minute, Letty, I can't compete with this.

(*He goes to shut the window, but Letty intercepts
him.*)

LETTY : I'll do it.

(*Arthur returns to the hallway and puts his hat and
papers on the hall table. Meanwhile, Letty crosses
to the window and closes the upper sashes, which
reduces the sound of the steam-organ to a tolerable
level.*)

ARTHUR : These wretched fair people, they seem determined to make more din every time they come here. High time something was done about it. It's becoming quite intolerable.

LETTY : There!

ARTHUR : That's better. No—what I was saying is, it means a lot of money—an awful lot of money, but it's the right decision, I'm certain.

LETTY : Oh, I'm sure it is, Arthur. You've been right so many times. The board knows that.

ARTHUR : What would you give to see Tremlett's face? He'll get it in the morning.

LETTY : I'd give more to have seen Father's. Oh, if only Father could have known this, Arthur.

ARTHUR : Yes. If someone had told him that in less than ten years Harnham's Brewery would be making a bid for Tremlett's he'd have thought they were barmy.

LETTY : It would have seemed utterly impossible to Father. But what will happen now, Arthur? Will there be a battle?

ARTHUR : Tremlett's getting old. He'll be ready to settle, but there's a son, you know, and I dare say the boy'll try to fight us as long as he can. But I don't care. That's my world and I know where I am in it. Ah, there you are, Edith. I was just telling Letty . . .

(*Edith Harnham, dressed to go out, has come down the stairs and now enters. Younger than Arthur, she is a gentle, attractive creature with a certain nervous vitality suggesting concealed tension.*)

EDITH : I'm sorry, Arthur. I heard you come in, but I'm just slipping over to the fair for a moment.

ARTHUR (*incredulous*): To the *fair*? What on earth for?

EDITH: To look for Anna.

ARTHUR: Anna? Oh, you mean the *new* girl. What's she doing over at the fair at this hour of the day?

EDITH: She had permission, but she should have been back long before this. I'm very cross with her.

LETTY: Arthur's had a most successful meeting, Edith.

EDITH: Have you, Arthur? Well, I won't stop now. You must tell me about it when I come in. I shan't be many minutes. It's really too bad of Anna.

(*Edith goes off and the front door is heard to close behind her.*)

ARTHUR: Hasn't this girl any work to do? The other servants aren't allowed to go gallivanting off whenever the fancy takes them.

LETTY: The other servants aren't quite—

ARTHUR: Well? Aren't quite what?

LETTY: Quite in Anna's position, I suppose.

ARTHUR: Either the girl's a servant or she's not. And if she's not, then what the devil's she doing here?

LETTY: Edith wanted her here. She was interested in the child, she said, and was anxious to help her.

ARTHUR: Oh? Help her do what?

LETTY: Why, better herself, I suppose you'd call it. It's easily understood when you consider both their families lived in that same village for so long. I gather Edith was friendly with the elder girl when Anna was just a toddler.

ARTHUR: That's all very well among village kids, but one doesn't usually continue with that sort of friendship in adult life, Letty.

100

LETTY: Edith says the child needs her, but it's quite clear to me that it's the other way round.

ARTHUR: What do you mean?

LETTY: Surely it's Edith who needs something to occupy *her*.

ARTHUR: After three years of marriage, I'd have thought she'd have found that among our own circle without having to cultivate the peasantry. (*With sudden irritation.*) Who said the girl could go off to the fair in the first place? Did you?

LETTY: I told her she couldn't go. So she went to Edith and in the end, of course, Edith said she could—just for twenty minutes. But that was over an hour ago.

ARTHUR: Do you mean that Edith gave her permission knowing that you'd already refused it?

LETTY (*avoiding a direct answer*): The trouble is, having let one go, now they all want to go, you see.

ARTHUR: That was very wrong of Edith, Letty, and I shall make a point of telling her so.

LETTY: But she's every right as your wife to expect to be mistress in her own house.

ARTHUR: Well, and so she is, isn't she?

LETTY: How can she be if she's not allowed the slightest responsibility in the running of it?

ARTHUR: Because that's something you've been doing since Mother died. Everything here runs like a clock.

LETTY: There's no need to butter me up. I'm not obliged to stay here. Edith's an immensely capable person, Arthur. You'd only to see the way she managed in that frightful old vicarage—practically on a shoe-string. And then, when her father was so ill, she more or less ran the entire parish as well.

ARTHUR (*growing exasperated*): But damn it all,

Letty, it was agreed right at the outset, wasn't it? Edith was delighted for you to stay and carry on. She agreed, didn't she? You both did.

LETTY: I only agreed then because I naturally expected there'd be babies coming along and that Edith would have her hands full. But that hasn't happened, has it?

ARTHUR (*a sore point*): No.

LETTY: And the result is, she simply hasn't enough to *do*, Arthur.

ARTHUR: Well, to me it's always seemed an ideal arrangement.

LETTY: Because you don't see further than the end of your nose. You never did.

(*Sarah, one of the housemaids, has appeared in the hall.*)

Yes, Sarah? What is it?

SARAH: Cook says shall she dish up for the master now, ma'am?

ARTHUR: Just five minutes, tell her. (*To Letty as he goes.*) You haven't waited, I hope?

LETTY: No—you did *say* you'd be late, Arthur.

(*Arthur goes off up the stairs.*)

SARAH: The water's boiling hot again in the cylinder, ma'am. I come out of the master's room and went into madam's to turn the bed down when it started up that horrible shaking noise. So down the back stairs I goes as fast as I could and shoved all the dampers in quick. Only I mean they keep saying about these boilers blowing up all over the place, don't they, ma'am?

LETTY: The fact is, Cook's never understood that old range. She pretends she does, but she doesn't.

(There is the sound of the front door opening and closing as Edith returns. Pulling off her gloves, she moves at once to the glass over her desk and unpins her hat, which, together with her bag and gloves, she hands to Sarah.)

EDITH : There! I wasn't long, was I? Was Arthur cross with me for going out?

LETTY : Well, of course not, Edith.

EDITH *(to Sarah)*: When Anna comes back, and she'll be in presently, you're to tell her I want to see her at once.

SARAH : Yes, ma'am.

EDITH : Here. And she's to come just as she is.

SARAH : Yes, ma'am. *(She goes out with Edith's things and off up the stairs.)*

LETTY : So you were able to find her?

EDITH : I guessed where she'd be, of course. The great attraction is this new steam roundabout, and I must say it's a most gorgeous sight, Letty. The horses are in threes, you know, and they really seem to actually gallop. As they go whirling round, each horse in turn rises up into the air and then sinks down again in the most graceful manner you could ever imagine. And all the colours are so new and bright—and of course everything's reflected a hundred times over in great mirrors. It's all done by steam. The whole effect is quite exhilarating. I found it very difficult to stand there and look cross.

LETTY : And was Anna . . . ?

EDITH : Anna was in paradise. I could tell from the look on her face. And the funny thing was, Letty, as I watched her perched up on the back of this great white horse, I suddenly realized that all the excitement and the strange sensations of motion, they were mine just as much as they were

103

Anna's. It was as if I'd been sitting up there beside her. Quite odd.

LETTY: But what excuse had she? Was she so carried away that she lost all sense of time?

EDITH: Not entirely. There was a young man involved.

LETTY: A young man? Really?

(Arthur has come briskly down the stairs and picked up the sheaf of papers from the hall table. He now enters.)

ARTHUR *(entering)*: Do you remember, Letty, the first time *we* ever went to the fair?

LETTY: Oh, dear me! That's nearly fifty years ago.

ARTHUR: Father took us, and I wasn't allowed to let go of his hand. That's how old *I* was.

LETTY: Yes—but everything was so different—no roundabouts or things of that sort. There were waxworks, I remember, and a peep-show and toys and gingerbread . . .

ARTHUR: And the quack-doctors. Wasn't there some fellow who reckoned to cure the cataract? They said he had his own special way of licking round a person's eyeball and his tongue was as rough as a tom-cat's.

EDITH: Arthur, how horrible!

ARTHUR: It worked for some of them—came clean away like the skin off a glass of hot milk. But what interested Father were the horses, of course. That was the real business of the fair then—horses. I was just saying to Letty, how Father would have enjoyed himself if he'd been at the meeting today.

LETTY: Oh, wouldn't he!

ARTHUR *(to Edith)*: You see, in Father's time, Tremlett's were on top—right on top. And didn't they let us know it? Well, now it's a different story.

LETTY: How you've worked, Arthur!

ARTHUR: It's never seemed like work to me. After all, they still say brewing's an art, don't they, despite all these clever fellers trying to turn it into a science. Mind you, they never will—not until they find out the secret of life itself, because that's what it's all about. There—on the floor of the maltings—it *is* life. And never mind what these chemists *say*, they can't tell you *how* it works and they can't tell you *why* it works.

LETTY: But you must feel a great sense of achievement, Arthur.

ARTHUR: Well—yes. These are early days, I know, but I must say it does look now as if the merger will go through.

EDITH (*tentatively*): That *is* good news, isn't it, Arthur?

ARTHUR: What? It certainly is. Damned good news.

EDITH: Well—then—I'm delighted for you.

ARTHUR: It'll make Harnham's the biggest brewery in the county. Isn't that something to be pleased about?

EDITH: I'm sure it is. I only wish I didn't find business affairs so—so incomprehensible.

ARTHUR: My dear girl, business is simply another word for common sense. You have to know your job, of course, and part of my job is to buy barley —at the right price. That's all it is.

(*Sarah has appeared in the hall.*)

LETTY: Yes, Sarah?

SARAH: The master's soup's on the table, ma'am.

ARTHUR: I'm coming, I'm coming.

SARAH : Only Cook's bursting herself to get done and get out, sir.

(*Arthur goes off towards the dining-room, followed by Sarah.*)

ARTHUR (*as he goes*) : I suppose it's the fair, eh? We all want to go to the fair, do we?

EDITH : Oh, dear! How difficult it is to say the right thing.

LETTY : You make it difficult, Edith. Harnham's has always been a family concern, and I'm sure all Arthur wants is that you should feel you're a part of it.

EDITH : I try to, Letty, I do try.

LETTY (*after a disapproving pause*) : You were telling me about Anna and a young man . . .

EDITH : That girl should certainly have come in by now. And one of the first things I mean to discover is just how they got to know each other.

LETTY : But surely young people of that class, enjoying themselves at the fair, don't wait on formal introductions.

EDITH : But you don't understand, Letty. This young man is not one of our local hobbledehoys.

LETTY : Oh?

EDITH : No, no. By no means. He's—well—quite . . .

LETTY : A gentleman?

EDITH : Oh, certainly that. And young, very young —but nice.

LETTY : You met him, then?

EDITH : What happened was that Anna's horse finally stopped quite near me, and as she climbed down, I said to her, 'How can you be such a wild girl, Anna? You know you were only to have twenty minutes.'

106

LETTY : And what did she say?

EDITH : She looked completely blank. I might have been someone from another world. Then this young man came from behind me and said, 'Please, don't blame her. It's entirely my fault. She looked so delightful on the horse that I persuaded her to go round again.'

LETTY : Anna wouldn't need much persuading.

EDITH : 'I assure you,' he said, 'she's been quite safe.' Well, what could I say?

LETTY : What did you say?

EDITH : I said, 'In that case, I'll leave her in your hands, but I expect her back directly'. What the young man must have thought of me, I daren't think.

LETTY : How do you mean?

EDITH : Well, I was cross. I spoke so sharply.

LETTY : But of course you did. And quite rightly so.

EDITH : I must have made a thoroughly disagreeable impression on him.

LETTY : I really don't think that need worry *you*, Edith.

EDITH : No—anyway—I'm sure she *will* be back directly.

ANNA : I am back, ma'am.

(*Both women turn quickly to find Anna, dressed in her best clothes and wearing hat and gloves, standing in the hall. She is a radiant eighteen.*)

EDITH : Come here, Anna. Why, you look quite flushed.

ANNA : I expect it was the horses, ma'am. You never felt nothing like it. (*She has advanced into the room, but remains standing.*)

107

EDITH (*correcting her*): You never felt *anything* like it.

ANNA: You never felt anything like it.

EDITH: That's better.

LETTY: Well, I'll just see that Arthur's got everything. He'll want some fresh coffee making. (*She picks up the coffee tray and goes off with it towards the dining-room.*)

EDITH: You may sit down, Anna.

ANNA (*sitting*): Thank you, ma'am.

EDITH: I began to be quite anxious. I'm responsible for you now, Anna, and if you should come to any harm I should never forgive myself. You do *see*, don't you?

ANNA: I see *that*, ma'am. But what I don't see, ma'am, is what harm could come to me at the fair where everyone's happy enjoying themselves.

EDITH: That's because you're too young yet to realize what lies under the surface of things. Tell me, that young man—he was a stranger until tonight?

ANNA: Yes, ma'am.

EDITH: Yet I suppose you told him your name and everything about yourself?

ANNA: He asked me.

EDITH: But he didn't tell you his, I warrant.

ANNA (*excitedly*): Yes, he did, ma'am. He did.

EDITH: Oh? Then what is it?

ANNA: It's Charles Bradford, ma'am, and he's down from London and he's asked me if he can see me again, ma'am.

EDITH: When?

ANNA: Tomorrow, ma'am.

EDITH: Yes—well, that is something we shall have to go into. How much have you told him—about yourself, I mean? About your situation?

ANNA : I told him about the village, ma'am, and how it was you sent for me to come here when my auntie died. And I told him you were the kindest lady I ever knew and the one true friend I had in all the world.

EDITH : It's really of no concern to anyone, Anna, but how did you come to strike up an acquaintance with this Mr—Bradford, is it—in the first place?

ANNA : I never did such a thing, ma'am. It was him who struck up with me. Wherever the horses stopped, he was always there waiting.

EDITH : And you allowed him to pay for you to go on again?

ANNA : Well, it was just—it was such a lovely ride, ma'am.

EDITH : Yes, yes, I dare say, but to be obliged to a stranger, Anna . . .

ANNA : Oh, I couldn't call him a stranger, not now, ma'am.

EDITH : Did he walk with you from the Square as far as the house?

ANNA : He asked to see me home.

EDITH : He took your arm?

ANNA : Crossing over the cobbles, yes, ma'am.

EDITH : And then—when he said good night—did he—did he make other advances?

ANNA : Advances, ma'am?

EDITH : Did he try to kiss you, child?

ANNA : Well—he said if I didn't *mind* . . .

EDITH : And you?

ANNA : He said it wouldn't do me no harm, and . . .

EDITH : It wouldn't do me *any* harm.

ANNA : It wouldn't do me any harm, he said, and him a great deal of good.

EDITH : And so you allowed him to kiss you, Anna?

ANNA : Well—yes.

EDITH : On the mouth?

ANNA (*innocently*) : Oh, yes. It was a real, proper kiss, ma'am.

EDITH : A young man you'd only just set eyes on?

ANNA : Well, *he'd* only just set eyes on *me*. Besides, his manners and the way he spoke, you could tell at once he wasn't just anybody. (*Pause.*) Couldn't you, ma'am?

EDITH (*taken aback*) : I—he seems quite respectable, I must admit, but—

ANNA : Did he smile at you, ma'am.

EDITH : He seems to have a certain charm, undoubtedly, but—

ANNA : And his eyes—did you look into his eyes, ma'am?

EDITH : I would agree his eyes are very pleasing, but do you seriously imagine a country-bred girl like you, Anna, who never lived in a town until two months ago, would be sharp enough to capture a young Londoner like him?

ANNA : I didn't try to capture him, ma'am. I didn't do anything. Anyhow, he likes country girls better than town girls. He told me so.

EDITH : You'd hardly expect him to tell you otherwise, would you?

ANNA : But he truly meant it, ma'am. You could see. (*Pleading.*) Oh, ma'am! He has to go back to London the day after tomorrow.

EDITH : Then isn't it rather foolish to try to further an acquaintance which must end so soon in any case?

ANNA : But it won't, ma'am, for he's quite often obliged to be down in these parts.

EDITH : Oh? Has he friends or relatives hereabouts?

ANNA : He comes on business, I think.

EDITH : What kind of business?

110

ANNA : I don't know, ma'am. I didn't ask him that. But I did say tomorrow was my regular afternoon off, ma'am, and I said you were always so kind I was sure it would be all right.

EDITH : I *try* to be kind, Anna, of course. We all try to be *kind*. But the important thing is to be sure we do what is best.

ANNA : Who for, ma'am?

EDITH : Why, for everybody, of course.

(*Letty enters with a tray bearing a coffee-pot and a single cup and saucer. These she sets down. Anna rises uneasily.*)

ANNA : Shall I—?

LETTY : It's all right, Anna. (*To Edith.*) Arthur says he'll have his coffee in here, Edith.

EDITH : Oh. Well, then, off you go, Anna.

ANNA : But, ma'am, you haven't said yet about tomorrow.

EDITH : Tomorrow, Anna, the fair will be gone and all the excitement with it. It'll be just another ordinary day. Now, don't you think the sensible thing would be to put this Mr Bradford out of your head?

ANNA : But I couldn't, ma'am. And I shouldn't want to either. Oh, no, I couldn't do that.

EDITH : Well, of course, you could. It was no more than a chance encounter and if I hadn't allowed you to go across to the fair it would never have happened, would it?

ANNA : But it has happened, ma'am. And somehow it's made everything seem—different. Oh, please, ma'am, please!

EDITH : Anna, I am not going to be stampeded into making a foolish decision. I want you to be happy

here, of course I do, but also it would be very
wrong of me to allow you to rush headlong into
a situation which could well prove, I won't say
disastrous, but certainly highly unsatisfactory. You
do *see*, don't you?

ANNA: I see some of it, ma'am. But what I don't
see is why it should turn out—unsatisfactory.

EDITH: That's because you let your heart run away
with your head, you silly girl. No, off you go, and
by the morning I shall have made up my mind
one way or the other.

(*Letty has unfastened the tantalus. She hands one
of the decanters to Anna.*)

LETTY: Take Mr Harnham the brandy, Anna.

ANNA: Yes, ma'am. (*She takes the decanter from
Letty and is about to move off when she suddenly
turns to face Edith.*) One thing, anyhow—Mr
Charles Bradford's a born and bred gentleman to
his finger-tips. That I can say.

EDITH (*coldly*): Good night, Anna.

(*Anna is about to reply, thinks better of it, turns
and goes off into the dining-room.*)

LETTY: That man wants to see her again, I gather?

EDITH: Poor Anna! Oh, dear! What the young
have to go through. I know exactly how she feels,
Letty—exactly.

LETTY (*with surprise*): *Do* you, Edith?

EDITH: Oh, I went through it all when I was her
age, and I expect you did, too. One was flattered
even to be noticed.

LETTY: So Anna's not to see him again?

EDITH: I should love to have said 'yes' to the child,

Letty, for nobody wants to nip a young affection in the bud, do they? But the circumstances are so —so unusual. Can you imagine what possible attraction a simple girl like Anna would have for a young man-of-the-world such as he?

LETTY (*with a laugh*): Really, Edith! That's not a difficult question to answer surely.

(*Arthur enters carrying a brandy in a goblet. Letty pours out his coffee.*)

ARTHUR: What's going on, Edith, what's the trouble?

EDITH: How do you mean, Arthur?

ARTHUR: I gather you've told that girl she's not to be allowed to see her young man tomorrow. Is that right? On her afternoon off?

EDITH: He's not her young man, Arthur.

ARTHUR: Well, she thinks he is—she was blubbing her eyes out.

EDITH: They only met for the first time this evening.

ARTHUR: Still, I suppose everybody has to make a start at some point, haven't they?

EDITH: Anna's been rather tiresome because, in fact, I haven't said one thing or the other.

ARTHUR: Then she must have got hold of the wrong end of the stick. Anyhow, she's all right now, as right as rain and gone up to bed smiling. (*He moves to the niche and from one of the lower shelves takes a Halma board on which a half-finished game is already set out.*) Here we are, that's right. We've still last night's game to finish, haven't we? And it was your turn, Edith, when we left off. (*He puts the board down on a low table in front*

113

of Edith.) There! Take your time, now. I can see a splendid move waiting for you. Don't miss it.

(*As Arthur moves away to select a cigar from a small cabinet, Sarah appears in the hallway carrying a lighted oil-lamp which she sets down on the hall table and then goes off.*)

EDITH : When you say Anna's right as rain now, Arthur, what do you mean exactly?

ARTHUR : Oh, I told her not to worry, of course.

EDITH : About what?

ARTHUR : About tomorrow. I told her it would be all right.

EDITH : Do you mean you told her she could see this man again?

ARTHUR : Certainly. After all, how she likes to spend her afternoons off is her affair, isn't it?

EDITH : But Arthur, I feel a personal responsibility for this girl.

ARTHUR : Not for her private life. That's no concern of ours.

EDITH : It would be—if she should get into trouble.

ARTHUR : For God's sake, Edith! Anna's a servant-girl—nothing more. And we've had a great many in and out of this house in the last twenty years. They know damn well that if they're unlucky enough to get themselves lumbered, then out they go. In any case, the fellows either pay up or marry 'em in the end.

EDITH : Not always.

ARTHUR : Anyhow, let's get on with our game.

EDITH : No, Arthur. If you don't mind, I won't play tonight, I—I don't feel I could concentrate. Good night, Letty.

LETTY : Oh—good night, Edith.

(Edith goes off up the stairs. There is a short silence during which Arthur, inwardly seething, lights his cigar. At the same time, he has his eye on Letty, watching for her reaction, but she continues with her needlework, refusing to catch his eye.)

ARTHUR : Well? I did the wrong thing, I suppose?
LETTY : Unless you intended to upset her, Arthur.
ARTHUR : Just because I told the girl she can please herself what she does on her afternoons off—what is there upsetting about that?
LETTY : Arthur, please. Don't go on about it. There's nothing to be gained, is there? Here— come along—I'll play Edith's corner for her.
ARTHUR : All right.

(Letty lays aside her needlework and sits at the Halma board.)

It's your move.

(Letty at once moves a piece. There is a pause as both study the board, but Arthur is not thinking of the game.)

All the same, I sometimes wonder, if I hadn't come along when I did, what would have become of Edith.
LETTY : Oh, I wouldn't have said you were the only pebble on the beach.
ARTHUR : They hadn't a penny, you know, not a penny.
LETTY : If you hadn't come along the answer's quite simple. She'd have married someone else.
ARTHUR : At her age? With that old father to nurse? Besides, in that God-forsaken village she hardly

115

saw a new face from one year's end to another. If I hadn't driven over that day to look at a few acres of barley . . .

LETTY: It's not a bit of good talking to me like that, Arthur, because I *know*. From the first moment you set eyes on her, it was you who made the running. Think of all the times you had me chasing up mutual friends—arranging things so that the pair of you would meet.

ARTHUR (*moving a piece on the board*.): Yes, you played the match-maker rather well.

LETTY: I simply tried to be helpful. To my mind, you've been extremely lucky. You're disappointed, of course, at not having a son, but you've only been married three years—Edith's still young enough. And how hard she's tried to make a success of everything.

ARTHUR: And haven't I? She's a comfortable home here, a very generous allowance. She's free to come and go as she likes, she shares our friends—all in all, she enjoys a most enviable existence. What more can she want?

LETTY: Shall I tell you, Arthur. She wants some of the things that I wanted when I was her age and never had.

ARTHUR: How do you mean? You'd only to ask and you could have had anything you wanted.

LETTY: No—not the things that matter because it was always taken for granted that I should stay at home and keep house.

ARTHUR: That was something you chose to do, Letty.

LETTY: Now—I sometimes feel I was never young —ever. But Edith *is*, Arthur, don't you see?

ARTHUR: Edith gets a damn sight more out of life *here* than she ever did in that village.

LETTY: You don't understand. She was needed there, Arthur, and what's more she could see that she was.

(*Sarah enters with a second lighted oil-lamp which she places in its customary position in the room and then moves to the windows to draw the curtains. For a moment she stands agape, captivated by the bright lights of the fair, until Arthur's voice brings her back to earth.*)

ARTHUR: It's your move.

(*With a shrug, Letty resumes her game as Sarah begins to untie the curtains.*)

Curtain

Scene 2

A sunny morning ten days later. The curtain rises as Sarah, pursued by Anna, darts into the room from the hall with a letter in her hand. To avoid surrendering it, she jumps up on to the seat of a chair, holding the letter high above her head while Anna vainly tries to reach for it. Both girls are wearing their morning print dresses and their caps and aprons. Brooms and a box of cleaning-gear are visible in the hall.

SARAH: Who's it from? Who's it from?
ANNA: Oh, Sarah! Give it me! Give it me!
SARAH: Who's it from? Who's it from?
ANNA: How can I tell you who it's from till I read

it, you stupid. Oh, do give it to me—*please*, Sarah.

(*With difficulty, because of Anna's clutching hands, Sarah reads out the superscription.*)

SARAH: 'Miss Anna Dunsford, at The Brewer's House, Market Square, Salisbury, Wiltshire.' I know who it's from!

ANNA: You do not.

SARAH: Yes, I do. Posted in London, it's from that feller.

ANNA: What feller.

SARAH: *What* feller? My! Aren't you cool? Why the feller at the fair, of course, what walked you out the earthworks Old Sarum way.

ANNA: It's not him, Sarah, no—truly it isn't. Oh, give it me. Go on, give it me.

SARAH (*teasing*): I don't suppose you ever had a letter from a feller before, did you?

ANNA: No—because I never had a feller before, that's why.

SARAH: You wait till you've been walking out as long as me and Bertie have.

(*Letty enters. She is dressed for a routine visit to the local shops and carries a basket.*)

LETTY: Sarah! Come down off the furniture. What *are* you doing?

(*Sarah quickly jumps down from the chair and thrusts the letter into Anna's hands.*)

SARAH: Nothing, ma'am.
LETTY: Nothing?
SARAH: No, ma'am.

118

LETTY : Well, you can't do much less than nothing, can you? The point is you should be at your work at this time of the morning, not larking about. What is it you have there, Anna?

ANNA : It's a letter, ma'am.

LETTY : I can see it's a letter, you silly girl. But who's it for?

ANNA : It's for me, ma'am.

LETTY : Oh? Let me look.

(*Reluctantly, Anna holds out the envelope so that Letty is able to read the face of it.*)

Hmm! So it is. Well? Aren't you going to open it?

ANNA : I don't want to open it, not yet, ma'am, if you'll excuse me. (*She stuffs the letter into the front of her dress beneath her apron.*) I just want to keep it a bit.

LETTY : You funny girl! (*To Sarah.*) Don't stand there with your mouth open, child. Now, get along, both of you. You should be quite finished downstairs by this time.

SARAH : So we are, ma'am. Come on, Anna.

(*Sarah goes off into the hallway, picks up the box of cleaning-gear and, followed by Anna with brooms and dusters, is about to climb the stairs as Edith starts to descend. Both girls wait side by side at the foot of the stairs until their mistress passes them.*)

EDITH : Good morning, Sarah—Anna.

SARAH } (*together, bobbing*): Good morning,
ANNA } ma'am.

(*Edith comes down to Letty, two lending-library books in her hand as the two girls hurry off up the*

119

stairs. She gives the books to Letty, who puts them into her shopping-basket.)

EDITH : If you can catch Miss Stevens, she knows what I like. (*Crossing to her desk.*) Oh—and I've a small list here for you, Letty—just a few odds and ends I need from Bowden's, if you wouldn't mind. And Arthur specially asked me to remind you to speak about the bacon. He said it was dreadfully salt again this morning.

LETTY : I didn't find it salty in the least. I suspect Arthur's just being rather faddy.

EDITH : He was so grumpy at breakfast, I began to wonder if it was something I'd said or done.

LETTY : I know exactly what it is. Yesterday, you see, Tremlett's turned down the offer from our firm. Didn't he tell you?

EDITH : No.

LETTY : Oh! Well, of course, he doesn't want you to have the worry.

EDITH : Somehow he makes me feel so inadequate.

LETTY : My dear Edith, Arthur thinks the world of you. He's always telling me so.

EDITH : He doesn't tell me.

LETTY : Ah, but he wouldn't. That's not his way. (*She picks up her basket.*) Now, there's nothing else, is there? I may be some little time because I have to visit two of our old work-people. There's one old dear of ninety-seven who still talks about Waterloo as if it were yesterday.

EDITH : Oh, then you must let me give you something, Letty. (*She open one of the drawers of the desk, takes out a small cash-box and from it a silver coin.*)

LETTY : Oh, there's really no need, Edith.

EDITH : But I'd like to. I insist. There ! Now, you

buy them each a box of those nice meat cubes.

LETTY (*accepting the money*): Well, thank you, Edith. They *will* appreciate it. It *is* so kind of you.

EDITH: Oh, nonsense! The truth is one can do so little.

LETTY: It won't seem so to them, Edith. That's why the poor are so useful. One can always help them without being unduly extravagant.

(*As Letty goes off towards the front door, Edith sits at her desk and prepares to attend to her correspondence. At the same time Anna appears on the stairs where she pauses until the front door has closed behind Letty. She then comes quickly down and into the room. For a moment Edith remains unaware of her presence.*)

ANNA: Oh, ma'am.

EDITH (*turning in her chair*): Yes, Anna? What is it?

ANNA (*fumbling in her dress*): I've had a letter come, ma'am.

EDITH: Well?

ANNA (*producing the now-opened envelope*): The trouble is—I can't read a single word in it.

EDITH: But of course you can. You've been getting on so well with your reading.

ANNA: But I can't, ma'am. You see, it's all in handwriting.

EDITH: Then you'd better ask Cook to read it to you when she has time.

ANNA: But this is from somebody—I don't want just anyone to read it, ma'am.

EDITH (*suddenly curious*): Is it from that young man?

ANNA: I think so, ma'am.

121

EDITH : Why, then I'll read it to you, child. You needn't worry, I shan't say a word to anyone.

(*Reluctantly, Anna takes the letter from its envelope and hands it to Edith.*)

ANNA (*fearfully*) : Oh, ma'am!
EDITH : What is it?
ANNA : I think it's you knowing, ma'am—things so —so private.
EDITH (*offering to return the letter*) : Well, if you feel that way about it then I *shan't* read it.
ANNA (*desperately*) : But I must know what he says, ma'am.
EDITH : You can't have it both ways, Anna, if you think it'll make you feel shy and bashful then go and stare out of the window while I read it out to you.
ANNA : Yes, ma'am. (*She moves upstage of Edith and faces the window.*)
EDITH (*unfolding the letter*) : Are you quite ready?
ANNA (*trembling*) : Yes, ma'am.

(*Edith reads the letter in a flat, hard, matter-of-fact voice.*)

EDITH (*reading*) : 174, Gray's Inn Road, London, Tuesday. Dearest, why—oh, why, have you not written? Did we not agree that you were to write first? Just imagine—for ten nights now I have lain awake trying to recapture the exact look of your sweet face as I first saw it that evening at the fair, sometimes succeeding, sometimes not, but always praying that tomorrow will bring me word from you until, as you see, I can wait no longer. I do so need you to tell me that what I believe to exist between us is true and not the wild imagining of a mind bewitched. To love vainly can be a torment, but to love and to know that one is loved in return is to breathe the very air of heaven. Do, therefore, dearest, write as soon as you are able and restore me to a more tolerable state of mind. For ever, C.B.

(*There is a pause. Edith folds up the letter.*)

ANNA (*turning from the window*): Thank you, ma'am.

EDITH: Were you quite able to follow it all?

ANNA (*doubtfully*): Yes, I think so, ma'am. It doesn't really say a lot, does it? (*More cheerfully.*) But it's a lovely letter, though.

EDITH (*dryly*): I should call it a remarkable letter. Considering that you've met only twice before, it could scarcely go much further.

ANNA: What I meant was, it doesn't say when he's next coming down this way, or if we're ever going to see each other again, or—or anything.

EDITH: Well, that'll be something for you to write about when you come to reply.

ANNA (*anxiously*): And you'll do that for me, ma'am, won't you?

EDITH: I?

ANNA: Please, ma'am, because I couldn't bear him to think I'm not able to do it myself. I'd sink into the earth with shame if he knew that.

EDITH: But you know all your letters now, Anna. At least, you can print them.

ANNA: That's not the same, ma'am. I mean, it's not real writing, is it? And whatever would he think of me?

EDITH: As it happens I was looking through your

123

copybook only yesterday. (*She takes a school copybook from the drawer of the desk.*) I have it here. See what a long way you've come since we first did these hooks and hangers together, haven't you?

ANNA : Yes, ma'am, but—

EDITH (*turning the pages*) : And there ! You see, you can write quite well when you put your mind to it. And here—look—you've written whole words together. (*Reading.*) 'Patience and Perseverance brought the snail to Jerusalem.'

ANNA : That's only copying, ma'am. I couldn't do it, not without something to go by. Anyway, it just looks like it was done by some little maid at school. I'm grown up.

EDITH : You're still only a girl, Anna.

ANNA : I'm a woman, ma'am—now.

(*There is a pause. Edith turns in her chair to look Anna full in the face. Anna boldly returns the stare. Edith drops her eyes and unfolds again the letter which is still in her hand.*)

EDITH : There was something in the letter I didn't quite— (*Reading.*) 'I do so need you to tell me that what I believe to exist between us is true . . .' 'What I believe to exist between us . . .' What does he believe? What do you take that to mean, Anna?

ANNA : It just means he believes we love each other, ma'am.

EDITH : And do *you* believe that?

ANNA : Yes, ma'am.

(*There is a pause. Edith rises from the desk and moves away from the desk, the letter still in her hand. Anna watches her anxiously.*)

124

EDITH : If I'm to help you with your letter, Anna
—and I say *if* because I'm not at all sure it's the
right and proper thing to do—but if I am to help
you, then I must know—certain things. You do see
that, don't you?

ANNA : Yes, ma'am.

EDITH : Now—on the day after the fair, you had
the afternoon off and this young man, this Mr
Bradford, he hired a fly, didn't he, to drive you
both out to the edge of the plain.

ANNA : To look at the old earthworks.

EDITH (*dryly*) : Yes—well, I don't suppose your
afternoon was spent discussing archaeology.

ANNA : We found ourselves a nice grassy little
hollow in the sun and out of the way of the wind.
And there we stopped till it was time for me to be
getting back.

EDITH (*uneasily*) : I see. And you—you talked, I
suppose.

ANNA : Some of the time, ma'am.

EDITH : About your future? I mean—did you come
to any sort of understanding?

ANNA : Not the sort you could put into words,
ma'am. Most of the time we just lay there.

EDITH (*sharply*) : Kissing and cuddling? (*Anna does
not answer.*) You remember that Betsy Hartnell in
the village and the nasty things they used to say
about *her*?

ANNA : I do, ma'am. But a girl can sometimes be
that hungry she don't always wait for the parson
to say grace. Besides, there was plenty of girls went
on worse than Betsy Hartnell and did better. And
they always say you're unlucky to get caught first
time, don't they, ma'am?

EDITH (*disturbed*) : Do they? I don't know, Anna.
I don't know what they say. But one thing's quite

clear—you've surrendered yourself body and soul to a man of whom you know nothing and after only the briefest acquaintance.

ANNA : I couldn't have done no other, ma'am. It would have gone against nature.

EDITH : But to commit the whole of your future happiness to the outcome of what may be only a passing attachment—Oh, Anna!

ANNA : If it was only that, he'd no need to write, had he?

EDITH : Unless it was just—no. No, I won't say it.

ANNA : What, ma'am? You can say.

EDITH : I was going to say, unless it was just curiosity.

ANNA : Oh, no! No, ma'am. I'm sure.

EDITH : He lives in London, remember, a hundred miles from here, Anna, in a gay society—theatres, concerts, dinner-parties—and there he has his friends, his occupation and, I dare say, countless other distractions as well. You may not see him again for weeks on end. Do you imagine his interest in you is going to survive all that?

ANNA (*agitated*) : Oh, I feel so, ma'am. It must do. And if you help me then it surely will. You're so good and kind, ma'am, and you know just how to put things in a nice way—a way that'll please him. I have the feelings, ma'am, but it's the saying of them when it comes to finding the words. Please, ma'am . . .

EDITH : Wait now, Anna. Just let us consider. To ignore the letter, if you could bring yourself to do such a thing, would make you utterly miserable, wouldn't it?

ANNA : Yes, it would so, ma'am.

EDITH : On the other hand, I agree that for me to leave you to write on your own as best you can might not, at this stage, produce the happiest result.

ANNA : No, it would not, ma'am.

EDITH : So I really have no alternative, have I? Very well then, Anna. I'll try to help you as far as I can.

ANNA (*fervently*) : Oh, thank you, ma'am. And shall we write it now while Miss Harnham's still out at the shop?

EDITH : But what about your duties, Anna? What are they this morning?

ANNA : Only the front bedroom, ma'am, sweeping and dusting. It had its proper turn-out yesterday and Sarah won't mind—she's nearly done already.

EDITH (*returning to her desk*) : But have you had time to think out just what you want to say?

ANNA : Oh, I know what to say, ma'am, if only you'll put it for me.

EDITH (*sitting at her desk*) : Well, then let us try. It'd be sensible I think, not to use my writing-paper. We'll use this plain scribbling-block which is just the sort of thing you might have yourself. Now—(*she takes up a pen*)—the address and the date, of course. What do you call your Mr Bradford?

ANNA : Charles, ma'am.

EDITH : Charles, I see. Then shall we begin 'My dear Charles' or 'Dearest Charles' or just simply 'Dear Charles'?

ANNA : I don't like none of those, ma'am.

EDITH (*needled*) : I don't like *any* of those, you should say.

ANNA : I don't like any of those. You see, what I want is for him to feel that I'm actually there right close beside him, ma'am.

EDITH (*coldly*) : Then what do you suggest?
ANNA : I'd like to start off 'To my own true love, my very dearest, most precious sweetheart'.

(*Edith puts down her pen.*)

EDITH : No, no, Anna. That is *not* the way to begin a letter.
ANNA : Why isn't it, ma'am?
EDITH : Because it's both so wildly extravagant and so clumsy. Letter-writing, you see, is hung about with certain conventions, which simply must be observed, and I'm sure Mr Bradford would expect you to have some knowledge of them however slight. The aim is to be simple, truthful and unaffected. Extravagance of any kind is always vulgar. You see that, don't you?
ANNA (*doubtfully*) : Well—yes, ma'am.
EDITH : In his letter to you, he begins very simply, 'dearest'. Just the one superlative. Quite enough. No one wants to be so smothered by words at the outset that there is nothing further to be said, let alone hinted at. And remember, too, although it may not always be the case, a gentleman likes to imagine he is pursuing the young lady and *not* the other way about. (*She picks up the pen.*) So—let us begin again.
ANNA : Then it'd better be just 'Dear Charles', ma'am.
EDITH : No one could find fault with that, Anna. On the other hand, the warmth of his own letter is such that you could afford to be a little more responsive. I think if I were writing for myself, which, of course, I'm not, I should begin— 'Beloved'. Just that—'Beloved'.
ANNA (*dismally*) : 'Beloved,' ma'am?

EDITH : Yes. I find it a tender, comforting word, Anna. It's a word that can be used without losing one's self-possession. One can retain a certain dignity, and yet still say so much. Yes, that's the word *I* would choose—'Beloved'.

ANNA : But I've heard them using that word in church, ma'am.

EDITH : I've no doubt you have. Love comes into everything, Anna.

ANNA : Well, if you think it *says* enough, ma'am, and think it's *right*, then I'll be guided by you.

EDITH : Good. Now—'why—oh, why have you not written?' he asks. Yes—well, we know very well why, don't we?

ANNA : But I don't want *him* to know, ma'am.

EDITH : Nevertheless, always answer questions, Anna. Nothing annoys a correspondent more than to have his queries ignored. But what is it you wish to say first?

ANNA : Say how worried I was, ma'am, not hearing, and what a blessed relief it was when his letter come this morning.

EDITH (*as she writes*) : Came this morning, Anna— *came*.

ANNA : Came this morning.

EDITH : Now—to the question why you haven't written before the answer is that, no matter what arrangement you may have agreed to, it was surely his place to write first.

ANNA : But I would have written the very next day, ma'am, if I'd been able to.

EDITH : Possibly. However, as things have turned out, I feel it's just as well you didn't. After all, the moment he got back to London it might so easily have become a case of 'out of sight, out of mind' on his side. And to have written under those circumstances would have done more harm than good.

ANNA : Why would it, ma'am?

EDITH : Because you could never have been sure that any response he might have made was not simply the result of a sense of obligation. You see that, don't you, Anna?

ANNA : I see that, ma'am, but I wouldn't like him to think I didn't write because I didn't care one way or the other.

EDITH : He won't get that impression.

(There is a pause. Anna peers anxiously over Edith's shoulder as the latter continues to write.)

The fact that, after time for reflection, he's declared his feelings so positively puts us on much firmer ground, Anna.

ANNA : Then I can say how much I love him, can't I, ma'am.

EDITH : The whole letter is saying that, Anna.

ANNA : Then say would he write soon and tell me when he'll be down this way next, ma'am.

(There is a pause. Edith continues writing.)

If I knew exactly when we'd see each other again the waiting wouldn't be so bad.

(Another pause. Edith goes on writing.)

It's when you can't see an end to waiting, that's what makes the days seem long.

(Another pause.)

And say I think of him all the time, ma'am—every blessed minute of the day.

(Finally, Edith lays down her pen and takes up the letter.)

EDITH : There! Now, I'll read it through to you, Anna, and if there's anything you don't like you must say so.

ANNA : Yes, ma'am.

(Anna shuts her eyes, clasps her hands up to her mouth and stands rigid. Edith reads carefully, modulating each phrase in an effort to make the meaning clear to Anna.)

EDITH *(reading)* : 'Beloved, your letter arrived this morning like a burst of sunlight and turned my foolish fears and anxieties to happiness and relief. Despite our arrangement, I hesitated to write myself in case you had found on your return to London that the sentiments you had expressed were less deeply felt than you supposed. A letter from me would then have been little more than a tiresome reminder of a chance encounter best forgotten. Although I am more than happy to learn that my fears are groundless, I live now only for the moment of our next meeting. I hope you will write soon and tell me when we can hope to see each other again. You are always in my thoughts—Anna.'

ANNA *(after a pause)* : Oh, I think it's beautiful, ma'am, really beautiful. I couldn't for the life of me have made that up out of my own head, but I feel it exactly now you've written it down.

EDITH : Then won't you, at least, put your name to it? You can write your own name perfectly well.

ANNA : Oh, no, ma'am! I should do it so bad. He'd be bound to notice at once. And then where should I be?

EDITH : Very well. Then you'd like it to go just as it stands?

ANNA : Yes, please, ma'am. And when you've done the envelope may I slip out and post it in the box myself? May I?

EDITH (*selecting an envelope*) : Oh, there's no need for that. Just leave it on the hall table. It can go with Mr Harnham's letters this evening.

ANNA : Somehow—I don't know—I'd like to post it myself, ma'am.

EDITH (*addressing the envelope*) : It won't get there any quicker.

ANNA : No, but it's the posting of it, ma'am. Only I've never posted a letter before, not of my own.

EDITH (*gently*) : Have you not, Anna?

ANNA : No, ma'am.

EDITH : Then you shall post this one.

ANNA : Oh, thank you, ma'am.

EDITH : *If* I have a stamp. (*She searches.*) Yes, I have. (*She affixes the stamp and thumps it with her fist.*) There!

(*She hands the letter to Anna who kisses it and is ready to fly.*)

You may slip out the front way, if you wish, but put your cloak on, mind, to go into the street.

ANNA : Yes, ma'am. I'll fetch it, ma'am. Thank you, ma'am.

(*Clutching the letter, Anna hurries out and goes off towards the back of the house to find her cloak. Edith starts to tidy her desk. Presently, she picks up Mr Bradford's letter. She studies it for a moment.*)

EDITH (*reading*) : To love and to know that one is loved in return is to breathe the very air of heaven . . .

(*Overcome by mixture of self-pity and genuine desire, she is unable to continue. At this point, Anna, her cloak flying, runs down the hall towards the front door which can be heard to open.*)

ARTHUR (*off*) : Careful, girl! Careful, now! Look where you're going!

ANNA (*off*) : Sorry, sir. Beg pardon, sir.

ARTHUR (*off*) : I should think so. I should think so.

(*The front door is heard to close. At the sound of Arthur's voice, Edith is thrown into a confusion of guilt. She quickly thrusts Mr Bradford's letter into a drawer of the desk and closes it, rising and turning her back to it as Arthur appears in the hall.*)

ARTHUR : Where the devil's that girl off to at this hour, Edith?

EDITH (*recovering her composure*) : Anna? Oh, she's just slipped out to post a letter for me, Arthur, that's all.

The lights fade.

Curtain.

Scene 3

It is a Sunday evening some six weeks later. Arthur stands sipping a glass of sherry. Sarah, having just turned down the beds, has descended almost to the foot of the stairs when the front door

*is heard to open. Edith and Letty appear in the
hallway, having just returned from Evensong at
the cathedral. Letty goes straight up the stairs to
take off her things.*

EDITH: Oh, Sarah! Please tell Anna I'd like to
see her.
SARAH: Anna's not back yet, ma'am.
EDITH: Not back yet? She's very late. Then
remember to tell her the moment she gets in.
SARAH: Very well, ma'am. (*She goes off towards
the rear of the house.*)

(*Edith, carrying her prayer-book and hymn-book,
both bound in ivory, comes down to Arthur.*)

EDITH: It *was* Canon Rawsley, Arthur. I said it
would be. And what a magnificent sermon! I do
wish you'd heard it.
ARTHUR: Yes.
EDITH: I found it most upsetting and I'm sure
Letty did, too.
ARTHUR: Oh? What was he on about?
EDITH: He was describing the dreadful conditions
that exist among the poor in the East End of
London. Do you know, he told us of finding the
little bodies of newly-born babies thrown out on
to the rubbish heaps. And these things are *true*,
Arthur. Canon Rawsley actually lives and works
amongst it all. It made me feel so ashamed.
ARTHUR: What have you to be ashamed of?
EDITH: I do so little.
ARTHUR: Nonsense!
EDITH: It isn't nonsense, Arthur. How *can* one turn
one's back on so much poverty and misery?
ARTHUR (*patiently*): My dear Edith, this world is

as it is. There's bound to be inequality. I was talking to our member of Parliament only last night, and he actually expressed the view that poverty is an economic necessity.

EDITH : Then he should have been there this evening to hear Canon Rawsley.

ARTHUR : Well, of course, Rawsley is obliged to lay it on pretty thick to get people to dig into their pockets, isn't he? But why stay on for the sermon if it upsets you so?

EDITH : A good sermon is meant to upset one.

ARTHUR (*amused*): What you mean is you thoroughly enjoyed it. Worth every penny of half a sovereign, I've no doubt.

EDITH : I didn't have half a sovereign in my purse unfortunately—only half a crown. But then when he spoke of the terrible drunkenness that prevails —the men like animals and the women even worse —I couldn't help thinking that we share some of the responsibility. You and I, Arthur!

ARTHUR : Eh? You mean on account of the brewery? But our beers don't reach the London market. I wish they did.

EDITH : But it's the same trade and our comfortable lives depend on it.

ARTHUR (*sharply*): Brewing is something more than a trade, Edith. (*Exploding.*) Good heavens! I've been into this I don't know how many times. Anything can be abused. Some people drink too much —yes—and other people eat too much. But you don't suggest farmers should stop growing food because of that, do you?

EDITH : I'm sorry, Arthur. I only meant . . .

ARTHUR : What do you suppose we should do? Give up and leave the whole field clear for Tremlett? What would happen to our work people? Some

have been with us ever since Father's time. Who'll
look after them if we go?

EDITH: Well—no, I see that you can't just . . .

ARTHUR: You're quite right, you can't. Nowadays,
in my opinion, there are far too many people about
trying to do good. Good means don't necessarily
lead to good ends, you know. Consequently, when
they leave off the sum total of human misery is
nearly always greater than when they began. Take
my advice, Edith—*be* good, if you can, but for
heaven's sake don't start trying to *do* good. Leave
that to the Almighty.

EDITH: But how can God work except through us,
His creatures? After all, we're only here to carry
out His will, aren't we?

ARTHUR: Yes, but the difficulty is to be sure it's
God's will and not the other feller's.

(*Letty, who has taken off her outdoor clothes, has
descended the stairs and she now enters.*)

LETTY: Oh, Anna's just back, Edith. I saw them
from my window and I *thought* I heard Mansell
shouting something about an accident . . .

EDITH (*alarmed*): An accident? Is Anna all right?
What happened?

LETTY: I don't know what happened, Edith. As
for Anna, she jumped down from the trap looking
as right as a trivet. It can't have been anything
serious.

EDITH: All the same, I'll just go and find out. (*As
she goes.*) Something must have happened or they
wouldn't have been so late. (*She hurries off.*)

ARTHUR: You'd think the whole world revolved
round that wretched girl. I tell you, Letty, I've a
damned good mind to send her home for good.

LETTY : Edith would be terribly upset if you did.

ARTHUR : She'd get over it. Something must be done. It's becoming quite absurd.

LETTY : I see no point in sending the girl away now. I'm surprised you even suggest it.

ARTHUR : Why?

LETTY : There's been such a difference in Edith these last few weeks.

ARTHUR : In what way?

LETTY : She's happy, Arthur.

ARTHUR : Happy?

LETTY : Yes, I'd say Edith's happier now than at any time since I've known her.

ARTHUR : Would you?

LETTY : Oh, *yes*! She looks younger, too, and she's so full of life and high spirits.

ARTHUR : Are you telling me now, then, that Edith's happiness is determined by this chit of a servant-girl?

LETTY : No, no, of course I'm not. After all, Anna was here before that. No, Arthur, I'd hoped this change in Edith was because—well—because things between you both were—better.

ARTHUR (*drily*) : Did you? Well, all I can tell you is that in these last few weeks Edith has seemed to me even more distant than usual. I'll not say any more.

LETTY : Oh. Well, there must be a reason. (*With a sigh.*) Oh, dear! Women *are* such complicated creatures. Perhaps you're beginning to realize that.

ARTHUR : It may surprise you, Letty, but I learnt a fair bit about women long before I met Edith, you know.

LETTY : Well, of course. I'm not saying . . .

ARTHUR : And I didn't take my lessons in the drawing-room, either. Does that shock you?

LETTY : I—I don't think so.

ARTHUR : I only mention it so you'll understand that I do know when a relationship is working satisfactorily and when it is not.

(*Edith comes quickly down the stairs, having taken off her outdoor clothes.*)

EDITH : Would you believe it? They'd hardly set out when a pheasant started up right under the horse's feet. They went over into the ditch and broke a wheel. Poor Mansell had to walk back for another.

ARTHUR : Nobody was hurt, I gather.

EDITH : Anna's looking rather pale, but Mansell's tucking into a plateful of cold beef and pickles, so I imagine it was no more than a shaking.

LETTY : Do you know what he's brought, Edith?

EDITH : New potatoes, broad beans, lettuce and spring onions.

LETTY : I'll go and settle up with him. He won't go until he gets his money.

(*As Letty goes off towards the rear of the house, Edith moves down to her desk, opens a drawer and then closes it again.*)

EDITH (*as she moves*) : Of course, Anna's only to be away from here for a night and a day to come back speaking almost as broadly as ever she did. It's really quite disheartening.

ARTHUR : But hardly surprising, Edith.

EDITH : How do you mean?

ARTHUR : I don't imagine she'd be encouraged to show off her airs and graces among her own people, would she?

EDITH : Why do you accuse her of putting on airs and graces, Arthur, just because she wants to learn to speak properly?

ARTHUR : I expect you think I'm stuffy and old-fashioned? But you see, to me a good servant is just as valuable as a good master. Try to turn one into the other and you lose both.

EDITH : Not always. And why *should* a girl have to miss the finer opportunities of life just because she doesn't know how to make the best of herself?

ARTHUR : Give her the chance, Edith, and she'll make her own opportunities. As it is, you're letting the girl and her affairs fill your entire life.

EDITH : No more than the brewery fills yours.

ARTHUR : But brewing is my vocation, Edith. It's something I care about. And when I think of Father and Grandfather and Great-Grandfather before that, I should feel ashamed if I *didn't* care. We all owe something to the past as well as to the future, don't we? Can't you see that? (*Pause.*) A glass of sherry?

EDITH (*miserably*) : No thank you, Arthur.

(*There is another awkward pause during which Arthur moves awkwardly and hesitantly towards Edith.*)

ARTHUR : Edith—my dear, I—things are not right between us, are they?

EDITH : What makes you say that now—at this particular moment?

ARTHUR : Don't think I'm reproaching you—I'm not. But you must be as well aware of what I mean as I am. Things were not—well—like this at the beginning, were they? (*Pause.*) What's happened?

EDITH : Nothing's happened, Arthur. It's just that . . .

ARTHUR : You see, if I didn't know that such a thing was inconceivable, I could so easily jump to quite the wrong conclusion.

EDITH : I don't know what you mean.

ARTHUR : I might easily imagine from the way you're behaving that—someone has come between us.

(*Anna, in her best Sunday dress, appears in the hallway and waits nervously.*)

EDITH (*with a nervous laugh*) : Now you're being quite absurd, Arthur. That's ridiculous. Really— it's unworthy of you. (*Suddenly and gratefully aware of Anna's presence.*) Yes, Anna?

ANNA (*moving down a little*) : My brother-in-law's just set off home, ma'am, and he said I was to say thank you for his supper which he much enjoyed.

EDITH : Thank you, Anna.

ANNA (*with a glance at Arthur*) : Shall I come back when it's more convenient, ma'am? Only you did say that as soon as . . . (*She breaks off.*)

(*Highly irritated by the interruption, Arthur strides towards his study, setting down his empty glass on the way.*)

ARTHUR (*as he moves up*) : We'll talk later, Edith.

(*Ignoring Anna, Arthur goes off into his study, closing the door sharply behind him. The moment he has gone, Anna moves down quickly to Edith.*)

ANNA : Oh, ma'am! Was there a letter?

EDITH : Yes, there was—by the afternoon post

yesterday. I *have* answered it for you already, so we'll talk about that in a moment. But first, tell me—are you sure you're quite recovered from your upset?

ANNA : Oh, yes, ma'am.

EDITH : You're still looking rather pale. You didn't bang your head on anything, I hope?

ANNA : No, ma'am. We went over nice and easy and tumbled out quite soft. But what does Charles say? And which train is he catching on Wednesday? And will he expect me to be waiting at the station, do you think?

(*Edith opens the drawer of the desk and takes from it the accumulation of Mr Bradford's letters which now number more than a dozen.*)

EDITH : Did it feel strange to be back in the village again?

ANNA : Oh, ma'am! Everything looks so small.

EDITH (*shuffling through the letters*): Then you didn't feel you'd rather be back there again?

ANNA : Not now, ma'am. I don't ever want to go back there now.

EDITH : Why not?

ANNA : I don't know—I just couldn't. They seem to live so rough, ma'am. You notice it more when you've been away. And life's ever so hard for them. Fifteen shillings a week, he gets, and four children to keep. Poor Rose, she's never got a minute she can call her own. The oldest girl, she's twelve, and they're hoping to find her a place up the vicarage this summer. That'd be a help, if she gets her legs under somebody else's table.

EDITH : Still, Rose was glad to see you, wasn't she, and hear all your news?

ANNA : Well, I doubt I'd have had that much of a welcome if you hadn't given me that lovely basket of good things to take, ma'am.

EDITH : Oh, nonsense, Anna.

ANNA : I don't mean that not in any nasty way, ma'am. It's just that there's not a mouthful to spare. She's my only close relation now, Rose, but she's not a person I could ever fall back on. Is that his letter, ma'am?

EDITH : Yes, this is the one—there. (*She hands Anna Mr Bradford's most recent letter and returns the rest to the drawer of the desk.*)

ANNA (*examining the envelope*) : But won't you read it out for me, ma'am?

EDITH : Surely by now you're able to read most of it for yourself, Anna, and it's time you began to make the effort. If you like to spell out the long words, I'll tell you how to say them.

ANNA : Very well, ma'am. (*She takes the letter from its envelope and begins to read.*) 'Dearest, I am quite . . .' (*She pauses, puzzled by a word.*) 'd-e-s-p-o-n . . .'

EDITH : Despondent.

ANNA (*saying the word*) : Despondent.

EDITH : That's right. What Mr Bradford's trying to tell you, Anna, is just how wretched and miserable he feels.

ANNA : But why, ma'am? Why should he?

EDITH : Well, read on, child, read on and you'll find out.

ANNA (*reading slowly*) : 'It is with a heevy . . .'

EDITH : Heavy.

ANNA : 'It is with a heavy heart that I find myself obliged to send you the dismal . . .' (*Pause.*) 'i-n-f-o-r-m . . .'

EDITH : Information. Here, give it to me, Anna.

You're not catching the sense of it at all. (*She takes the letter and begins to read briskly.*) 'It is with a heavy heart that I find myself obliged to send you the dismal information that circumstances, all unforeseen, have suddenly arisen which make it impossible for me to travel to the West on Wednesday as I had planned.'

ANNA (*fearfully*): Does it mean he's not coming, ma'am?

EDITH: It means he's not coming on Wednesday, Anna. Listen how it goes on: 'Will you ever forgive me, I wonder? Will I ever forgive myself? But I can see no opportunity at the moment of my being able to leave London much before the end of next month, so your letters will be all . . .'

ANNA (*faintly*): Next month? Oh, ma'am! (*Her knees give way and she sinks to the floor in a faint.*)

EDITH: Anna! Child! What is it? Anna! (*She goes down on her knees beside Anna and begins to slap her on the hand.*) Oh, Anna! I said you should have gone straight up to bed the moment you came in, and I should have sent Sarah for Dr Warren. Anna! Anna!

(*There is no immediate response from Anna. Edith gets to her feet and starts for the hall then, changing her mind, hurries to the desk. From one of the smaller drawers, she takes a bottle of smelling-salts and returns to the prostrate Anna. Kneeling, she raises the girl's head and holds the smelling-salts under her nose.*)

ANNA: Oh, ma'am. What—?

EDITH: You've been in a faint, Anna. Now, take a good sniff at these.

(*Anna does so.*)

Once again. There—that's better, isn't it? They
make the eyes water, but they clear the brain. I'll
help you up and you can sit quietly in that chair
for a little. Can you manage?
ANNA : I think so, ma'am.

(*With Edith's help, Anna gets to her feet and sinks
into a nearby chair.*)

EDITH : You see, I was perfectly right. That accident
gave you more of a shock than you imagined. You
must go upstairs and get into bed, and in the morning we'll ask Dr Warren to give you a thorough
examination.
ANNA : No, ma'am, no. I—I don't need to see a
doctor, ma'am.
EDITH : But if there's something wrong, Anna, why
not?
ANNA : It's not a doctor I *need*, ma'am, it's Charles.
EDITH : Oh?
ANNA : You won't turn me out, ma'am, will you?
Please—please say you won't turn me out. Only I
can't keep it to myself, not for another whole
month, can I?
EDITH (*after a pause*) : How can you be so sure?
ANNA : I've had all the signs, ma'am. And Rose,
she knows all about *them*.

(*Towards the rear of the house the gong is
sounded.*)

EDITH : I hardly know what to say, Anna, still less
what to do.

144

(*Arthur emerges from the study and crosses in silence to the dining-room. Letty comes down the stairs.*)

LETTY (*entering*): There's the gong, Edith—oh, you have Anna with you.

EDITH: Arthur's just gone in, Letty. I shall be along presently. Don't wait for me.

LETTY: Oh, very well. (*She looks curiously from one to the other.*) Is there something the matter?

EDITH: Anna's not feeling quite herself, but it's nothing serious, we hope.

LETTY: It might have been serious. You've been very lucky, Anna. Don't be too long, Edith, will you? (*She goes off into the dining-room.*)

ANNA (*after a pause*): If you was to turn me out now, ma'am, whatever would become of me?

EDITH (*sharply*): Don't be stupid, child! There's no question of that at the moment. But quite soon your condition will become increasingly difficult to conceal, and I know very well what Mr Harnham's attitude will be.

ANNA: But when Charles knows what's happened to me, he'll stand by me—won't he. ma'am?

EDITH (*instinctively*): Stand by you? Do you mean *marry* you, Anna? Oh, but he can't do *that*!

ANNA: But he must! Why not? Why can't he, ma'am?

EDITH: Because—well, because that kind of young man—no, no, Anna, it's most improbable.

ANNA: But if he loves me? And he's always saying he loves me.

EDITH: A man may say many things in the course of a casual attachment, Anna, but he can be just as quick to repudiate them the moment he faces any real responsibility.

ANNA : Then whatever shall I do? Oh, ma'am!

EDITH : Try not to upset yourself, Anna. What we must do is to decide on our own course of action as calmly and as rationally as we can. Now, it seems to me that the best we can hope for is that he may be persuaded to make proper financial provision for you.

ANNA : Oh, he'll do more for me than that, my Charles, ma'am. I know he will.

EDITH : Well, certainly his letters would lead one to think so, but . . . You see, although we've had quite a number, they tell us so little. Of his family, his situation, his financial position, he's never said a word.

ANNA : I wouldn't care who he was or what he was, ma'am, so long as he still loved me.

EDITH (*pacing about*): Obviously, he'll have to be told sooner or later. The pity is that he's not coming on Wednesday as we'd hoped for then you would have instinctively chosen the right moment to tell him. As things are, what we must decide is whether to say nothing until his visit in a month's time, or whether to inform him by letter immediately.

ANNA : Oh, I want to tell him now, ma'am. I couldn't wait all that time not knowing what his feelings are, could I?

EDITH : I dare say not. But it won't be an easy letter to write, Anna.

ANNA : Why, ma'am?

EDITH : Because for one thing, I—I've never known myself what it is to be in your situation.

ANNA : But you can put yourself in my place, ma'am, like you do. And you do it so truly.

EDITH : There's another thing. We must remember that our letter will probably reach him at his breakfast-table—hardly the time or place one would choose to make such an intimate disclosure. Oh, dear! These things are so much easier to say than they are to put down on paper.

ANNA: You don't have to mince matters, ma'am. After all, it's me that's having the baby—not him.

EDITH: I'm quite aware of that, Anna.

ANNA: He knows what happened between us that day just as well as I do, so you can be as plain-spoken as you want.

EDITH: I shall see no misunderstandings arise, if that's what you mean.

ANNA: Yes, and say he's to come down at once, ma'am, so we can make our arrangements and settle things, and that'll help put my mind at rest for a bit.

EDITH: But Anna, if I'm to write convincingly, I'm obliged to write as I feel, and so far I've always done so. I shall try to put myself in your place, of course, but to change now would be to become quite a different person, perhaps not at all to Mr Bradford's liking.

ANNA: But I want him to know I'm worried out of my wits, and I will be until I know what he's going to do.

EDITH: No, Anna, no. I'm sure that's not the attitude we should adopt. Surely the important thing at this stage is not to let him feel you're going to be a burden to him in any way. You want him to know what's happened, of course, but you don't want him to think you a great nuisance, do you, and put him to a lot of inconvenience. Aren't I right?

ANNA (*doubtfully*): Well, I don't want to cause no

147

more trouble than I need, ma'am, so long as he's not going to try and wriggle out of it.

EDITH : What we have to aim at is to keep his interest alive—the interest he already has for you. So I shall tell him what's happened and I shall say that he must go on writing as tenderly as ever, and if he *could* come in a month's time—well—that'll be soon enough to discuss what had better be done.

ANNA : But not asking for anything, won't he think I don't know my rights, ma'am? Is that saying enough, I mean?

EDITH : It's what I would say, Anna.

ANNA : All right, ma'am. I'll do what you think's best. Only you've a nicer way with it all than I should have.

EDITH : Then off you go up to bed, Anna, and I'll speak to Sarah. When she's been up, I'll come and read you the letter.

ANNA : Oh, thank you, ma'am. (*She seizes Edith's hand and kisses it.*) You've been ever so kind.

EDITH (*pulling her hand away*) : That'll do, Anna. I'm only trying to do what's best. Off you go now.

ANNA (*moving up*) : Yes, ma'am, and I feel better already just having you knowing. (*Turning back.*) When you come to the end of the letter, will you say I love him still very much—please?

EDITH : Of course, Anna.

(*Anna goes out towards the rear of the house. After a moment's pause, Edith moves thoughtfully to her desk. She opens the writing-pad, takes up her pen and sits thinking for a moment. Suddenly, she drops the pen and buries her face in her hands, her whole body shaking with sobs. Presently, Letty enters.*)

148

LETTY: Edith—Arthur says if you don't . . . My dear! Whatever's the matter?

EDITH (*dabbing her eyes*): It's nothing.

LETTY: Nothing?

EDITH: I shall be all right in a moment.

LETTY: Is it—Arthur?

EDITH: No, no.

LETTY: Then that girl. Is it Anna? Something she's said? What is it, Edith?

EDITH: Letty—don't say a word to Arthur—but—the fact is Anna is going to have a child.

LETTY: Oh, no! Oh, my dear! Do we know who the father is?

EDITH: You remember the young man she met at the fair?

LETTY: But she only saw him twice. He was only here for two days.

EDITH: Nevertheless . . .

LETTY: Well! No wonder you're upset. And after all you've tried to do for the girl. But you mustn't be, Edith, you mustn't be. They're not worth it, you know. They're simply not worth it.

EDITH: It's not that. You don't understand. I'm not upset with Anna—I envy her.

LETTY: Edith!

EDITH: I envy her, Letty.

LETTY: Edith, what *are* you saying?

EDITH: I wish it had been me.

LETTY: You wish—? But—oh, I *see*! Of course, I see. You mean you wish it was your child—yours and Arthur's.

(*Edith rises.*)

EDITH (*choking on the word*): Arthur's!

149

LETTY: My poor, dear Edith, of course you do!

(*Edith hurries from the room and up the stairs. Letty follows her as far as the foot of the stairs.*)

And so it will be. It will be one of these days, Edith, I'm sure it will.

Curtain.

ACT TWO

Scene 1

A Saturday afternoon nearly two weeks later. As the curtain rises, Edith moves across the room and pulls the bell-crank. A bell is heard to ring quite loudly at the rear of the house. Edith returns to her desk and begins to put away the letters she has just been re-reading. Presently Sarah enters, wearing a clean, afternoon cap and apron. Edith rises.

EDITH: Oh, Sarah. I'm expecting a gentleman to call very shortly—a Mr Charles Bradford.

SARAH: Yes, ma'am.

EDITH: You're to show him in here, then come and tell me. I shall be in the breakfast-room.

SARAH: Very well, ma'am.

EDITH: Oh—and you can make the tea as soon as he arrives.

SARAH: Tea for—three, ma'am?

EDITH: No, Sarah—just for two. Don't wait for me to ring. Bring it in as soon as it's ready.

(Letty has descended the stairs and enters with some show of eagerness.)

SARAH: Yes, ma'am.

LETTY: I've just thought of something else, Edith.

EDITH: That'll do then, Sarah.

SARAH: Thank you, ma'am. *(She goes off.)*

EDITH: Yes, Letty?

LETTY: Won't he be expecting to see Anna?

EDITH: Oh, he knows she's not here today. He's arranged a meeting with Anna for tomorrow. Indeed, that's why he's chosen to come. It was all in his letter to Arthur.

LETTY *(suddenly)*: Why, Edith, I've just realized— you've put on your new dress.

151

EDITH (*making a slow pirouette*): Do you like it?

LETTY: Oh, I *do*. It's *most* becoming. Has Arthur seen it?

EDITH: Not yet.

LETTY: Incidentally, he was so pleased and so *touched*, I think, when you suggested that as he was busy just now, you and I should receive this Mr Bradford.

EDITH: I've never felt this was a matter for Arthur to deal with, Letty. I know exactly what his reaction would be. The moment he learnt of Anna's condition, he'd pack her off back to the village and wash his hands of the whole affair.

LETTY: Oh, I don't think so, Edith.

EDITH: But he's practically said as much, hasn't he?

LETTY: Arthur sometimes *says* things like that, but he doesn't really mean them, you know. He didn't show me the young man's letter, but I gather there was nothing in it to indicate the *real* reason for this visit, was there?

EDITH: Fortunately, no. It simply said that with Anna away in the country, here was a convenient opportunity to discuss her future well-being. That was the phrase he used.

LETTY: It really is a most peculiar situation, isn't it?

EDITH: How do you mean?

LETTY: Well, I mean here we are, about to confront a young man, a complete stranger, who's quite unaware that we already know what his relations with Anna must have been and who, in any case, is expecting to meet Arthur.

EDITH: I see no problem there, Letty.

LETTY: What I mean is—to talk to Arthur, another

man, is one thing, but faced by us he may well decide to avoid the issue entirely.

EDITH : In that case, we shall be obliged at some stage to tell him exactly what we know and ask him point blank what he proposes to do about it.

LETTY : I suppose so, but how embarrassing it could be. One can only hope he already has something in mind. Perhaps he'll put down a lump sum and set up a trust for the child. That's often done, I believe.

EDITH : Yes—well, in any event, he's obliged by law to make some provision for the child until it reaches a certain age. And if he doesn't do that, then he can be brought before the court to answer.

LETTY : But I imagine the sum of money the law would insist on is really quite small.

EDITH : It's totally inadequate. A few shillings a week.

LETTY : You seem to know a great deal about the subject, Edith.

EDITH : I should do. Yesterday, I spent a whole hour in the public library reading it up.

LETTY : Oh, I see. Well, in that case, I think I'd better leave most of the talking to you.

EDITH : I was just thinking, Letty . . .

LETTY : Yes?

EDITH : There's really no need for both of us to confront Mr Bradford, is there? I was just wondering if it wouldn't be kinder, and perhaps less humiliating for him, if he had only one of us to contend with.

LETTY : Oh, no, Edith—that's not fair at all. It's essential that you should be present. I should feel most uncomfortable left on my own. I'm sure it'll be embarrassing enough as it is. No, no, you can't get out of it now, Edith. It's far too late for that.

EDITH : I'm not trying to get out of anything Letty.
In fact, if you're going to be so uncomfortable all
the time, I should be quite happy to deal with Mr
Bradford myself.
LETTY : You mean—see him alone?
EDITH : If it'll make things easier for us all, why
not?
LETTY : A tête-à-tête in these particular circum-
stances, Edith, would seem to me to be highly
improper.
EDITH : Surely the question is, simply, how can
Anna's interests best be served, isn't it?
LETTY : Nevertheless, I'm quite certain Arthur
would never have agreed . . .
EDITH : This has nothing whatever to do with
Arthur . . .
LETTY : And I'd have thought the presence of a
third party and an older person at that would
have . . .

(*Suddenly a bell jangles towards the rear of the
house.*)

Oh, dear! Do you think—?
EDITH : Come along, Letty—quickly! (*She hurries
off and along the hall, leaving Letty alone.*)
LETTY : But I know Arthur expects me to be
present, Edith, so I'm afraid I shall just have to
insist. (*She goes off in Edith's wake.*)
EDITH (*off*) : But don't you feel in this situation
that one head would be better than two?
LETTY (*off*) : No, I don't. I'm sorry, but I can't
agree.

(*The sound of their voices is suddenly cut off as the
breakfast-room door closes on the two women.
Presently, Sarah passes along the hall to the front*)

door. There is a brief, unintelligible exchange of voices as she admits the visitor and takes his things. Sarah then enters, followed by Charles.)

SARAH : If you'll just wait here, sir.
CHARLES : Thank you.

(Sarah goes off. Charles looks about the room with interest. He is a well-built young man of pleasing appearance. He moves to examine one of the silver trophies, pausing to read the inscription on its base. Then, moving to the windows, he stands gazing out across the market square. Edith enters.)

EDITH : Good afternoon.
CHARLES *(swinging round)*: Oh—Mrs Harnham?
EDITH : Yes.
CHARLES : My name's Bradford—Charles Bradford.
EDITH : How do you do, Mr Bradford? We did meet, I think, just for a moment, didn't we—when the fair was here last?
CHARLES *(flattered)*: Ah—so you remember?
EDITH : Perhaps because Anna's mentioned your name once or twice since. Do sit down.
CHARLES : Thank you. I'm sorry if I seem a nuisance, but I did write to Mr Harnham, as I expect you know ...
EDITH : Of course. Unfortunately, just now my husband's entirely taken up with his business affairs, Mr Bradford, and it so happens, you see, that I've known Anna's family for donkey's years and Anna in particular since she was quite tiny. So my husband felt that perhaps I could be of more help to you that he could.
CHARLES : I see. Of course, I know from what Anna's told me how kind you've been, not only to her, but to the whole family.

EDITH : I've tried to do what little I could. The Dunsfords were a part of the village and well-respected. Farmers, of course, and had been for generations. But when the bad times came in the late seventies, like so many others, they lost practically everything.

CHARLES : And you made Anna your—your protégé, so to speak?

EDITH : When the parents died, there was an old aunt—and there was me. So I continued to take an interest in Anna, yes. And eventually I was able to find a place for her here.

CHARLES : As a servant?

EDITH : As a servant, Mr Bradford. Of course, I still look on her as a mere child, although every now and then I realize, with something of a shock, that she's really quite grown-up.

CHARLES : Oh, indeed—yes, she is. She's quite grown-up.

EDITH : In certain respects, at all events.

(*Sarah enters with a silver tray of tea things, which she arranges on a small table between Edith and Charles.*)

Do you know Salisbury at all well, Mr Bradford?

CHARLES : Not really well, I'm afraid, although I've made several visits recently, that is before I—er—

EDITH : Before the day of the fair, I expect you mean.

CHARLES : Exactly.

EDITH : The cathedral is very fine, isn't it? Thank you, Sarah.

(*Sarah goes out.*)

They say it has the tallest spire in the whole of England.

CHARLES : And I'm perfectly happy to agree with them, Mrs. Harnham. (*Rising.*) May we return to Anna?

EDITH : By all means.

CHARLES : It would seem, so far as she's concerned, that you're acting *in loco parentis*. Isn't that so?

EDITH : Well, in the sense that, to some extent, I've made her interest my own, yes—but, of course, I've no legal standing whatsoever.

CHARLES : No, no, but for all practical purposes such is the case. And that is why I'm here.

EDITH : Where is all this leading us, Mr Bradford?

CHARLES : I'll come to that in a moment. But first, I think I should tell you something about myself. May I?

EDITH : Please do.

CHARLES : I am, by profession, a barrister.

EDITH (*surprised*) : A barrister?

CHARLES : Yes—but only just. At the moment I'm a junior in chambers, barely existing on the few crumbs that fall from the high table. However, this is only a beginning. It won't always be so, I can assure you. It's not for me to say whether I'm brilliant or not, but I work hard, and on my feet I've a certain fluency which has already earned me several useful commendations. So I'm not without prospects. In short, I mean to get on, as they say.

EDITH : Sugar, Mr Bradford? How many?

CHARLES (*thrown*) : Oh—two lumps, if you please.

EDITH : But why are you telling me all this? And what has it to do with Anna?

CHARLES : I'm coming to that now, Mrs Harnham. You see, when I first saw her that evening at the fair, I'd not the slightest intention of ever becoming—oh, thank you. (*He accepts a cup of tea from Edith and sits.*) No—I went there simply to while away an hour or so, but having spent a miserable and lonely day, you'll understand it wasn't difficult to fall into conversation with Anna.

EDITH: Anna is a very natural girl, Mr Bradford.

CHARLES (*eagerly*): Yes, isn't she?

EDITH: Some would perhaps call her—ingenuous.

CHARLES: If you mean there's a certain innocence about her, I agree. That's what I found so engaging. Then, as you probably know, we had a further meeting, Anna and I.

EDITH: The day after the fair?

CHARLES: Yes—let me tell you what happened . . .

EDITH (*hurriedly*): You're letting your tea get cold, Mr Bradford.

(*He gulps some of his tea, then resumes.*)

CHARLES: Well, we spent a delightful afternoon together. But such encounters in this enlightened age are not altogether uncommon and normally, in a day or two, I'd have forgotten the whole incident. (*Pause.*) But I didn't.

EDITH: No?

CHARLES: Oh, I can understand very well that to you Anna must seem just another little girl from the village, with all the limitations that implies. But you see, I've had the good fortune to discover qualities in Anna which I'm sure you're quite unaware of.

EDITH: How can you have done? You were only . . .

CHARLES: I know what you're going to say. I was only here for two days. But since then, Mrs Harnham, Anna and I have been writing to each other.

EDITH: Really?

CHARLES : Yes—twice a week at least—sometimes more often than that. If you'll allow me to . . . (*He rises and from an inside pocket of his jacket produces a fat bundle of letters tied with pink tape.*) There! And I'm not ashamed to admit that I know several of them by heart.

EDITH : Your correspondent would be highly flattered to hear that.

CHARLES : It's perfectly true. I could recite one now, if you wish.

EDITH : Oh, please! It's just that I'm a little surprised to learn that Anna has the ability to express herself so effectively.

CHARLES : Quite frankly, so was I. But that's what I find so delightful. Her sentiments, you see, are so fresh, so obviously those of a young girl of such —well—such tenderness and generosity that only a fellow with a heart of stone could fail to respond.

EDITH : You make her sound a paragon, Mr Bradford.

CHARLES : Ah, I see what it is. You think I'm overstating the case, don't you?

EDITH : I'm really in no position to judge that, am I?

CHARLES : Then in one moment you will be, Mrs Harnham. (*He tugs at the pink tape, untying the bundle of letters.*) I'd like, if I may, to show you just one letter.

EDITH (*protesting*) : Oh, but surely . . .

CHARLES (*selecting one of the letters*) : Absolutely in confidence, of course. It won't embarrass you in any way, I can promise. It's one of the early ones. But it will give you an idea. There . . .

(*He unfolds the chosen letter, hands it to Edith, then moves away to the windows. Edith glances at the letter merely to identify it, then puts a hand over her eyes in a gesture compounded of embarrassment and desperation. Presently, Charles turns to her.)*

Well?

EDITH: It's certainly literate. I think I can say that much.

CHARLES: Oh, come now. You can say much more than that, Mrs Harnham. Don't you agree she writes very prettily?

EDITH: If she's pleased you—well, there's your answer, isn't it?

CHARLES: Mrs Harnham—let me come to the point. For weeks past now, Anna's hardly been out of my thoughts for a moment, so you'll understand that what I'm going to say is carefully considered and comes only after much heart-searching.

EDITH: Well, of course.

CHARLES: I won't pretend there haven't been times when I had doubts, but not any longer. Those doubts were finally swept away by one particular letter which I have here. It's quite recent.

EDITH: Oh?

CHARLES: It concerns a matter which I won't bother *you* with, Mrs Harnham, but in this letter Anna shows an unselfishness, indeed a nobility of character which I, for one, never dreamt of finding in *any* woman.

EDITH (*nervously*): Oh, come, Mr Bradford! Obviously, you haven't looked very far, have you?

CHARLES: It was this letter which decided me to come down here and make my intentions clear to those most concerned with Anna's welfare, because —tomorrow I mean to ask her to marry me.

EDITH: Marry you, Mr Bradford?

CHARLES : Yes—as soon as it can be conveniently arranged.

EDITH (*rising*) : Oh, but really—I—

CHARLES : You don't approve?

(*Edith, agitated, moves away to the windows.*)

EDITH : I didn't say *that*. I should be delighted, of course, for Anna to make a suitable match. Her future happiness is very much my concern. (*Turning.*) On the other hand . . .

CHARLES : On the other hand?

EDITH : Anna is what she is—a simple girl with little or no knowledge of the world at large, while you, I now learn, are a professional man with your whole career in front of you.

CHARLES (*cheerfully*) : Mrs Harnham, if I thought it was necessary, for the sake of Anna, I'd give up my profession tomorrow.

EDITH (*appalled*) : Sacrifice your career? For Anna?

CHARLES (*laughing*) : Oh, please don't be alarmed. I see no necessity to do any such thing. But I think I know what's disturbing you.

EDITH : Do you, Mr Bradford?

CHARLES : Yes—you're afraid that I may be asking too much of her.

EDITH : And aren't you?

CHARLES : I don't think so.

EDITH : But as you rise in your profession, Mr Bradford, do you think Anna will be able to meet all the requirements of her position as your wife.

CHARLES : I can't see why not. With her powers of development, and perhaps after a little coaching in the social forms of life in London, she'll make as good a professional man's wife as anyone could hope for.

EDITH : And then there's your family. You have your family to consider, surely? What do they think?

CHARLES : Apart from an unmarried sister a lot older than I am, I've no close ties now.

EDITH : But the fact remains, the pair of you are barely acquainted, you've seen so little of each other . . .

CHARLES : For the very good reason that I've had to keep my nose to the grindstone, but if the knowledge one has of another person is essentially a matter of communication, which it undoubtedly is, then there can be no two people who know each other better than Anna and I do at this moment.

(*Edith has moved down to her desk. With seeming casualness, she pulls open the drawer and looks down at the letters from Charles which lie there. She is almost at the point of confession.*)

Aren't I right?

EDITH : Oh, I know just how much letters can mean to one—but—but surely they can never take the place of the actual—the loved one?

CHARLES : No—but sometimes, I think, it's good for us to have to put our thoughts into words, Mrs Harnham. We learn things about ourselves we'd never have believed. I know I have. And I'm sure Anna has, too.

EDITH : Has she?—yes . . . I . . .

CHARLES : It's not easy, perhaps, for us to put ourselves in her place—a girl of her age. Perhaps we've forgotten how exciting it all was.

EDITH : How do you mean?

CHARLES : That growing wonder of waking up into a new world for the first time and realizing that

until now one has only been half alive. I find it all
here in her letters to me.

EDITH (*shaken*): Do you?

CHARLES: Oh, yes—quite clearly.

(*Edith closes the drawer then, to recover her composure, moves back to the tea-table.*)

EDITH: Some more tea, Mr Bradford?

CHARLES: No, thank you. Then—may I take it
you're not wholly against the plan, Mrs Harnham?

EDITH: I'm not wholly against it—no—it's just
that I—I've hardly had time to consider it. But
any decision, of course, must be Anna's.

CHARLES: Of course. Judging by the letters, I fancy
her mind is already made up. Now, if I may
trespass a little further on your kindness and ask
for your co-operation.

EDITH: Co-operation?

CHARLES: Yes. (*He produces a small pocket-diary
and sits close beside her.*)
Let's see . . .(*Briskly.*) Now I thought a suitable day
for the wedding would be 5th August, which this
year falls on a Saturday. That allows us four weeks
precisely in which to make our arrangements. But
would that be a convenient day for you?

EDITH: Do you mean you wish her to be married
from here—from this house?

CHARLES: If you agree. It's sensible, isn't it?

EDITH (*weakly*): I don't know whether my husband . . . ?

CHARLES: It'll only be a civil ceremony, of course.

EDITH: Oh—not in church?

CHARLES: I know Anna's circumstances, Mrs
Harnham—her financial circumstances, I mean—
and I know my own. We're going to need every

penny we can scrape together. The Registrar's Office is not far from here, I imagine?

EDITH: It's just across the square.

CHARLES: Good. I shall stay overnight at The White Horse. I dare say Anna would like to have some few friends or relatives of her own present at the ceremony—what do you think?

EDITH: There'll certainly have to be witnesses. And then, Mr Bradford?

CHARLES (*with self-mockery*): And then, Mrs Harnham? Why, then we shall catch the train back to London and there live happily ever after.

EDITH: I see. And do you intend to set up house in London?

CHARLES: Ah! I'm afraid funds won't run to that—not immediately, that is. But I have my eye on some very comfortable rooms in Bloomsbury.

EDITH: I'm afraid I don't know London at all.

CHARLES: No? Well, Bloomsbury's just between the West End and the City. I'm sure Anna will be delighted with Bloomsbury.

EDITH (*with feeling*): Anna will be in paradise, Mr Bradford.

CHARLES (*pleased*): You think so? Of course, I know a lot of people would say that to start married life with no money in the bank is sheer madness. But when one's in love one's already a little mad, don't you think?

EDITH: Oh, yes.

CHARLES: In a rather exciting way. And to have someone who'll gladly put up with the lean years is to build two lives on a firmer foundation than mere pounds, shillings and pence. Then, after a year or two, when one's a success and comes to look back, surely it's to find that the early worries and

164

disappointments have only served to strengthen the love each has for the other.

EDITH (*slowly*): Yes—that—that is how marriage should be.

(*There is a pause. Charles rises, then Edith.*)

CHARLES: Well, I must thank you, Mrs Harnham, for letting me take up so much of your time.

EDITH: You return to London tomorrow, Mr Bradford?

CHARLES: Late tomorrow. Naturally, I'm hoping to see something of Anna before I go.

EDITH: Naturally. (*She turns away and pulls the bell-crank.*) And she's expecting to see you. Mansell will be bringing her back this evening.

CHARLES: Then thank you again, Mrs Harnham. Oh—one small thing. You won't—I mean—I know you'll understand, but I'd like to be the one to *tell* Anna.

EDITH: Of course. And I hope you'll be down here again soon, now that—now that you've made up your mind.

CHARLES: I'd like very much to think so, but I doubt if it'll be possible before the wedding.

EDITH: Oh, dear! Why not?

CHARLES (*with a wry laugh*): Mainly because I'm obliged to keep on good terms with our clerk in chambers.

EDITH: How on earth does your clerk come into it?

CHARLES: He fixes me up with work, you see— usually out of town and on Fridays—briefs that nobody else can be bothered with. But if you're never seen, you'll never get known; so, with an eye to the future, I take what comes and as solicitors are already beginning to ask for me by name, I feel I'm heading in the right direction.

EDITH : Then you'll see nothing of Anna?

CHARLES : I'm afraid not. We shall just have to continue our courtship by correspondence.

(*Sarah appears in the hallway.*)

EDITH (*worried*) : Yes, I—I suppose you will.

CHARLES : Good-bye, Mrs Harnham—and thank you.

EDITH : Good-bye, Mr Bradford.

(*Charles goes out and off towards the front door, followed by Sarah. For a moment, Edith remains quite still then, as she hears the sound of the door opening, she hurries to the window, pressing close to the glass to catch a last glimpse of the departing Charles.*

So engrossed is she that when Sarah returns for the tea-tray, she fails to notice her. Sarah gives her mistress a curious look and goes off as Letty enters.)

LETTY : Well?

EDITH (*turning from the window*) : Oh, I was just—

LETTY : What happened, Edith? Did you come to a satisfactory arrangement?

EDITH : A satisfactory arrangement? Yes, I suppose one could call it that, Letty.

LETTY : Oh, Then he's agreed to make reasonable provision for the child?

EDITH (*flatly*) : He's going to marry her.

LETTY : Marry her? Did you say marry her?

EDITH : Yes.

LETTY : Well! Good gracious! You do surprise me, Edith. *Marry* her. I never expected to hear that.

Of course, it's perfectly right that he should, but it so seldom turns out that way, especially when there are such differences of background. I wonder *why* he decided to marry her?

EDITH : I imagine because he thinks he's in love with her.

LETTY : And isn't he?

EDITH : No.

LETTY : How can you be so certain?

EDITH : I know Anna.

LETTY : I don't understand.

EDITH : He's in love with the person he *imagines* her to be.

LETTY : Edith, dear, don't be so fanciful. There's nothing imaginary about the girl's condition, is there?

EDITH (*moving to her desk*) : If it's not to prove a disaster, Anna must be turned into something nearer to that young man's idea of her.

LETTY : But surely the ceremony will have to be quite soon—in the circumstances, won't it?

EDITH : Yes, the wedding is to take place exactly four weeks to-day.

LETTY : Four weeks! Do you seriously imagine that Anna can be transformed quite so rapidly?

EDITH (*as she sits*) : She must be, Letty. She must be.

The lights fade.

Curtain.

Scene 2

A Tuesday morning, three days later. Anna, in cap and apron over her print dress, sits at the desk,

167

*pen in hand, labouring over her copy-book. Sarah,
similarly dressed, moves quickly about the room
returning recently cleaned silver pieces to their
various positions.*

SARAH : . . . so I said why don't you ask if you
can speak to Mr Philips, the manager at the maltings? But Bertie's ever so shy that way. He never
wants to step out of line or nothing. Only I kept
on nagging at him and it was a lucky thing I did.

ANNA (*not looking up*) : So?

SARAH : Well, he did get to see him in the end.
And Mr Philips says there's bound to be a house
come up *if* this business with Tremlett's goes all
right. I mean Bertie's done over twelve years at
Harnham's and he's right up the list, so now we
just got to keep our fingers crossed.

ANNA (*turning on her chair to face the room*) : But
how lovely though, Sarah, when you *do* get a house.

SARAH : Walking out's all right in the summer
time, but in the winter where can you go to? You
can't. You've been lucky—being so quick. You
don't hardly know you're born, you don't.

ANNA : Yes, I do, Sarah. My Charles isn't rich or
anything like that. We'll have to go ever so carefully—to start with anyway.

SARAH : Still, he isn't exactly what I'd call poor
though, is he?

ANNA : Well, *we're* not having a house—only fur-
nished rooms.

SARAH : Never mind that, you'll be living like a
lady, won't you? So what will you do all day?

ANNA : One thing, I shan't be lonely. Charles has
ever such a lot of nice friends and, in time, I shall
get to know all of them. Charles says, if I like, I
can have an afternoon tea-party every day until I do.

SARAH: Every *day*?

ANNA: Well—perhaps not *every* day. I expect some days I shall be out paying calls myself.

SARAH (*impressed*): Paying calls, eh? My! Aren't you cool!

ANNA: But that's what life's like in London, Sarah. Everybody pays calls. Charles did try to explain it to me. Some things are done, he says, and some things are not done. So I should think to begin with, I shall be quite busy trying to find out which is which.

SARAH: I should say! But suppose you go and make a mistake?

ANNA: Then what happens is next time you walk down the street all the people look the other way and nobody says good morning.

SARAH: Ooh! The stuck-up lot! I wouldn't like that sort of going on.

ANNA: No—only with Charles there helping me and telling me what's what, I shan't feel too bad. (*Turning back to the desk.*) Here, look out, Sarah —she'll be down in a moment and I'm meant to have this whole page of writing done by then.

SARAH (*approaching Anna*): Let's have a look.

ANNA: No, go on—it's private.

SARAH: No, it's not. That's only your old copy-book, that's all that is.

ANNA (*covering up*): All the same, it's private, if you don't mind.

SARAH: Oh, come on—let's have a look.

ANNA: It's not even interesting—truly. It's nothing really—only words.

SARAH: Then what's it matter? Let's see.

ANNA: You won't be no wiser if I let you. Oh, all right then—there.

SARAH (*peering over Anna's shoulder*): What's it

say? (*Reading.*) 'Charles Bradford. Charles Brad-ford. Charles Bradford.' That first line there's not your writing, Anna—that's madam's.

ANNA : Because it's the copy, stupid.

SARAH (*reading*) : 'Belov'd. Belov'd. Belov'd.' And that's her writing, too.

ANNA : I *told* you! She sets me the words, then I copy them out over and over.

SARAH : Why? Are you trying to get to write just like madam does?

ANNA : That's what she wants, but I'll never be able to, not if I was to sit here till kingdom come.

SARAH (*head on one side*) : I see what it is. *She* writes pointed. Yours is more round. I like the way she does her big B's though. She does her big B's lovely, only that's a funny word—belov'd.

ANNA : Belo*ved*. It's what I call him in the letters.

SARAH : Oh? I see. It's still funny though, isn't it?

ANNA : I never really liked it a lot, but she thought it was nice, so . . .

SARAH : Madam did? Then what's he call you—if I'm not being too nosey?

ANNA : He calls me dearest.

SARAH : Dearest. Is that *all*?

ANNA : Well—in the letters. He's different, of course, when . . . What's Bertie call you?

SARAH : Bertie? Now what does he call me? Oh, all sorts really. Sometimes he'll call me love. 'Hello, me old love,' he'll say. Or sometimes he'll just call me Sal, like, 'Well, how's me old Sal today?' That's his style. Oh, he's quite a card.

(*Arthur emerges from the study. He is about to leave for the brewery and carries a sheaf of documents.*)

ARTHUR : Ah! Mrs Harnham about anywhere?

ANNA ⎫
      ⎬ *(together)* : She's upstairs, sir, in the sew-
SARAH ⎭   ing room.

              She's upstairs, marking the new
              linen, sir.

ARTHUR *(to Sarah)* : Then slip up and tell her I'm just off, would you, Sarah.

SARAH : Yes, sir. (*She goes out and up the stairs.*)

ARTHUR : Well, Anna? So Mrs Harnham tells me you'll soon be leaving us.

ANNA : Yes, sir. Three weeks on Saturday, sir.

ARTHUR : Wedding-bells, eh? I'm delighted to hear it.

ANNA : Yes, sir.

ARTHUR : And you've made a pretty good catch, I understand.

ANNA : I hope so, sir.

ARTHUR : Hope so? No good living in hopes, you know. You need to be damned sure.

ANNA : Yes, sir. I am, sir.

ARTHUR : Good. Now I don't know what your arrangements are, Anna, but when our girls leave to get married, what usually happens is that, after the ceremony, we have the friends and relations back here, to drink a toast to the happy couple and that sort of thing.

ANNA : Oh, I think that would be lovely, sir.

ARTHUR : Then I'll have a word with Mrs Harnham. We let Cook take over the breakfast-room and I must say she usually does it rather well.

ANNA : How kind of you, sir. Thank you, sir.

ARTHUR : Come to think of it, you've both got a lot to thank me for—the pair of you.

ANNA : Have we, sir?

ARTHUR : It *is* the young feller you met at the fair, isn't it?

ANNA : Oh, yes, sir.

ARTHUR : Well, then. Don't you remember crying your eyes out because madam wasn't going to let you follow it up? Why, if I hadn't come along when I did, you might never have seen him again.

ANNA : I know, sir. Thank you, sir.

(Sarah starts down the stairs.)

ARTHUR : Anyhow, it all ended happily, that's the main thing. But that doesn't always happen, you know.

SARAH *(from the hallway)* : Madam's just coming, sir.

ARTHUR : Thank you, Sarah.

(Sarah goes off towards the rear of the house.)

(With a nod at the desk.) What are you supposed to be doing now? Writing?

ANNA : Yes, sir. Madam's set me a whole page of writing to do.

ARTHUR : I'd have thought you got enough practice writing letters to your young man.

(Edith starts down the stairs.)

ANNA : Oh, I don't write those, sir.

ARTHUR : Oh?

ANNA : No, sir. Madam writes those, sir.

ARTHUR : Madam does?

ANNA : Yes, sir.

ARTHUR : Madam does. I *see*.

(Edith enters.)

Oh, there you are, Edith. I was just telling Anna

that after the wedding, if she likes, she can bring
her friends and relations back here.

EDITH : Oh? But—

ARTHUR : It's something we've always done—not
perhaps in your time, but we've always done it—
given our girls something of a send-off.

EDITH : But there'll be no occasion for that, Arthur.
There'll barely be time for them to catch the
London train as it is.

ARTHUR : Then let them catch a later train.

EDITH : I don't think that, under the circumstances . . .

ARTHUR : You ask Letty. She'll tell you. (*Laughing.*) I remember once we put up a barrel of our
special home brew for them and the next morning—the next morning—Letty found one old man
still fast asleep under the sideboard.

EDITH (*not amused*) : Really?

ARTHUR : You ask her. Anyhow, we'll see. Plenty
of time to talk about that later.

EDITH : Yes. Have you finished, Anna.

ANNA : Not quite, ma'am.

EDITH : You should be by now. What on earth have
you been doing?

ARTHUR : Yes—well, I'm just off, Edith. All I
wanted to say was that I'm lunching with Tremlett
before the meeting and it's likely to be a long one.
We're giving him a seat on the board, of course,
but it's the end of the road so far as he's concerned. And yet he can't see it, you know—can't
see it. Poor fellow.

(*He goes into the hall, picks up his hat and during
the following goes off towards the front door.*)

EDITH : Let me see what you've done.

173

(*Anna hands the copy-book to Edith, who studies it for a moment.*)

Anna, this is *not* good enough. It really isn't. I can't believe you're even trying.

ANNA : I am, ma'am, truly I am. It's just that I can't do it like you, ma'am.

EDITH : But surely with the copy staring you in the face it's not too much to expect you to *spell* the words correctly. Look—you've left the *e* out of Charles all the way down the page.

ANNA : Have I, ma'am?

EDITH : Yes, you have.

ANNA : I didn't mean to, ma'am.

EDITH : It's just carelessness. The fact is you're not giving your mind to it. (*Desperately.*) And you must, Anna, you must! I'd have thought, for the sake of someone you say you love, you'd have been only too anxious to work hard at your writing. If you're not prepared to make even this small sacrifice, then what kind of a wife are you going to be, Anna?

ANNA (*rather sullenly*) : Once we're married, what'll it all matter?

EDITH : That may well be something you've yet to discover. But you're *not* married, Anna—not yet. There're nearly four weeks until the wedding-day and that means at least seven or eight more letters have still to be written. *Who* is going to write *them*?

ANNA : Well—you'll have to, ma'am, I suppose.

EDITH : Oh, if only you'd made more progress, Anna. Even if I'd had to help you with the sentiments, at least by now you could have written the letters yourself. As it is— (*She drops the copy-book on to the desk.*) there's only one thing I can do.

174

ANNA : How do you mean, ma'am?

EDITH : He must be told, of course. He must be told everything.

ANNA (*alarmed*) : No, ma'am.

EDITH (*firmly*) : He must be told that all this time, I've been answering his letters for you.

ANNA : But why, ma'am? Why do you have to tell him?

EDITH : Because, after you're married, he's bound to find out—sooner or later. Then think of all the miserable recriminations that would begin . . .

ANNA : But if you tell him now, ma'am, he might change his mind and not marry me at all.

EDITH : That should be for him to decide, Anna. And the poor fellow must have the opportunity to do so in the full knowledge of all the circumstances.

ANNA (*distressed*) : Oh, ma'am! But whatever would I *do*? What would *happen* to me? I think if he was to change his mind now I'd—I'd make an end to myself.

EDITH : Anna! Don't ever say such a wicked thing!

ANNA : I would, ma'am. For what kind of a life should I look forward to?

EDITH : But can't you see that a marriage built on a deceit—on a mere trick, if you like—which is how it'll seem to him—could so easily become the most bitter and loveless existence imaginable?

ANNA : But once we're married, I shan't need to worry about the old letters because I know, from going with him, I can make him happy. I know that. And at those times, ma'am, he's never bothering himself about grammar or spellin' or fine words or any things like that.

EDITH (*stung*) : There are other times to consider, Anna. And let me tell you this : it was the *letters*

175

and *only* the letters that made him decide to marry you.

ANNA: No! No, it wasn't, ma'am, it wasn't.

EDITH: My letters, Anna.

ANNA: But it's me he wants—not letters. Over and over, he's told me that. It's *me*.

EDITH: Oh, in a physical sense, I'm sure he finds you wholly desirable. I don't doubt that for a moment. But to give his sudden passion some sense of lasting value, he was looking for something more. Well, he found it—in my letters.

ANNA: You *say* that.

EDITH: He told me.

ANNA (*deeply upset*): Oh, ma'am!

EDITH: So now you see, don't you, how terribly wicked it would be not to tell him the truth?

(*A sullen silence from Anna.*)

You do see, don't you?

ANNA (*stoutly*): No, I *don't* see, ma'am. How can the letters matter, whatever you put, set beside what the two of us have been to each other?

EDITH: If you'd shown more concern for what was *said* in the letters instead of leaving it all to me, you'd not ask such a foolish question.

ANNA: I did try to at the start, ma'am, only in the end they was always written your way.

EDITH: But *his* letters? Why, apart from wanting to know when he was coming again, you've not shown the slightest interest in his letters either.

ANNA: It's just that I've grown to feel they're nothing to do with me, ma'am.

EDITH: No. And in a sense, they're not. But Mr Bradford doesn't feel that. Each letter from him has marked a step forward to which I always had

176

to respond. So it's not you he's come to know, Anna, but me.

ANNA : Only in his head, ma'am. He's never even touched you, has he? But me—he knows me. He *really* knows me.

EDITH : I don't care, Anna. I cannot go on. I shouldn't go on. And it's not only him I'm thinking of—I'm thinking of the effect it's having on me.

ANNA : On you, ma'am?

EDITH : Yes.

ANNA : But it can't have any effect on *you*, ma'am.

EDITH : How can you say that?

ANNA : Because—

EDITH : Well?

ANNA : Because you're married already.

EDITH : Oh, you poor, stupid little fool! Can't you see what it's meant to me to have had to write to this man for weeks on end? And to write in terms which are now virtually those of a wife? Can't you see? To have had to lay bare my deepest, most intimate feelings and then—oh, God!—pretend— pretend to a physical condition which, in fact, isn't mine at all? Can you imagine what that's meant and still say it can't have had any effect on me?

ANNA : Oh, no!

EDITH : Every letter from him, I read as if it were meant for me. Every letter I wrote was written from *my* heart and nobody's else's. And I won him, Anna, *I* won him.

ANNA (*desperately*) : You didn't! You didn't!

EDITH : Do you imagine a man like him would have let himself be captured by a common, ignorant servant girl?

(*Anna flinches and hides her face.*)

177

They were *my* thoughts and *my* feelings he
responded to, and for the first time in my life I
feel I'm no longer alone. I've someone to love and
care about—even though to him I'm hardly so
much as a name. But it cannot go on . . . it cannot.

(*Edith, overcome, sinks down and wipes her eyes.
For a moment Anna struggles mentally with the
dimly perceived implications of Edith's words, then
she moves quickly to her mistress and kneels beside
her chair.*)

ANNA : Oh, ma'am! I see what it is. I *am* a common,
ignorant girl and I haven't rightly understood.
But now I see—of course. (*Pause.*) You love him,
too, don't you?

(*Edith averts her face, a movement which Anna
rightly interprets to be an affirmation.*)

Oh, ma'am!

(*The two women remain silent for a moment,
pressed close, grasping each other, seeking comfort.*)

EDITH : Forgive me, Anna. Forgive me.
ANNA : Don't be upset so, ma'am. You've been so
good and kind to me . . .
EDITH : But I haven't. I haven't.
ANNA : . . . there's nothing to forgive.
EDITH : I've been selfish and foolish. I am to blame
for everything—everything.
ANNA : No, ma'am, no.
EDITH : Yes—I should have seen what was hap-
pening, but I wouldn't. And I wouldn't because—
because I *wanted* to go on. And . . . oh, I still do.
ANNA (*after a pause*): It was only because I asked

178

for your help, ma'am, that it all started. You were only trying to do what was best for everyone.

EDITH : Of course. For who else *could* have helped you, Anna? You had nobody. At the start, you were my only concern.

ANNA : Am I not still, ma'am?

EDITH : Yes, yes, of course you are, but . . .

ANNA : Then I know you'll not forsake me now, ma'am.

EDITH : But now we have to think of him, too, Anna.

ANNA : I do think of him—all the time, ma'am.

EDITH : Then surely you'd never wish to deceive him?

ANNA : But, ma'am, I'm not. Whatever nice things you put in the letters, you could never have put anything nicer than what I'm thinking every blessed minute of the day—for I've a niceness of my own when it comes to thinking of him.

EDITH : Of course you have, Anna.

ANNA : And I'm sure, if I'd been able, what I'd have put down for myself would have meant just the same as what you put, ma'am.

EDITH : If you'd been *able*—that's the very point, Anna. As it is, he believes you to have an ability which you simply don't possess.

ANNA : And because I haven't, is that why you think I'm not good enough for him?

EDITH : I shouldn't have said that, Anna. I was upset. But that's what the world will think.

ANNA : Then—I suppose—that's what he'll think, too.

EDITH : He may not.

ANNA : Ma'am—if you was to write and tell him everything—now—this very minute—do you truly believe, right deep down, that he'd ever marry me?

EDITH : How can either of us know what he'd do, Anna? On the one hand, I have his letters—on the other hand, you . . .
ANNA : I have his baby, ma'am.

(*There is the sound of the front door opening and closing. Anna gets to her feet quickly and moves away from Edith, as Letty, carrying a full shopping basket, passes down the hallway towards the rear of the house.*)

Oh, please don't tell him, ma'am. If we was to go on as we did for just a little longer, it can't make so much difference to you, but—oh, ma'am, the difference to me !

(*Edith remains impassive. Anna tries again.*)

If I should marry him I'll be as good as gold to him. I'll work and slave for him, I swear I will, and put myself out to learn all the things I need to know. That, I promise, ma'am.

(*Pause.*)

Perhaps he won't find out about the letters, not to start off with. Why should he? Perhaps by then, ma'am, I'll have had the baby and he'll have seen it. He's not the sort to turn against his own, is he? Not *him*.

(*Pause.*)

So why shouldn't he be happy, ma'am, up there in Bloomsbury with me to do the rooms out and keep everything nice and cosy for him and not go daft spending money like water as some do who've never had it.

(*Pause.*)

And if he *is* happy, ma'am, then that's what we both want isn't it?

EDITH (*speaking from a preoccupation of her own*): Do you realize, Anna, that you'll be asked to sign your name by the Registrar?

ANNA: Will I, ma'am?

EDITH (*rising*): So you'd better concentrate your attention on learning to write it the way I do.

ANNA (*slowly*): You mean—you—you'll go on with writing the letters, ma'am?

EDITH: I shall hate myself, but I shall go on—for your sake, Anna.

ANNA: Oh, ma'am! I can't ever thank you enough, but—oh, I do thank you, ma'am, for now I'm sure everything'll come right because you always know what's best to do. (*She seizes Edith's hand and kisses it.*)

EDITH: Anna, Anna! If one knew that . . .

Both remain motionless as the lights fade.

Curtain.

Scene 3

The morning of the wedding, the first Saturday in August. Letty is arranging, in a handsome silver bowl, some roses which have just arrived from the florist. Arthur, in high spirits, emerges from the study carrying a copy of The Times.

ARTHUR: I say, Letty, look at this. We're in *The Times*. Quite a decent bit. (*He hands Letty the paper, folded in such a way that she can read the column heading.)*

LETTY: Why, so we are! (*Reading.*) 'Tremlett's to merge with Harnham's. Further rationalization of brewing interests in the South West.'

ARTHUR: Go on.

LETTY (*reading*): 'The chairman of Harnham's, Mr Arthur Harnham, told our representative, "This merger will make Harnham's not only the oldest but by far the largest firm of brewers in the south west of England".'

ARTHUR: Not bad, is it? The whole of the South West. Hello? Where've those come from?

LETTY: Anna's young man—the bridegroom.

ARTHUR: Oh! Who are they for?

LETTY: They were addressed to all of us, but I suspect they're really meant for Edith.

ARTHUR: Well, that's very civil of the feller—very civil. (*He moves to the windows.*) I suppose they'll be back any moment now, won't they?

LETTY: Yes, it doesn't take many minutes in a Registry Office.

ARTHUR (*gazing out at the square*): No.

LETTY: You've seen the masterpiece Cook's brought forth, I suppose?

ARTHUR (*his thoughts elsewhere*): Yes, I have— yes. How they love that sort of thing, don't they? (*There is a pause, then he suddenly turns to Letty.*) I don't blame the girl, of course I don't, but I must admit I'm damn glad to see her go.

LETTY: It'll upset Edith terribly at first. You'll have to be very gentle with her for a little while.

ARTHUR: If I ever have the chance to get near her!

LETTY: You'll have more chance now, Arthur. It's going to be very much easier for you both.

ARTHUR: How do you mean?

LETTY: I'm going away.

ARTHUR: What?

LETTY: I'm leaving here, Arthur.

ARTHUR: You don't mean that.

LETTY: Yes, I do. I'm going to live in Weymouth near Cousin Maisie.

ARTHUR: But why?

LETTY: She tells me the winters are relatively mild in Weymouth.

ARTHUR (*after a pause*): That's not why you're going, is it?

LETTY: No. I shall be happier, I think. You see, you have Edith, and Edith doesn't need *me*, I assure you.

ARTHUR: But who's going to look after everything? I mean . . .

LETTY: She will, of course. You'll find her far more competent than ever I was, Arthur.

ARTHUR: But—does she know you're going?

LETTY: Not yet. It's been a very emotional time for Edith, so I thought I'd wait until the wedding was over.

ARTHUR: I see. (*Pause.*) She locks her bedroom-door now. Did you know that?

LETTY: No, Arthur. I—I'm sorry.

ARTHUR: Do you think it would do any good, once Anna's gone, if you were to talk to Edith?

LETTY (*firmly*): No, Arthur.

ARTHUR: She might tell *you* things that . . .

LETTY: Arthur, you once said I played the matchmaker rather well. Perhaps I played it too well and for rather too long.

ARTHUR: How do you mean?

LETTY: If I'd been sensible, I should have gone from here the day you got married.

ARTHUR: Why?

LETTY : Because we all of us have to learn to live our own lives—not other people's.

(*Sarah, breathless and excited, bursts noisily through the front door and appears in the hallway. She wears a hat, gloves and her best summer dress with a spray of flowers pinned to it. She puts down an overnight bag belonging to Mr Bradford by the hall table, then comes down to Letty unaware that Arthur is by the windows.*)

SARAH : Oh, he's such a lovely feller, ma'am. You'd never believe. A real gentleman, he is, but ever so nice and friendly with it. (*Suddenly aware of Arthur.*) Oh, beg pardon, sir.

ARTHUR : So it's all over, is it? Man and wife now, eh?

SARAH : Yes, sir.

ARTHUR : Well, I must try to think of something suitable to say. They'll expect a few well-chosen words, no doubt.

LETTY : Of course they will, Arthur.

ARTHUR : I'll be in the study.

(*Arthur goes off into the study.*)

SARAH : And look—look what he give us, ma'am. (*She indicates her spray of flowers.*) He give 'em to all the ladies.

LETTY : How very pretty, Sarah.

SARAH : And a white carnation each for the gentlemen—all done up in silver paper.

LETTY : Did everything go quite smoothly at the ceremony?

SARAH : Oh, perfect, ma'am. Mind, it's not like in church, is it? You don't get none of that feeling come over you and it's so lovely you want to cry.

You don't get none of that. But it was a dear little wedding all the same.

LETTY: They'll be here any minute, I suppose?

SARAH: Madam wanted me back here to show the others where to go, so I rushed on over while they're having the photograph.

LETTY: Well, that shouldn't take long.

SARAH: No—only I come straight across the square, ma'am, but I expect the others'll go the long way round because they're still putting up the stalls and the swings and that.

LETTY: I'd forgotten about the fair. Really—it seems no time at all since it was last here.

SARAH: August Bank Holiday on Monday, ma'am. And the new steam roundabout, that's back here again. Do you think Cook and me will be able to slip out for a short while on Monday, ma'am?

LETTY: I dare say, but that's something you'll have to ask Mrs Harnham, Sarah.

SARAH: Cook's made ever such a lovely little wedding cake, ma'am, with a pink horse-shoe right in the middle.

LETTY: I'm sure Anna will be delighted.

SARAH: She was ever so nervous, ma'am. When it come for her to sign the form, her hand was shaking so she could hardly write.

LETTY: I expect you'll be just as nervous on your wedding day, Sarah.

SARAH: *My* wedding day! I hope I live to see it, ma'am, the way things are.

LETTY: Nonsense! It'll be your turn next, I expect.

SARAH: Mr Harnham hasn't said nothing more about a house for us, has he?

LETTY: He's been so busy lately. But now that this Tremlett affair is settled there'll be several houses falling vacant. I'll speak to him again.

185

SARAH : Oh, thank you, ma'am. Only Bert says he thinks Mr Philips has forgotten all about it, too.

(*Noise and movement in the street outside catch Sarah's attention and she moves quickly to the windows.*)

It's them, ma'am. They've come in a fly. Just the two of them. And he's helping her out.
LETTY : Then you go and show them in, Sarah.
SARAH : Yes, ma'am.

(*Sarah darts off into the hall to open the front door while Letty, having finished arranging the roses, carefully carries the bowl back to its customary place in the room. Presently, Anna and Charles then Sarah appear in the hallway. Anna, carrying a bouquet of flowers, is hesitant to enter.*)

LETTY : Well, Anna? Come in, my dear, and tell me how it feels to be Mrs Charles Bradford.
ANNA (*coming down*): It feels very nice, ma'am. This is Charles, ma'am.
LETTY : Oh, how do you do, Mr Bradford? I'm Mrs Harnham's sister-in-law.
CHARLES : How do you do?
LETTY (*grasping his hand with both of hers*) : Please allow me to wish you both every happiness for the future and many, many golden years together.
CHARLES : Thank you—that's most kind of you. (*He glances at Anna.*) I fancy we're both still feeling somewhat tongue-tied, perhaps even a little bewildered by our sudden change of status. Aren't we, Anna, my dear?
ANNA : Yes, Charles.

CHARLES : But I'm told that is something we'll grow accustomed to quite soon enough.

LETTY : Is Mrs Harnham ... ?

ANNA : She should be here any moment, ma'am.

CHARLES : She insisted on walking, I may say, but only so that Anna and I would be alone together in the fly.

ANNA : As we drove round the square, we could see the workmen putting up the new steam round-about, couldn't we, Charles?

CHARLES : We saw the very horse Anna was riding that evening last May when we met for the first time.

ANNA : A big white one with a long, black mane.

CHARLES : Unhappily, it was in a rather undignified position lying on its back with its legs in the air waiting to be attended to.

(*Everyone laughs.*)

LETTY : How very unromantic of it !

SARAH (*from the hallway*) : Here's madam now.

(*Edith appears in the hallway. Like Sarah, she wears a spray of flowers pinned to her dress. Briskly, she at once takes charge.*)

EDITH (*as she comes down*) : Is everything ready in the breakfast-room, Sarah?

SARAH : Yes, ma'am.

EDITH : Then I think we should go along now. (*To Charles and Anna.*) There's not a great deal of time before you two must set out for the station.

CHARLES (*looking at his pocket-watch*) : Not to cut it too fine, Mrs Harnham, I've told the fellow on the fly that he's to wait for us.

EDITH : Yes, it's sometimes difficult to find one on

a Saturday. Now, go along, Sarah—Anna. Cook
has a lovely surprise waiting for you.

(*As the two girls move off along the hall towards
the breakfast-room, Anna is showing her wedding
ring to Sarah.*)

(*To Letty.*) Does Arthur know we're back?
LETTY : Oh, he's bound to have heard, Edith. He's
only in the study.
EDITH : Then come along, Mr Bradford.

(*Edith and Letty move up into the hall, followed
by Charles. As the two women move off towards
the breakfast-room, the study door opens and
Arthur appears in time to detain Charles.*)

ARTHUR : Ah, Bradford? I'm Harnham.
CHARLES : How do you do, sir?
ARTHUR : Everything went off all right, I hope?
CHARLES : Oh, splendidly, sir.
ARTHUR : Good. Then I think, before the revels
start, my lad, we'd better just have a word together,
you and I, eh?
CHARLES : Certainly, sir.

(*Arthur grips Charles by the arm in a friendly
manner and leads him down into the room.*)

ARTHUR : Don't be afraid. I'm not proposing to
make a long speech or anything of that sort. I know
you've a train to catch, but they're expecting a
few words from me, of course. And you'll have to
reply.
CHARLES : I think I can manage that, sir.
ARTHUR : But the thing is, in the ordinary way, these
affairs are entirely local and everybody knows

everybody else. But this is different. Down here, you're what we call a foreigner—a bit of a dark horse. So I thought it might be a good idea if I could tell 'em a bit about you.

CHARLES : Such as?

ARTHUR : Well, now—you're a Londoner, aren't you?

ARTHUR : I was born in London, yes.

ARTHUR : Then what *are* you? What do you do for a living?

CHARLES : I'm a barrister, but—er—

ARTHUR : Eh? What?

CHARLES : A barrister, sir.

ARTHUR (*incredulous*) : A barrister?

CHARLES : Of Lincoln's Inn.

ARTHUR : Lincoln's Inn? A barrister? (*His whole attitude changes.*) My dear fellow, I'd no idea you were a professional man. No idea at all. Nobody told me that. Good heavens! But how extraordinary!

CHARLES (*sharply*) : In what way, sir?

ARTHUR : You're the same young man that Anna met at the fair, aren't you?

CHARLES : I imagine so. We did first meet at the fair.

(*At this moment, the remainder of the wedding-party passes down the hall from the front door towards the breakfast-room. All sidle past shyly and awkwardly, two men in ill-cut suits of some heavy material wearing white carnations, three women wearing sprays of flowers pinned to their voluminous but shapeless gowns.*)

ARTHUR : Yes—well—when I say extraordinary, all I mean is it's extraordinary that Anna should have

—er—been fortunate enough to encounter someone in such good standing as you on a fairground. That's all I mean.

CHARLES : It was quite fortuitous, I agree, but for my part, sir, a very *happy* encounter.

ARTHUR : Oh, but of course. And one that has led on to an equally happy conclusion. Well, you've certainly given me plenty to talk about, but don't worry, my dear fellow, I shall keep it short and sweet. And you, I realize, must be well accustomed to getting on your feet.

CHARLES : Naturally, I shall welcome an opportunity to thank everyone for all their kindness, and in particular, of course, Mrs Harnham.

ARTHUR : Yes—well, it's quite fair to say that if it hadn't been for Mrs Harnham it's most unlikely that you'd be here today.

CHARLES : I don't doubt that at all, sir.

ARTHUR : There's no blame attaching to Anna, of course—none whatsoever. But the aunt must have been a stupid woman.

CHARLES : I don't quite—?

ARTHUR : I blame the aunt entirely.

CHARLES : What for, sir?

ARTHUR : Why, for not seeing that Anna went to school and learnt to read and write.

(*Sarah enters, carrying a silver tray on which are several glasses of champagne.*)

SARAH (*suppressing a giggle*) : Mrs Bradford says she's waiting to cut the cake, sir.

ARTHUR : We're just coming. (*To Charles.*) A glass of champagne, my dear fellow?

CHARLES (*who has been thinking hard*) : I beg your pardon?

ARTHUR : A glass of champagne?

CHARLES : Oh! (*Taking a glass.*) Oh, thank you.

ARTHUR (*also taking a glass*) : But let me tell you you're not the only one with something to celebrate, is he, Sarah?

SARAH : Oh, no, sir.

ARTHUR : This has been a memorable week for Harnham's, too. We are now not only the oldest and the best, but also the biggest brewery in the whole of the south west of England. There! What do you think of that?

CHARLES : I'm interested in what you were saying about the aunt, sir.

(*Edith enters.*)

EDITH : Oh, do come along, Arthur. Their glasses are all filled. Everybody's waiting.

ARTHUR : We're coming, we're coming. Let's get it over, my dear fellow. Come along. Yes, the biggest in the whole of the south west of England—that's something, isn't it?

(*Taking their glasses with them, Arthur and Charles go off towards the breakfast-room.*)

SARAH : *You* haven't had a glass of champagne yet, ma'am.

EDITH (*moving to the windows*) : No, thank you, Sarah. I don't want anything just at the moment.

SARAH : Mr Mansell's brought a great bag of rice in his pocket, ma'am, so I told him, I said, if *one single speck* of that stuff gets into my hall, I'll scratch your eyes out, I said.

EDITH (*from the window*) : There's that poor man waiting outside with the fly. If you like, Sarah, you may take *him* a glass of champagne.

SARAH : Ooh! It won't make him squiffy, ma'am, will it?

EDITH : I should hardly think so.

SARAH : All the same, I expect he'll say he'd rather have a glass of beer any day, although champagne'll make a nice change for him, won't it, ma'am?

(*As Sarah moves up into the hall with her tray of glasses, there is a burst of laughter from the wedding-party in the breakfast-room. Sarah puts the tray on the hall table, picks up a single glass and goes off with it to the front door. Letty enters.*)

LETTY : Arthur's now in full spate, Edith. Do you want to hear him?

EDITH : All I want is for them to go. The thing's done. It's over. If only they'd go.

LETTY (*gently*) : They'll be off presently, Edith.

EDITH : They should never have come back here. They could so easily have gone straight to the station.

LETTY : It wouldn't have been quite the same, would it?

EDITH : It was Arthur, of course. He insisted.

LETTY : I think he was curious to see the young man. And I must confess so was I. He's—he's very handsome, Edith.

EDITH : Well, I've done my best for Anna. Now, there's no more I *can* do.

LETTY : And how pretty she looks, too. Of course, I think it's a pity they weren't married in church, but I suppose times are changing.

(*There is a burst of clapping from the wedding-party in the breakfast-room.*)

Oh, but I do so love to see a white wedding with

the organ and the choir and the bells and the carriages—like yours was, Edith. Do you remember?

(Sarah appears in the hall. She returns the empty glass to the tray which she then picks up.)

It's hard to believe it was only three years ago.

(Sarah, carrying her tray, comes down into the room a step or so.)

SARAH : I give him the champagne, ma'am, and he drunk it down. And do you know what he said? He said, 'Very nice, but I'd sooner have a glass of beer any day?' I knew that's what he'd say, ma'am. Didn't I say he would? *(She goes off with her tray towards the breakfast-room.)*

LETTY : Does that girl sound to you as if she's been helping herself rather too freely, Edith?

EDITH : So far as I'm concerned, she can fall down in a stupor, if she likes. *(Moving towards the hall.)* I shall come down to wish Anna goodbye.

LETTY : Oh, but won't that look rather . . .

EDITH : You go and join the others, Letty.

LETTY : Very well, Edith, but . . .

(Edith goes off up the stairs. For a moment, Letty watches her go anxiously. At the same time, from the wedding-party comes a sustained burst of applause, followed by a buzz of general chatter, laughter and the clink of glasses. Letty is about to return to the breakfast-room when Charles suddenly appears.)

CHARLES : Oh, Miss Harnham—?

LETTY : Can I help you, Mr Bradford?

CHARLES : The fact is, I'm looking for Mrs Harnham. She seems to have quite disappeared.

LETTY : She's gone up to her room, but she'll be down presently, Mr Bradford. Is there anything I can do?

CHARLES : I think not, thank you. It's just that Anna and I—well—we've a little surprise for her.

LETTY : Oh?

(*Anna enters.*)

ANNA : What is it, Charles?

CHARLES : Ah, Anna. My dear, I want you to do something for me.

ANNA : Anything, Charles—anything in the world.

CHARLES : If Miss Harnham will excuse us both for a moment?

LETTY : Of course. I should be helping with the guests, in any case. (*She goes out to rejoin the wedding-party.*)

ANNA : Well? What am I to do?

CHARLES : First, let me show you something.

(*From his pocket, Charles produces a jeweller's box which he opens, showing Anna the contents—a pendant of paste and semi-precious stones.*)

Look—isn't that pretty?

ANNA : Oh, Charles! It's lovely. But—oh, my dear, you shouldn't—you've already given me so much.

CHARLES : It's not meant for you, Anna, no.

ANNA : No? Then who is it for?

CHARLES : It's a present for Mrs Harnham. For all her kindness, a present from us both.

ANNA : For Mrs Harnham? Yes, yes! Oh, I'm so glad you remembered her, Charles. She'll be so pleased. Now I know what you want me to do. You want me to give it to her.

CHARLES : Not that exactly, Anna.

ANNA : Oh?

CHARLES : What I'd like you to do is write a little note . . .

ANNA (*fearfully*) : Write a little note?

CHARLES : Yes—to go with it.

ANNA : But if we're going to give it to her ourselves, there's no need. We can *say* . . .

CHARLES (*firmly*) : I would like you to write a few lines, Anna. It shows a proper concern and it'll please Mrs Harnham, too. Besides, you can do it so charmingly. (*He moves to the desk and sets the chair for her.*) Come and sit here, Anna. It'll only take you a moment, and then we shall have to start thinking about our train.

(*Like a person going to the scaffold, Anna walks to the desk and sits.*)

That's it. There, now—just a few words of thanks for all her past kindnesses. And try to work in one of those little turns of phrase which I used to find so delightful.

(*Miserably, Anna takes up the pen. There is a burst of laughter from the wedding-party in the breakfast-room. Charles moves to look out of the window. Anna begins to write, but her eyes fill with tears. At length, she lets her head fall on her arms and breaks into loud, uninhibited sobs. Charles moves to her quickly.*)

Why, Anna—my dear—what on earth's the matter?

ANNA (*through her sobs*) : I can't do it. I can't.

CHARLES : Oh, nonsense! Of course you can.

ANNA (*through her sobs*): I can't. I can't.

CHARLES: Here, let me see what you've done.

(*Charles takes up Anna's abortive note, an action which triggers off a further outburst of sobbing, and looks at it.*)

ANNA (*through her sobs*): Oh, Charles! I—I didn't write those letters, Charles. She did. (*She twists herself round in the chair and grasps Charles about the waist, hiding her face against him.*) I'm learning though. I *am* learning, my dear. You'll forgive me, won't you? You'll forgive me for not telling you before?

(*Pause.*)

CHARLES (*gently*): You mustn't cry on your wedding day, Anna. It's unlucky, they say.

(*Anna rises and puts her arms round his neck.*)

ANNA: Oh, Charles, I feel so bad about it. Oh, my dear!

(*Charles gently removes her arms.*)

CHARLES: You have some things to bring down from upstairs, haven't you?

ANNA: Yes.

CHARLES: Then dry your eyes, my dear, and go and get ready, for we must be off shortly.

ANNA: I knew. I knew I was right. I knew it wasn't those old letters.

(*Tearful still, Anna goes off towards the rear of the house as her room is reached by the back stairs. Charles turns back to the desk and picks up the*

*sheet of writing-paper which bears Anna's few
clumsy words. Edith starts down the stairs. Charles
drops the paper on the desk as she enters.)*

EDITH : Oh. Anna's not with you, Mr Bradford?
CHARLES : She's just gone to gather her belongings
together. It's nearly time for us to go.
EDITH : Yes, I suppose it must be.
CHARLES : Mrs Harnham—I find it hard to thank
you for all you've done, not only for Anna, but for
me also.
EDITH : Please don't try. I—I've done little enough.
CHARLES *(producing the pendant in its box)* : Both
Anna and I would be most happy if you'd accept
this very inadequate . . .
EDITH *(taking the box)* : Mr Bradford, this is quite
unnecessary. *(Opening the box.)* Oh, how
lovely!
CHARLES : It's not genuine, I'm afraid, but it looks
pretty, I think.
EDITH : It's most beautiful. I shall always treasure it.
CHARLES : Anna began a little note to go with it.
(He picks it up from the desk) Unhappily, she
didn't get very far.

*(Edith takes the note from him, glances at it, then
their eyes remain fixed on each other. At length,
Edith turns away and puts down both the note and
the pendant on one of the small tables. Charles
moves after her.)*

So . . . *(Pause.)* The letters were yours?
EDITH : Yes.
CHARLES : No part of them was Anna's?
EDITH : They were written *for* Anna.
CHARLES : But you wrote them without her—alone?

197

EDITH: Some of them. Yes—many. But only on her behalf. I was trying to help her.

CHARLES: Then the thoughts and feelings expressed were yours—not Anna's?

EDITH: I put down what I would have written had I been in her position.

CHARLES: I see—yes. I think I understand. You had such concern for her.

EDITH (*clutching at a straw*): Yes, I had. I *was* concerned for her.

CHARLES: And—quite naturally—you'd no concern for me.

EDITH: Oh, but I had!

CHARLES (*shaking his head*): No concern. So—you deceived me.

EDITH: But it wasn't—I didn't mean—

CHARLES (*interrupting firmly*): You deceived me, Mrs Harnham.

EDITH (*almost a whisper*): Yes.

CHARLES: Cleverly. Successfully.

EDITH: Cleverly? It wasn't clever—no, no—it wasn't that.

CHARLES: To have chained me to a little—peasant—

EDITH: No!

CHARLES: —a pretty, little peasant.

EDITH: Don't!

CHARLES: That was very clever, Mrs Harnham.

EDITH: It wasn't. It was wrong of me. I'd no intention of hurting you—not *you* . . .

CHARLES: Then why did you do it? (*Pause.*) Why?

EDITH: I began—I think I began in simple kindness. Kindness to her—to Anna. What else could I have done, knowing the girl was in trouble? But I admit I—I went on—for other reasons.

CHARLES : Other reasons?

EDITH : Yes.

CHARLES : What other reasons?

EDITH : Writing freely to someone—brought me a sort of—happiness, I think.

CHARLES : Why?

EDITH : Because—no. No, I mustn't say.

CHARLES : But you must say, Mrs Harnham. Why?

EDITH : Because—to open my heart to someone—and to find a response—was something I'd never known.

CHARLES (*after a pause*) : Do you mean your letters to me were not all make-believe, that you were not just pretending? Is that what you're saying?

EDITH : Yes.

CHARLES : You were expressing your true feelings—your true feelings towards me?

EDITH : Yes.

CHARLES : You meant every word you wrote?

EDITH : Every word.

CHARLES : And you still do?

EDITH : With all my heart.

CHARLES : I see. (*Pause.*) Well, then—it would seem that you and I are lovers. Lovers by correspondence. In fact, more than that now.

EDITH : Now?

CHARLES : Legally, I've married Anna—God help us both—but in soul and spirit I've married the writer of those letters and no other woman in the world.

EDITH : But I couldn't—you must know that we could never—ever—

CHARLES (*interrupting*) : Why try to dodge the whole truth? You've admitted half of it. I've married you. So let me now make one claim.

199

(*He draws her to him. She hesitates.*)

For the first time—and the last.

(*He kisses her fiercely. As he does so, a burst of rough laughter is heard from the breakfast-room. Edith breaks away from the embrace, bewildered by its ferocity and uncertain of Charles' real feelings.*)

EDITH : Then—you forgive me?
CHARLES : Forgive you, Mrs Harnham?
EDITH : Can you?
CHARLES : No. I can never forgive you.
EDITH : But—perhaps—in time—with Anna, you may find . . .
CHARLES : Never. And with Anna there to remind me it's unlikely I shall ever forget.

(*Anna appears in the hallway. She carries her belongings in a small, basket-like trunk held together by a leather strap.*)

Ah—here she is. Are you ready, my dear?
ANNA : Yes, Charles.
CHARLES : Then we must make a start. Good-bye, Mrs Harnham.

(*Edith remains silent. Charles moves up and takes Anna's luggage from her. Anna runs down to Edith and flings her arms about her. The two women hold each other tightly for a moment while off-stage Sarah's voice is heard.*

SARAH (*off*) : They're going! They're going—everybody! Mr and Mrs Bradford are just going. Come and see them off! Come on, everybody! They're leaving for the station now!

(Charles picks up his own bag as Anna joins him in the hallway and both move off quickly.

The wedding-party, their former inhibitions now softened by alcohol, troop through the hall laughing and chattering.

Edith remains motionless as to cries of 'Good luck!' and 'Every happiness!' and much shouting and laughing, the newly-married pair prepare to set forth.

Suddenly, as the fly is heard to pull away to a ragged cheer, the new steam roundabout emits three short blasts on its whistle and the organ bursts into gay, martial music.

As the wedding-party begins to retrace its steps towards the breakfast-room and the drinks, Arthur comes bustling into the room. He proceeds at once to close the upper sashes of the open windows, thus reducing the sound of the music to a reasonable level.)

ARTHUR : High time they put a stop to this. Can't hear yourself speak. Let them hold it somewhere out in the country.

(Arthur is moving towards the hallway when a thought strikes him and he turns back to Edith.)

I daresay the others will be here for quite a while yet, you know. They're expecting to see something of *you*, Edith, so come along and join in the fun.

Arthur goes off towards the breakfast-room. Edith remains as though turned to stone. The music from the steam-organ swells a little. After a moment the curtains fall quickly.

WILLIE ROUGH

A Play by
BILL BRYDEN

First published, with the aid of a Scottish Arts Council grant, Edinburgh, 1972, by Southside (Publishers) Ltd.

All professional and amateur companies wishing to perform this play must apply for permission to Felix de Wolfe & Associates, 1 Robert Street, Adelphi, London WC2N 6BH.

Willie Rough appeared at the Lyceum Theatre, Edinburgh, on 10 February, 1972, with the following cast:

MR PENROSE	*John Shedden*
GEORDIE MACLEOD	*James Kennedy*
SAM THOMSON	*Paul Young*
WILLIE ROUGH	*James Grant*
HUGHIE	*Fulton Mackay*
EDDIE	*Callum Mill*
JAKE ADAMS	*Roddy McMillan*
PAT GATENS	*Joseph Brady*
APPRENTICE	*Andrew Byatt*
KATE	*Eileen McCallum*
BERNADETTE	*Clare Richards*
POLICEMAN 1 (SANNY)	*Bill McCabe*
POLICEMAN 2 (PETER)	*James Gavigan*
CHARLIE MCGRATH	*John Cairney*
NURSE	*Christine McKenna*
WORKERS	*Harry Fox, Ray Rennie, Mike Roberts*

Directed by Bill Bryden

Designed by Geoffrey Scott

There were the following changes in the company when the play came to the Shaw Theatre, London, on 17 January, 1973:

POLICEMAN 1 (SANNY)	*Ian Stewart*
POLICEMAN 2 (PETER)	*William Armour*
NURSE	*Ann Maley*

I carry a brick on my shoulder in order that people
may know what my house was like.

BERT BRECHT

GREENOCK

This grey town
That pipes the morning up before the lark
With shrieking steam, and from a hundred stalks
Lacquers the sooty sky; where hammers clang
On iron hulls, and cranes in harbours creak,
Rattle and swing, whole cargoes on their necks;
Where men sweat gold that others hoard or spend,
And lurk like vermin in their narrow streets:
This old grey town
Is world enough for me.

JOHN DAVIDSON

CHARACTERS

MR PENROSE, *clerk*

GEORDIE MACLEOD

SAM THOMSON

WILLIE ROUGH

HUGHIE

PAT GATENS

EDDIE, *publican*

JAKE ADAMS, *foreman*

APPRENTICE

KATE, *Willie's wife*

BERNADETTE, *Pat's wife*

SANNY, *policeman*

PETER, *policeman*

CHARLIE MCGRATH

NURSE

WORKERS

The action is set in Greenock, Scotland, between February 1914 and June 1916.

ACT ONE

1. *Shipyard Employment Office: February 1914*

The shipyard horn blasts loud and long. Three men are sitting on a simple wooden bench opposite a cluttered wooden desk with an empty chair behind it. Willie is reading a newspaper. Beside him Sam is rolling a cigarette. Next to Sam sits Geordie. Sam lights his cigarette, and, while they wait, Geordie begins whistling impatiently. Mr Penrose, the clerk, comes in, ignoring their reaction to his arrival. He sits down on the empty chair, and rearranges his papers.

MR PENROSE : Who's first? (*Geordie stops whistling, gets up quickly, and goes over to the desk.*) Name?

GEORDIE : I've tae see Jake Adams.

MR PENROSE : I asked you your name.

GEORDIE : My name? George R. MacLeod, an' I've tae see Jake Adams.

MR PENROSE (*giving up trying to fill in the form*): You'll find him down the yard. Ask somebody where the tanker is.

GEORDIE : What's it cried, like?

MR PENROSE : Pardon?

GEORDIE : What's its name, pal?

MR PENROSE : It hasn't got one yet. You'll have to build it first.

GEORDIE : I'll find 'im O.K. Thanks, pal. (*He goes out.*)

MR PENROSE : Next? (*Sam rises and goes to the desk, still smoking his roll-up.*)

MR PENROSE : Name?

SAM : Same as him.

MR PENROSE : I suppose you're George R. . . .

SAM : Not at all. Jake.

MR PENROSE : And what's Jake short for?

SAM : I'm no Jake. I'm Sam. I'm lookin for Jake, but. Jake Adams. I've come tae the right place, I hope.

MR PENROSE : Yes.

SAM : Jake Adams is the foreman, right?

MR PENROSE : He's one of our foremen, yes.

SAM : Well, I want tae see 'im. He's startin me this mornin. I'm Sam Thomson.

MR PENROSE : You'll find him down the yard. Ask somebody where the tanker is.

SAM : Thanks for nothin', Jimmy. (*He goes to the door. He opens it, then turns to face Mr Penrose again.*) Hey?

MR PENROSE : Yes.

SAM : Is it as hard tae get out o here as it is tae get in?

MR PENROSE : I beg your pardon?

SAM : Just a wee joke. Cheer up. (*He goes out.*)

MR PENROSE (*not pleased*): Next! (*Willie folds up his newspaper, rises, walks over to the desk, and takes off his cap.*) I suppose you're looking for Jake Adams as well?

WILLIE : Who's Jake Adams?

MR PENROSE : Name?

WILLIE : Rough. R, O, U, G, H.

MR PENROSE : I can spell.

WILLIE : Sorry. I wis just tryin tae help.

MR PENROSE (*delighted that at last he can fill in a form*): Rough by name and rough by nature, eh?

WILLIE : Aye.

MR PENROSE : First name?

WILLIE : William.

MR PENROSE : Any others?

WILLIE : The wife an' two weans.

MR PENROSE : Names, I mean. Any middle names?

WILLIE : No . . . just thae two. . . . Willie Rough.

MR PENROSE : Date of birth?

WILLIE : The eighteenth o January 1883.

MR PENROSE : That makes ye ... ?

WILLIE : Thirty-wan.

MR PENROSE : How long have you been idle?

WILLIE : The last job stopped the week o Christmas.

MR PENROSE : Tough luck.

WILLIE : We still had Christmas.

MR PENROSE : It's getting so that it doesn't mean a thing, Christmas.

WILLIE : I can see you've nae weans.

MR PENROSE (*less familiar*) : Do you have your lines?

WILLIE : Aye. (*Taking some papers out of his pocket, he hands them to the Clerk. The Clerk reads them.*) . . . My time's been out a good while nou. . . . I'm a good tradesman. I've got references.

MR PENROSE : Organised, I see.

WILLIE : Oh, ye *must*, Mr . . . eh?

MR PENROSE : Penrose. Religion?

WILLIE : Prod'sant.

MR PENROSE : Do you go?

WILLIE : Aye. I'll need tae find a good kirk doun here.

MR PENROSE : You're not a Greenock man, then?

WILLIE : Na. I walked frae Johnstone this mornin.

MR PENROSE : That's fifteen miles.

WILLIE : Felt like fifty in the dark.

MR PENROSE : Oh.

WILLIE : I left early in case there was any chance o a start.

MR PENROSE : Well. . . . I don't see how I can help you, Mr Rough.

WILLIE : What dae ye mean?

MR PENROSE : We've nothing at present.

WILLIE : I thought I'd get a start.

MR PENROSE : There's no work.

WILLIE : What dae ye mean, nae work? Them other two men got a start. Nae fillin in any forms. Nae nothing! I'm no stupit. What's the password, Mr Penrose?

MR PENROSE : I don't know what you're talking about. Look, if you call in at the end of the week there just might be something. I'll see what I can do.

WILLIE : I left the house at half-four this mornin. I walked tae Greenock tae get a job, and I'm no goin home 'ithout wan!

MR PENROSE : Hot-headedness will get you nowhere, Rough. It's nothing to do with me.

WILLIE : Who's it tae dae wi, then?

MR PENROSE : I'm not the management. I'm a clerk. Shouting at me won't affect the issue one way or another.

WILLIE : I think I've been wastin my time talkin tae you. Who's the heid man?

MR PENROSE : I'm sorry.

WILLIE : You're no. You don't even know me. What does an application form tell ye about a man? You're no the least bit sorry.

MR PENROSE : If I could help you, I would.

WILLIE : Let us see the top man, then.

MR PENROSE : Mr Cosgrave isn't interested in the problems of employing one riveter, and you know it.

WILLIE : Aye, he should be, but.

MR PENROSE : That's as may be.

WILLIE : I'm a good man, Mr Penrose.

MR PENROSE : Look, I'll tell you what.

WILLIE : What?

MR PENROSE : Find one of the foremen. Preferably one that's a Protestant. Talk to him. He might be able to start you.

WILLIE : How can he start me when you cannae?

MR PENROSE : Because

WILLIE : Because what?

MR PENROSE : Because that's the way things are. Every yard on the Clyde does things that way, and we're no exception.

WILLIE : What a state o affairs!

MR PENROSE : That's the way it is.

WILLIE : Well, what dae I dae first? Join the Masons, or something?

MR PENROSE : I don't think it need come to that. You'll find one of the foremen in the James Watt Bar across the road at dinner-time. Name of Jake Adams. He's never out of there.

WILLIE : Right y'are. I've never got a start in a pub afore. (*He moves towards the door.*)

MR PENROSE : Have you got any money?

WILLIE : How?

MR PENROSE : You might have to buy him a refreshment.

WILLIE : I've got four an' a tanner.

MR PENROSE : You're fine, then.

WILLIE : Aye. (*He goes to the door, but turns back before leaving.*) I must thank ye very much.

MR PENROSE : You haven't got a start yet.

WILLIE : I will, but. I've got tae.

(*Willie goes out. Mr Penrose pulls the application form into a bundle and throws it into the wastepaper basket.*)

2. *The James Watt Bar: February 1914 (same day)*

(*The Public Bar is so small that when a few workers come in it will seem crowded. The bar is on one*

*side. At the other side there are two round tables,
and a long bench against the wall provides seating
for both. The entrance to the Family Department
is beside the bar, and a door at the back opens on
to the street.*

*Eddie, the publican, behind the bar, is studying
the racing form. Two other men are seated on the
long bench behind one of the round tables, talking.
Pat is in his late thirties; Hughie, a small, wiry man,
must be nearly sixty, but it's difficult to tell exactly
how old he is. They are arguing chiefly to pass the
time; and, though they tend to shout, their dispute
is neither violent nor serious.)*

PAT : He is!

HUGHIE : He isnae! Ye don't know.

PAT : I know aa-right. He's my wean, in't 'e?

HUGHIE : Aye, but he's only six months auld. Ye
cannae tell yit.

PAT : I can tell.

HUGHIE : How can ye tell 'at a wean's gonna be
clever at that age?

PAT : He's got a big heid. That's a sign o intelli-
gence.

HUGHIE : It's no!

PAT : I'm tellin ye it is!

HUGHIE : An' I'm tellin you it's no! Listen tae me.
There's a wumman lives doun ablow me. She's got
a boy wi a big heid, and he's daft!

PAT : Aye, but that's different. Och, ye cannae
argyie wi you, Hughie!

*(An Apprentice comes in. He's about fourteen years
old.)*

EDDIE : Hey, get out!

214

APPRENTICE : Keep your hair on, wigs are dear.

EDDIE : You're too young tae be in here. What dae ye want?

APPRENTICE : I'm over wi the gaffer's line.

EDDIE : Who's your gaffer?

APPRENTICE : Jake Adams.

EDDIE : That's all right, then, son.

(*The Apprentice crosses to the bar, and gives Eddie a piece of paper.*)

APPRENTICE : He says there should be somethin' back frae yesterday.

EDDIE : Oh. Just let me check up. (*He looks at his list of bets.*) Aye, he has, right enough. (*Sadly.*) He had a winner at Hamilton, and a place as well, but Ballykameen wis naewhere. They're still out lookin for it wi a bale o hay. That's (*counting*) eh . . . five tae wan at a tanner's hauf a croun, and he's a tanner back's, three shillins, an' wan an' three for the place. Four an' three, son. Is that what Jake said it would be?

APPRENTICE : He didnae tell me.

EDDIE : That's what it is, well. Nou, what's he on the day? (*He looks at the slip of paper.*) Confident, I see. Two bob each way on the favourite in the first race at Ayr, an' a shillin tae win on Chansin Damour. Five bob. By Jeese, he's breakin out the-day. Look son, gie us ninepence, and he's on. (*The Apprentice gives him the money.*) Right ye are, son. Ye can have a drink, if ye want.

APPRENTICE : Never touch it. My faither's a Rekkabite. (*He goes out.*)

EDDIE : Hey, Hughie!

HUGHIE : What's that, Eddie?

EDDIE : Will ye go a wee message for us?

HUGHIE : Is there a drink in it?

EDDIE : I'll gie ye a hauf.

HUGHIE : I never say 'No' to a wee refreshment, Edward. . . . . There's no too much walkin in it, is there?

EDDIE : Just run over an' get me the *Outlook*.

HUGHIE : I don't know whether I'll be runnin

EDDIE : Ach, ye know what I mean. Just get us the paper. I want tae see the latest price o that horse Jake Adams is on. It's no even in the bettin in this wan.

(*Hughie, whose left leg has been amputated just above the knee, picks up a heavy wooden crutch from under the table, gets up, and hobbles over to the bar to get the money from Eddie, then crosses quickly to the door which opens on to the street.*)

HUGHIE : I'd pour out that hauf, Eddie. It's great how the prospect o a wee goldie fairly gies a man acceleration. (*He goes out into the street.*)

EDDIE (*pouring out Hughie's drink*): How about you, Pat?

PAT : Na, I'm fine, Eddie. I'll need tae get back tae the job. I'm supposed tae be out for a message.

(*Willie comes in and crosses to the bar.*)

EDDIE : Yes?

WILLIE : A hauf gill o Bell's.

(*Willie gives him money. Eddie gives Willie his change, then returns to the racing page. Pat looks at Willie; Willie waits, drinking his whisky.*)

EDDIE : . . . Chansin Damour . . . it's funny, it's no in the bettin.

PAT : I know what you want, Eddie.

EDDIE : What's that?

PAT : You want everybody's horse tae go on the bing. By the law o averages somebody's got tae win sometime.

EDDIE : What dae you know about Chansin Damour, Pat Gatens?

WILLIE : It's by Pride and Prejudice out o French Dressin. It was a close fourth at Bogside a while back. It woulda won if I hadnae been on it. It's due a win. There's an apprentice on it the day.

(Hughie comes back into the Public Bar with the newspaper.)

PAT : You're too late, Hughie.

HUGHIE : How?

PAT : We know aa about Jake Adams' horse nou. This fella tellt us.

HUGHIE : Dae I still get my drink?

EDDIE : Aye.

HUGHIE : That's aa-right, then. *(He lifts Willie's glass and drinks his whisky.)*

EDDIE : Hey, Hughie, that's his.

HUGHIE : Hell of a sorry. *(He lifts his own glass and drinks that down, then dances over to join Pat.)*

EDDIE : You're a bettin man, I see. . . . eh . . .

WILLIE : Willie. Willie Rough. No, I wouldnae say that. I'm just interested in horses an' dugs. I only bet when I'm at the meetin. Sometimes I can pick a winner in the flesh. I've nae luck wi the papers.

EDDIE : Is 'at a fact?

PAT : He's no wan o the mugs, Eddie.

EDDIE *(to Willie)* : Ye local, like?

WILLIE : Na, I'm frae Johnstone. Came doun this mornin tae try tae get a start ower by.

ACT ONE

(*Sam and Geordie come in from the street.*)

EDDIE : What'll it be, boys?
SAM : Two pints.

(*Willie looks at Sam and Geordie, then moves over
to the empty table and sits down. Pat slides along
the bench to be beside him, and Hughie follows
suit.*)

PAT : I couldnae help owerhearin your, eh, con-
versation, like. . . . Tryin tae get started, are ye?
WILLIE : Aye. It's like gettin out o prison.
HUGHIE : It's harder without your faculties, believe
me.
PAT : Shut it, Hughie!
HUGHIE : It's aa-right for some folk.
PAT (*to Willie*) : You want tae speak tae wan o the
gaffers. That's the system.
WILLIE : I know.
PAT : You've come tae the right place.
WILLIE : Will ye point 'im out tae us when he comes
in?
PAT : Aye, sure.
WILLIE : You workin?
PAT : I'm at the hole-borin. Pat Gatens.
WILLIE : Willie Rough.
PAT : This is Hughie.
WILLIE : Hello.
HUGHIE : Pleased tae meet ye.

(*They shake hands. Several workers come into the
pub. Most of them order a whisky and a bottle of
beer; and when they have been served, they begin
chatting in groups round the bar. They are dirty,*

*and have obviously been working. All of them wear
caps (which they call 'bunnets'). The small bar
soon begins to look crowded.)*

WILLIE : Thae two ower there. They got a stairt
this mornin. Aa I got was a lecture frae the time-
keeper.
PAT : Penrose?
WILLIE : Aye.
PAT : Holy Willie. He's a Wee Free or something.
He disnae drink or onything !
HUGHIE : Some folk's no wise.

*(They drink. Jake comes in. He is about forty-five
years old. He wears a suit and matching bunnet.
He looks cleaner than the rest. He is not tall but
powerfully built.)*

GEORDIE : Can I buy ye a drink?
JAKE : That's very good o ye, Geordie. I'll have
a hauf gill o Bells.
EDDIE : Right ye are ! *(He pours out the drinks.)*
HUGHIE *(confidentially)* : That's your man there,
Willie . . . the gaffer.
PAT : Shut it, Hughie. He might be frae Johnstone,
but he's no stupit.
HUGHIE : Sorry I spoke.
JAKE *(to Eddie)* : My boy was tellin me ye're no
too pleased about my win yesterday.
EDDIE : Naebody likes tae lose.
JAKE : Come on, Eddie, the bookie never loses, and
you know it. Got a tip frae the course the day—
Chansin Dammer.
EDDIE : Outside chance.
JAKE *(laughing)* : It'll walk hame. I've a good mind
tae get the whole yard on it just tae spite ye, Eddie.

EDDIE : Hey! Steady on, Jake! Ye want tae bank-rupt us aathegither?

JAKE : Aye, likely. Take mair than wan cert tae dae that.

EDDIE : Remember, we've a maximum pey-out here, Jake.

JAKE : I'm sure the lads would take payment in kind frae the likes o you, Eddie. They've a gey long time tae wait tae next New Year, an' thay'll be some that's no daein much drinkin, or first-fittin either, this time.

EDDIE : How no?

JAKE : King and Country, Eddie.

EDDIE : Aye, ye might be right.

JAKE : I'm bloody sure I'm right. They'll be run-nin doun tae the Toun Hall tae enlist like the R.Cs. queuein up for their wee bit o soot on Ash Wednesday. Just you wait.

(*Leaving the bar, Jake goes towards the entrance to the Family Department, passing Willie's table.*)

PAT : Hello-rerr, Jake. Got that wee message for ye.

JAKE : Ye werenae long gettin back.

PAT : This is Willie Rough—Jake Adams.

JAKE : Fine day.

PAT : He's eh . . . wonderin, like, if there's any chance o a start, Jake.

JAKE : Impossible at the moment, son. I started a couple o new men this mornin.

PAT : He's wan o yours, Jake.

JAKE : I see. I cannae promise. I'm goin in there. (*He goes out into the Family Department.*)

HUGHIE (*to Willie*) : There ye are, then.

WILLIE : What?

HUGHIE : G'in and see 'im.

220

WILLIE : I'm no deif, Hughie, he said it was impossible.

HUGHIE : That'll be right, I don't think !

WILLIE : O.K. What dae I dae nou?

(Pat produces a packet of Gold Flake cigarettes and offers one to Willie.)

PAT : Fag?

WILLIE : Ta.

HUGHIE *(seizing one before Willie can)* : You're a gentleman, Patrick.

PAT : When are you gonna buy some?

HUGHIE : The next hallecaplump Tuesday 'at faas on a Wednesday.

PAT : I havenae got a light, Willie. Go an' ask Jake Adams for a match.

WILLIE : Haud on. I've got a box in my pocket.

PAT : Just dae what I tell ye.

(Willie gets up and goes into the Family Department. Pat gives Hughie a light and then lights his own cigarette.)

HUGHIE : It's a bit slow on the uptak. Just doun frae the hills, ye ask me.

PAT : It's aa-right for us. We know the gemm. But how onybody's expectit tae know how ye go about it beats me.

HUGHIE : It's hardly worth 'is while onywey. The likes o him'll be itchin under 'is khaki afore ye can say 'Jock Robinson'.

(Willie comes back into the Public Bar.)

HUGHIE : Well?

WILLIE : Well what?

PAT : What happened?

WILLIE : Nothin'. I asked him for a light. He gies me a box o matches an' says, 'Keep the box. There's only wan in it.'

(*Hughie and Pat exchange looks. They have a secret.*)

HUGHIE : Light your fag, then.

WILLIE (*opening the matchbox*) : Christ! Ther' money in here. Hauf-a-croun.

HUGHIE : Pat, what did I tell ye afore? He's daft, an' he *hasnae* got a big heid. Look, Willie, ye don't expect Jake Adams tae gie somebody a light like any other body, dae ye?

PAT : Have ye got a hauf-crown?

WILLIE : Aye.

PAT : Well, pit it in the box wi the other wan, an' gae ben there, an' gie 'im the box back. Tell him there were three in it, and ye used wan.

HUGHIE : That's safe enough. Walls have ears, Willie.

WILLIE : Bribery and corruption.

PAT : Well, ye want the job, dan't ye?

WILLIE : Aye.

PAT : That's aa-right, well.

WILLIE : It's *no* right.

PAT : Listen tae me, pal. I don't know you. I only met ye five minutes ago. Ye tellt me ye wantit a job, right?

WILLIE : Right.

PAT : Well, will ye shut that fuckin box an' tak it ben there an' get wan? You're no the only wan idle, ye know. Maist folk think it's worth a few bob tae get a start these days.

222

HUGHIE : Pat knows, Willie . . .
WILLIE : Gie's a light.

(*Pat lights Willie's cigarette. Willie rises and goes out into the Family Department.*)

PAT : . . . Want a drink, Hughie?
HUGHIE : You know me, Patrick. Refuse naething but blows.
PAT : You get them up then.

(*Pat gives Hughie money. Hughie gets up and goes over to the bar.*)

HUGHIE : Three Bell's, Eddie.
EDDIE : Three Bell's. Aa-right for beer?
HUGHIE : Aye.

(*Willie comes back into the bar and sits down again beside Pat.*)

WILLIE : What happens nou?
PAT : Ye wait, Hughie's gettin 'em up.
HUGHIE (*to Sam, who stands at the bar reading a newspaper*): Is that the wan o'clock *Telegraph*?
SAM : What dae ye think it is? Scotch mist?
HUGHIE : Can I hae a wee scan at it?
SAM : Buy your ain.
HUGHIE : Keep the heid. Civility costs naething.
SAM : Away ye go. I'm studyin form here.
HUGHIE : Ye can keep that page. Gie's the rest.
SAM : Oh, is that aa? Here ye are. (*He hands over most of the newspaper.*) I thought ye wantit the runners.
HUGHIE : Na, I just want tae see if they've set a date for it yet.

223

SAM : For what?

HUGHIE : The war, what dae ye think?

SAM : You're no thinkin o volunteerin, are ye, Hughie?

HUGHIE : I've had mine. You wait. It's no a Sunday School Picnic tae fuckin Largs.

EDDIE (*handing over drinks*) : That'll be wan an' nine.

HUGHIE : It's on the counter. (*He takes the drinks over to the table, making two trips.*)

PAT : Look, I'm tellin ye. It's no money doun the drain. Ye'll be aa-right.

WILLIE : I'd better be. I'm skint . . .

(*Pat and Willie begin drinking, while Hughie is fetching the rest of their drinks.*

PAT : Ye mairrit, like?

WILLIE : Aye. I've got two weans. A boy and a wee lassie.

PAT : I've got five.

HUGHIE (*bringing the last of the drinks*) : He's tryin tae win the Pope's medal.

PAT : Shut your face, you! What's in the paper?

HUGHIE : The usual.

PAT : Dae ye think ye'll be joinin up, Willie?

WILLIE : Na.

PAT : How no?

WILLIE : It's no my war when it does come. Nor yours, neither.

HUGHIE : Aye, but ye've got tae go but. I mean, I didnae start the last wan, but I had tae go. An' look what happened tae me. I left wan leg in a midden bin in fuckin Africa, bi-fuck!

WILLIE : But naething cam out o't at aa, did it? Can ye no see? What's five weans gonna dae

'ithout their faither? Ye see . . . it's aa arranged
frae start tae finish. It's been worked out, like. The
time-tables o trains that'll tak the boys back an'
furrit frae the Front have aa been organised. Ye
wouldnae believe it. The war's got tae come nou,
because folk want it. An' it's no only the politicians,
either.

PAT : Naebody wants war.

HUGHIE : Naebody wise, onywey.

WILLIE : You're wrang there. Just tak a look at thae
men ower at the counter there.

PAT : What about them?

WILLIE : They'll volunteer tae a man when the
time comes. Some o them are learnin tae march
at nights up our way aaready.

PAT : Aye. I go mysel' . . . the odd time.

WILLIE : Sorry I spoke, then.

HUGHIE : Hey, you . . . Willie, for Christ's sake,
ye're no a German spy, are ye?

PAT : Och, Hughie, wheesht! (*To Willie*) So what
dae ye suggest we dae . . . supposin . . . just supposin the war breaks out? Take a fortnight's
holidays an' take the weans tae Rothesay for a
dip?

WILLIE : Stay where ye are. Here in Greenock,
where ye belang. Sure, we've got tae try our
hardest tae prevent this imperialist war. (*rhetori-
cally*): but if it starts, as start, God help us, it surely
will, it's our duty to oppose it. Out of the crisis of
the war we must find the means to bring an end
tae capitalism.

HUGHIE : A Red Flagger, for fuck's sake!

PAT : Hey! Keep the heid, Willie. Ye sound like
wan o they manifestos, or somethin' lik that. Drink
up. It might never happen.

HUGHIE : What cam intae ye at aa?

WILLIE (*smiling*): Nothin' cam intae me. Ye ever hear o John McLean's meetins up in Paisley?

HUGHIE: John McLean . . . for fuck's sake. . . .

WILLIE: He's a great man. I really believe that. His meetins are the only thing I've got tae look forward tae 'cept gaun hame tae the wife an' the weans at night. An' just look at me nou. I'm sore ashamed o mysel, sae I am! Willie Rough sittin here waitin tae see if he's bought 'imsel' a job.

PAT: Look, your politics is naething tae dae wi me. I'm no clever enough tae hav politics. I just vote Labour lik everybody else. But listen tae me. Ye're no exactly whisperin, an' if ye say much mair, ye'll be out o that yaird afore ye're in it!

HUGHIE: Aye. Come see, come saa, Willie.

PAT: You've got a wife an' weans tae feed. Remember that.

WILLIE: Aye. Sae I'll sit quiet. I'll drink my drink an' say nothing! I'll say nothing, no because I'm feart, but because I don't know what I want tae say. I'll wait. . . .

HUGHIE: I'll say wan thing, Willie. Ye've kinna put the tin lid on the conversation. We're lik three folk at a funeral waitin' tae see if the widow wumman's teetotal. I mean

(*Jake comes out of the Family Department, and Hughie stops talking. Jake walks past their table towards the street door, stops, and turns to Willie, who goes on looking straight ahead.*)

JAKE: Hey, Rough! (*Willie turns to face him.*) Ye start in the mornin. (*He goes out.*)

WILLIE: Thanks, eh . . . Mr Adams.

(*Pat and Hughie are delighted: Willie now owes them a drink.*)

226

PAT : What did I tell ye?

HUGHIE : Pat knows. Pat's the wee boy.

WILLIE : I should buy the baith o ye a hauf, but I've just got my bus fare hame for the night an' the morra left.

HUGHIE : Nae dout we'll all congregate at this very spot for a few refreshments at a later date, Willie. I'm free when ye get your pay next Saturday.

WILLIE (*to Pat*) : Dae ye work a week's lyin time?

PAT : Aye.

WILLIE : A week on Saturday, then. (*He rises.*) I must thank ye very much, Pat. I suppose I'd better get up hame an' tell the wife.

PAT : Aye, ye'll need tae find a house doun here

WILLIE : I'll go and see some factor the-morra.

PAT : Willie?

WILLIE : Aye?

PAT : Hope ye don't mind, like, but I've got a wee bit o advice. Keep aa that John McLean propaganda tae yoursel', for Christ's sake. At least, wait till ye've taen your jaicket aff an' worked a few hours.

WILLIE (*getting ready to go*) : I know what ye mean.

PAT : I go tae the drillin an' that, but I don't think I'm gonna go tae the Front either.

HUGHIE : Ye've baith naething tae worry about. Even if they get tae the stage of sendin the Press Gang out, you'll baith be on work of national importance.

WILLIE : I don't know what's worse.

HUGHIE : Better a live coward nor a deid hera.

PAT : Aye.

HUGHIE : Well, cheerybye, Willie.

WILLIE : Cheerio. (*He goes out.*)

HUGHIE : . . . Fairly gies ye 'is life story, dan't he?

PAT : Nice enough fella.

HUGHIE : Aye . . . the-nou. But you wait. Just you watch that yin. He'll be mair confident wi a pound or two in 'is pocket. He'll be haunin out leaflets and pamphlets an' God kens what aa else. Wait tae ye see.

PAT : Well, it'll be a chynge frae the *War Cry*.

HUGHIE : He'll just hav tae watch he disnae get 'is jotters . . . or worse . . . he'll get his heid bashed in and find himsel' six fit doun below South Street.

PAT : Aye . . . mebbie you're right, Hughie. . . .

EDDIE : Hughie!

HUGHIE : What?

EDDIE : Will ye go a wee message for us?

HUGHIE : It'll cost ye a pint.

EDDIE : I'd be better goin mysel'.

HUGHIE : Please yoursel'.

EDDIE : Half a pint.

HUGHIE : I'll hav tae talk tae the Message Boys' Union about this. A pint's the rate for the job. Ye'll hae a strike on your hauns.

EDDIE : Don't joke about the likes o that, Hughie, for Christ's sake. A strike's no funny.

HUGHIE : Aye. It isnae, is it? They'd be nae mair doubles, trebles, an' roll-ups then, Eddie, and naebody would be able tae afford the price o a pint, either. Ye'd hav tae gie't awa.

EDDIE : I'd raither sit here an' drink it mysel'.

HUGHIE : That's the sort o thing you would dae!

EDDIE : Would you come in an' help me finish up the stock, Hughie?

HUGHIE : Gie me plenty o warnin so's I can get intae trainin.

EDDIE : Aye. That'll be right. Look, Hughie, go over tae Timpson's and pick up my shoe repairs. It's their half-day.

HUGHIE : Gie's the money. (*He goes over to the bar.*)
EDDIE : Haud on.

(*Eddie takes out his purse. He looks inside it carefully to find the money, then takes it out, coin by coin. Hughie is leaning against the bar. Suddenly he swipes the air with his crutch as if it were a club.*)

EDDIE : What ye daein?
HUGHIE : *GOT IT!*
EDDIE : Got what?
HUGHIE : Just a wee moth, Eddie.

3. *The Shipyard: May 1914*

(*The horn blows. Pat, Sam and Geordie march in step down the yard. The Apprentice follows, watching them with admiration.*)

GEORDIE : Squa-a-a-d . . . halt!

(*Raggedly, they halt.*)

PAT : It's wan-two, *HALT*, wan-two. Ye don't just stop. What dae they learn ye up at the drillin?

(*Willie comes in and stands looking at them.*)

SAM : It's aa-right for you. You were at the back.
GEORDIE : Aye. We couldnae see you.
APPRENTICE : He's as bad.
PAT : Shut up, you!

WILLIE : Pat?

PAT : Aye.

WILLIE : What ye daein?

PAT : Marchin.

WILLIE : Thought ye'd chucked aa-that.

PAT : Keepin my haun' in. Just in case.

WILLIE : Ye're aa aff your heids.

GEORDIE : Who dae ye think you are?

WILLIE : I know I'm as well haudin my breath wi the likes o you, Geordie. When's 'is union meetin?

SAM : Quarter an hour.

WILLIE : They couldnae run a minauge, so they couldnae.

APPRENTICE : I've got a baa. Gie's your jaicket for a goal, Willie.

(Willie gives the Apprentice his jacket. The Apprentice makes a goal with his own jacket and Willie's.)

GEORDIE : Aa-right. Two-a-side.

APPRENTICE : I'll go goalie.

SAM : You're no playin.

APPRENTICE : It's my baa!

SAM : In ye go, then.

PAT : Me an' Willie against the rest.

SAM : Fair enough.

GEORDIE : Right! To me, son.

(The Apprentice throws the ball to Geordie. The game begins. The tackling is quite tough.)

APPRENTICE : Come on, the Rangers!

(The game gets rough. Eventually Pat scores a goal.)

PAT : Goal!

GEORDIE : That's no fair. Ye held my jaicket.

APPRENTICE : Na, he didnae!

GEORDIE : He did, Sam! Nae kiddin.

SAM : Thae Fenians is aa the same.

PAT : Mind your mouth, son.

SAM : What'll you dae about it?

PAT : I'll dae plenty.

GEORDIE : You, an' what army?

PAT : Two against wan, is it?

GEORDIE : Na. A square go, anytime ye like. Haud my jaicket, Willie.

WILLIE : Ye no feart ye'll catch the cauld?

PAT : Haud 'is jaicket, Willie. I'll mangalate 'im!

WILLIE : Ye'd be better mangalatin your piece. What happens when the gaffer comes roun? Bagged on the spot, the baith o ye.

PAT : I suppose ye're right, Willie.

GEORDIE : Ye crappin it?

PAT : If ye're serious. . . . Roun the back aifter the meetin.

WILLIE : Ye're like a couple o weans on the school play-ground.

GEORDIE : You stay out o this. We'll settle it.

WILLIE : Settle what?

GEORDIE : Eh?

WILLIE : What are ye fightin about? If Jake Adams wisnae about, I'd tak on the baith of ye mysel'.

APPRENTICE : Let's see ye, Willie.

WILLIE (*kicking him in the backside*) : You get tae fuck an' boil my can. Get me ten Capstan full strenth, tae. I gied ye the cash.

(*The Apprentice goes. Willie picks up his jacket. Geordie passes the ball to Sam. Slowly the game*

231

begins again. Pat sits down exhausted. Jake walks down the yard.)

JAKE : Hav ye got nothin' better tae dae wi your time than kickin a baa about?

WILLIE : Waitin for the Union meetin tae start, Jake.

JAKE : That'll dae yez a lot o good, I don't think!

WILLIE : Twopence an hour rise. Forty-five bob a week frae nou on.

JAKE : An' what did the band play? *(He goes out.)*

(Geordie and Sam continue to kick the ball to each other, once they are sure that Jake is gone.)

WILLIE : Pat?

PAT : What?

(Willie goes over to Pat, who is stretched on the ground.)

WILLIE : I know Jake's no in the Union.

PAT : You stupit?

WILLIE : I wish tae hell he wis.

PAT : What good would it dae the likes o him?

WILLIE : Time we got tae the meetin. I can see some o the boys goin doun nou.

SAM : Aye. We'd better shift.

(Geordie and Sam go out carrying the ball. The Apprentice comes in carrying Willie's can of tea.)

APPRENTICE : Hey! Where dae youz think ye're goin wi my baa? *(He gives Willie his tea.)*

APPRENTICE : Come back wi my baa, ye thievin bastarts!

232

(The Apprentice runs off after Sam and Geordie. Willie sips his tea. Pat gets up.)

PAT: Takin your tea in wi ye, then?

WILLIE: Keeps me awake when the shop steward's forgot 'is glesses an' cannae read the treasurer's report.

PAT: Aye. He's a bit auld for it. Know what?

WILLIE: What?

PAT: I'm gonna propose you.

WILLIE: What for?

PAT: Election o office-bearers the-day. 'S about time we had a chynge. Don't look sae pleased about it. Ye might no get it, an' if ye dae, it'll be 'cause naebody else wants it.

WILLIE: Ye're hell of a good tae me, Pat. I don't deserve it.

PAT: It's nae bother at aa. *(Pat makes a smart "about turn")*

WILLIE: Are ye for mairchin intae the meetin, like?

PAT: Can ye no take a joke? You're that serious about everythin'.

WILLIE: They cannae wait for the war tae break out.

PAT: Neither can you. *(They go off to the meeting.)*

4. *A Street: July 1914*

(Kate, Willie's wife, is waiting for him. At her feet are two bags full of shopping. Willie comes along the street, in a hurry.)

KATE: You're a fine yin. That's three tramcars we've missed. It's bad enough when ye're workin, but ye've knocked aff for the Fair, an' you're still late.

233

WILLIE : I wis daein my correspondence.

KATE : I don't want tae go tae Rothesay the-morra. Ye've pit me aff the notion.

WILLIE : Ye'd think I liked bein Shop Steward, tae hear you.

KATE : It's a chynge from McLean, anyhow. At least ye can dae it in your ain toun.

WILLIE (picking up the shopping-bags) : The weans aa-right?

KATE : A lot you care. They'll be wonderin what their faither looks like.

WILLIE : I'll tak them for a douk the-morra. I like a wee paddle mysel'.

KATE : What about me? Hav I tae sit up the lum as usual?

WILLIE : I'm takin ye out the-night. We're goin tae Pat Gatens's club.

KATE : I don't like goin out wi other folk.

WILLIE : Bernadette's nice.

KATE : I know, but I mairrit you. Sometimes I wish I wis back hame, in Campbeltown.

WILLIE : Campbeltown wis too quiet when ye were in it.

KATE : Aye. But there's nae meetins there. Ye don't hav tae read pamphlets doun there. People tell ye aa ye need tae know.

WILLIE : Three fishin-boats an' a distillery.

KATE : At least your man comes hame the odd night.

WILLIE : You'll no be sayin that when we get the twopence-an-hour rise.

KATE : I'll believe that when ye lea me forty-five shillins on the table wan Friday night. You're awful askin us out wi the Gatenses. People'll think we're turnin our coats. Is it that club up the Port?

WILLIE : Aye.

KATE : Ye'll be at the Chapel next.

WILLIE : What's the maitter wi you? I've got my holiday pay in my pocket. Dae ye blame me for wantin tae gie you a night out? I don't know. When ye're in, ye want out, an' when ye're out ye want tae gae hame again.

KATE : Mebbie ye shoulda mairrit somebody else.

WILLIE : What's got intae you?

KATE : Ye know I'm no very good at talkin tae folk.

WILLIE : Ye're as good as onybody. We're as good as onybody.

KATE : Just don't you get above your station, Willie Rough.

WILLIE : Would ye stop criticizin me aa the time! I left the yard happy. I'm on holiday. I've got my pay in my pocket. I'm takin the wife an' the weans doun the watter the-morra. I wis as happy as Larry till I met you.

KATE : Have you ever tried tae get throu the shops on Fair Friday?

WILLIE : So that's it.

KATE : What a crush! I havenae got hauf the things I need.

WILLIE : Come on up hame, an' I'll gie ye a wee hauf afore we go out.

KATE : I didnae mean it, Willie. I'm just exhausted. I could dae wi goin tae my bed.

(*They hear a tramcar approaching. They lift the bags and look at the approaching vehicle.*)

WILLIE : We'll come hame early.

KATE : Ye know what happens then?

WILLIE : Ye werenae complainin' last night.

KATE : Oh, you!

(*The noise of the tramcar comes nearer and nearer.*)

235

5. *The James Watt Bar: September 1914*

Patriotic posters are now displayed in the Public
Bar—'YOUR KING & COUNTRY NEED
YOU!' and 'WOMEN OF BRITAIN SAY
"GO"!' The bar is crowded. Many of the men
are either drunk or well on the way to it. Eddie is
behind the bar, as usual. Across it from him is Jake.
Round one of the tables Hughie has gathered his
troops. All of them are singing. Amongst them
are Sam and Geordie, who have volunteered and
are already wearing khaki uniforms. Hughie and
his mob are wearing spectacles of many different
shapes and sizes, swapping them with each other,
and trying them on. Willie and Pat are sitting
together at the other table trying to ignore Hughie's
gang. Willie himself has had too much to drink;
he's in an aggressive mood.

Hughie and his cronies sing at the top of their
voices, each in their own key, of course.

HUGHIE (*with all his gang, singing*) :
Oh, Greenock's no a bonnie toun, you'll hear some
    folk complain
For when they go tae Greenock there is nothing
    else but rain;
Da da da da da da da da da da da da da DEEEE!
For I'm proud that I'm a branch of the *GREEN-*
    OAK TREE!

Here's tae the Green Oak that stands doun by the
    Square
Here's tae its tounsfolk a-slumbering there :
Here's tae its tounsfolk wherever they may be—
For I'm proud that I'm a branch of the *GREEN-*
    OAK TREE!

(*A triumphant cheer goes up from the singers as they reach the end of their song.*)

SAM : Best of order there! Best of order!

GEORDIE : Aye. Best of order for Shughie!

HUGHIE : Boys. We know what we're here for the-night, an' it's no joke. As an auld sodger that done his bit in the last wan, I'd just like tae say that I'm proud tae be in the company of these brave young fellas that are about tae do their bit in the defence o the Realm—Geordie MacLeod an' Sammy Thomson (*cheers*). . . . An' I'd just like tae add that the first blow in the battle against the Hun has been struck. It was struck the-night. An' we struck it, so we did! (*Prolonged cheers.*)

EDDIE : You'll no be sayin that when the Polis come.

HUGHIE : There might be a few German sympathisers in this toun, Eddie MacCausland, but not in the Force. Patriots! Patriots to a man! Now lads, while we're talkin serious, who's buyin the beer?

GEORDIE : My turn, lads.

HUGHIE : Same all round, Geordie. Same all round.

(*Geordie goes over to the bar. Eddie begins pouring out the large order of drinks.*)

JAKE (*to Geordie*) : Where the fuck did ye get thae glasses?

GEORDIE : The spoils of war, Jake.

JAKE : Ye're no at the Front yet, Geordie, tell us where ye got them?

GEORDIE : How? Dae ye want a pair?

JAKE : There's nae use talkin tae you. You're para-lytic.

GEORDIE : Here, take a pair. (*He gives Jake some spectacles.*) Take two!

JAKE (*handing them back*) : I'm havin nothing tae dae wi it.

GEORDIE : Aye. Ye were kinda conspicuous by your absence. Hauf the toun was there, but I never seen you.

JAKE : What's that supposed tae mean?

GEORDIE : If the cap fits.

JAKE : Ony mair o that, Geordie MacLeod, an' ye'll have two big keekers that ye'll no be able tae see out o wi ten pair of specs.

GEORDIE : Keep the heid, Jake. It's a free country.

JAKE : Mebbie—but no for long when we're dependin on the likes o you tae defend it!

GEORDIE : I take exception tae that remark!

JAKE : Ye can take fuckin Syrup o Figs, if ye like.

EDDIE : Easy, lads. Here ye are, Geordie, away over there, an' lea Jake alane.

GEORDIE : If I wisnae drunk

EDDIE : If ye werenae drunk, ye'd be flat on your back at Jake's feet, an' you know it. Nou, here's your drink. Take them over.

(*Geordie pays for the drinks and carries them over to Hughie and the others. Hughie moves over to the bar.*)

HUGHIE : Wis Geordie giein' ye a wee bit o trouble, Eddie? It's the blood-lust, I think. He cannae wait tae go.

EDDIE : What side are you on, Hughie?

HUGHIE : How dae ye mean?

EDDIE : Well, afore the war broke out, ye were never done stickin' up for Willie Rough over there.

HUGHIE : Well the-night it suits me tae be patriotic. The-morn, we'll see.

EDDIE : Look, tak aa your cronies ben there tae the ither bar, will ye? I'm no wantin ony trouble if the Polis come.

HUGHIE : Anything tae oblidge, Eddie.

(Hughie goes over and begins to herd his cronies through the door into the Family Department.)

HUGHIE : Come on, boys, we're tae muve.

SAM : How?

HUGHIE : Eddie says it, that's how. Come on, Sam.

SAM : I'm nice and comfortable sittin here.

EDDIE : Next door, or outside!

(Sam rises, staggers to the door, and walks through. Hughie steadies him on his way, and is just about to go through himself.)

PAT : Hughie!

HUGHIE : What?

PAT : Come 'ere, Willie an' me want tae talk tae ye.

(Hughie comes up to Willie and Pat.)

PAT *(to Hughie)* : You want tae look at yoursel'.

HUGHIE : If you were me, would you want tae look at yoursel'?

WILLIE : Ye're steamboats.

HUGHIE : Ye're no lookin sae sober yoursel', Willie.

WILLIE : That may be. But I'm ashamed, that's how *I'm* drunk. You're just drunk.

HUGHIE : I never need a reason tae be drunk, Willie.

PAT : Hughie, where did aa thae glasses come frae? The whole pub's weirin them.

HUGHIE : We done Lizars.

JAKE : Ye what?

HUGHIE : Lizars. Ye ken the opticians in West Blackhall Street?

WILLIE : Aye.

HUGHIE : Well a big crowd o the lads, like. . . . Aye, a rare crowd, an' wee boys, tae . . . we broke the windae an' climbed in an' wrecked the place. The only pairs of glesses 'at arenae broke are the wans ye see in here tonight.

PAT : But, what did ye dae it for?

HUGHIE : They're fuckin Germans! I mean . . . we just cannae tolerate German sympathisers in this toun. Case you don't know, there's a war on, Pat. We've got tae fight the enemy within.

WILLIE : So that's it. Christ, ye've nae sense, the haill lot o ye. Wan minute they're signin on for the Army, an' the next they're paradin about Cathcart Square lik a shower o bloody clowns, an' nou ye're breakin shop windaes. Hav ye nae sense? Has the war demented the whole toun?

HUGHIE : I didnae start it, Willie.

WILLIE : Who did?

HUGHIE : I don't know.

WILLIE : Na. Naebody ever knows who starts the like o this. They're aa in at the finish, tho.

HUGHIE : I didnae think ye'd be sae het up about it, Willie.

WILLIE : Well, I am. Pat and me. We've been at meetins aa week. We're tryin tae get a rise in two months. Dae you know what twopence an hour means tae this toun? We're tryin tae prove that we're no representin a bunch o loonies, an just when ye're gettin somewhere, they're out throwin bricks through windaes. This on tap o everything else.

HUGHIE : What else?

PAT : McLean was arrested at a rally in Glesga. The School Board hav bagged him nou.

HUGHIE : That's hard lines.

WILLIE : What dae *you* care?

HUGHIE : I care aa-right. I see that you care, an'
I care about you, so I *care*. I can see that ye're no
sae sober, either.

WILLIE : But Lizars isnae a German shop, even, is
it?

PAT : Not at all. He's frae Stirling or somewhere.

HUGHIE : What dae ye mean, frae Stirling? Lizar.
Lie Zar—frae Stirling, my arse! He's frae fuckin
Berlin!

PAT : Ye mighta checked up afore ye done 'is shop.

HUGHIE : It's no a Greenock name, is it? Even I
know that. Lie-Zar. Sounds foreign enough. He's
a fuckin Gerry aa-right.

WILLIE : Ach away an' join your gang! It's a pity
ye cannae drink specs, in't it?

HUGHIE : It is that, Willie.

PAT : What about the Polis?

HUGHIE : What about them?

PAT : Dae they no know about ye wreckin the shop?

HUGHIE : If ye ask me, I think they knew an' just
let us enjoy wirsel's.

WILLIE : Oh, Pat, are we the only two sane men
in this madhouse?

HUGHIE : Mebbie you're the loonies, boys. Hav ye
thought about that?

*(Hughie goes next door to join his friends. Cheers,
within, followed intermittently by snatches of
shouting and singing.)*

PAT : I'd better get ye hame, Willie.

WILLIE : Wan for the road, Pat.

PAT : Are ye sure ye want wan?

WILLIE : A wee Bell's, Pat.

PAT : Right. (*He gets up and goes to the bar to get the drinks.*)

JAKE (*to no one in particular*) : So they done the opticians?

PAT : Two John Bell's, Eddie. Jake, what'll ye hav?

JAKE : Na, I'm fine.

EDDIE : I see Willie's well on. It's no usual for him.

PAT : I think he thinks he's been let doun.

EDDIE : How dae ye mean?

PAT : Well, he's that serious about everythin', ye know.

EDDIE : Aye, I know.

(*Jake moves over towards Willie's table.*)

PAT : An' wi the negotiations about the rise goin on, an' aa the rest o't, he wants the men tae keep the slate clean, like.

JAKE (*at Willie's table*) : Hello, Willie.

WILLIE : Sit doun, Jake. Dae ye think there's three o us?

JAKE : What?

WILLIE : 'At's no stupit?

PAT (*to Eddie*) : An' McLean's in the jyle.

EDDIE : Aye. I've often heard Willie go on about 'im. 'War against the warmongers', an' aa that. If ye ask me, jyle's the best place for 'im.

PAT (*refusing to be involved in a conversation with Eddie*) : Naebody's asking you, Eddie. (*He puts down money for the drinks.*)

(*Pat returns to Willie's table with their drinks.*)

JAKE : How's the weans, Pat?

PAT : No bad, Jake. No bad. But . . . the wee lassie's no daein sae good.

JAKE: You've a couple o weans, dan't ye, Willie?

WILLIE: Aye. A boy an' lassie.

JAKE: That's nice.

WILLIE: I havenae seen much o them lately.

JAKE: Aye, ye've been kept busy.

WILLIE: You any weans, Jake?

JAKE: No. We had wan, but it was still-born, the wife cannae hav any mair.

WILLIE: Oh. . . . (*They drink.*) I always meant tae thank ye, Jake.

JAKE: Thank me for what?

WILLIE: You know what for. I bought a job off ye like everybody else.

JAKE: Ye mean the graftin?

WILLIE: Aye. What made ye stop?

JAKE: Ye cannae depend on a couple o bob in a match-box aa your days.

WILLIE: That's no aa I wis gettin at, Jake. I wis talkin about your attitude. Even although ye're a gaffer, ye're solid behind a hunner-per-cent union shop.

JAKE: So'd anybody be that's wise.

PAT: What brought ye roun?

JAKE: I can read as well, ye know.

PAT: Aye, I suppose ye can.

(*They drink. Geordie comes in from the Family Department, and passes Willie's table on his way to the bar to place his order.*)

GEORDIE (*to Eddie*): Same again, Eddie.

EDDIE: Have ye no had enough?

GEORDIE: First time I've heard o a publican no wantin tae sell a man a drink.

EDDIE: Nou I didnae say that, did I?

(*Eddie pours out the drinks. Geordie waits. Willie rises, then moves over towards Geordie.*)

WILLIE : Geordie MacLeod. I never thought ye could be sae stupit. Ye're stupit!

PAT : Willie, you're drunk.

WILLIE : Just look at yoursel'. Tommy fuckin Atkins, Defender of the Realm!

GEORDIE : Just watch what ye're sayin, Willie. I'll mangalate you.

WILLIE : Ye know what? I think that's what I want ye tae dae. I want tae see stars, an' I wouldnae care if I never saw anither khaki jacket.

GEORDIE : Well, ye're goin the right wey about it.

EDDIE : Easy, boys. No fightin. Outside, if ye want tae have a set-to!

GEORDIE : Don't worry yoursel', Eddie! He couldnae punch a hole in a wet paper.

(*Willie is nearer to Geordie now, but less aggressive.*)

WILLIE : Tell me wan thing, Geordie.

GEORDIE : What?

WILLIE : When I brought McLean doun here, an' he tellt ye the truth about this war, I looked at ye, an' your mouth was wide open. Ye were spellbound, bi-Christ, listenin tae that man. Ye believed 'im. I know ye believed 'im. An' then Willie Gallacher cam doun frae the Albion. Ye were there that night as well. He tellt ye, an' McLean tellt ye, an' at wan meetin after another I've tellt ye mysel', an' here ye are like a whippet strainin at the leash. Over the top! Tell me where we went wrong, Geordie, 'cause I've got tae know. Honest, I've got tae know!

GEORDIE : Mebbie I got fed up wi your Red Flags an' songs an' aa that shite. You can stay here an' sing the 'Internationale', an' the 'Red Flag', tae, but when ye're daein it, remember that me an folk like me are fightin for ye. Ye cannae be serious tae think that I'd miss the chance o goin tae the Front. Ye'll change your mind, but by that time it'll be all over.

WILLIE : Would ye believe me, Geordie, if I tellt ye I hope it will?

GEORDIE : Just answer me this, Willie Rough.

WILLIE : What?

GEORDIE : Supposin somebody attacks me wi a big stick on the way hame the-night.

WILLIE : What?

GEORDIE : Just supposin that happened. Would I be justified in usin a big stick tae defend mysel'?

WILLIE : Aye.

GEORDIE : Well, then?

WILLIE : Well, what?

GEORDIE : That's the war, in't it, an' the British Army's the big stick against the Germans?

WILLIE : I don't know who you've been talkin tae the-day, but that's kinna fancy for the like o you.

GEORDIE : I asked ye the question, an' you answered it.

WILLIE : Look, Geordie. If somebody attacks ye on the road hame the-night I've nae objection tae you usin a big stick—two, if ye can handle the baith o them. An' if Bethmann Hollweg uses a big stick tae attack Sir Edward Grey, I cannae complain if Sir Edward Grey uses a big stick back tae Bethmann Hollweg, but there's wan thing I'm fuckin sure o, an' that is that I'm no gonna be the big stick, an' I've done aa I can tae stop the workin class bein used as the big stick. You're in

the wrong fight, Geordie. Sure I want ye tae win.
If ye want bands playin, we'll hav bands playin,
but the victory shouldnae be for the Imperialist
Allies. It should be *your* victory. I'm talkin about
Geordie MacLeod, the hauder-on, no Private
MacLeod, G. !

GEORDIE : I'm no kiddin ye, Willie. Any mair o
that talk, an' they'll be lockin ye up for treason.

WILLIE : You'll be in beside me for breakin an'
enterin if ye don't tak these stupit glesses aff !

GEORDIE : Can I tak my drinks, Eddie? Next door
they'll be thinkin it's a dry area.

EDDIE : Here ye are.

(*Geordie takes the drinks through to the Family
Department. Willie sits down beside Jake and Pat.*)

JAKE : What wis aa that about?

PAT : I'm gonna get you hame.

WILLIE : I've just thought o something.

PAT : What?

WILLIE : I might never see Geordie MacLeod again.

JAKE : Christ, you're cheery !

(*Two policemen, Sanny and Peter, come in. They
walk to the bar. Hughie steps out of the Family
Department, still wearing his stolen spectacles: but,
seeing the policemen, he pops back into the Family
Department very, very quickly.*)

HUGHIE (*off*) : Act normal.

VOICES (*off*) : It's the Polis. . . . Shut up. . . . They'll
no know we're here if ye haud your wheest. . . .

SANNY (*a Highlander, to Eddie*) : Where's Hughie?

EDDIE : What's he done?

PETER : He was seen at Lizars the-night. Hauf the toun done the shop.

EDDIE : Hughie's no hauf the toun.

PETER : Mebbie no, but his wan leg wis recognised.

EDDIE : Aye. It would be, wouldn'it?

SANNY : Is 'e been in or no?

EDDIE : 'E'll no get time or anything, will 'e?

SANNY : Not at all. We'll let 'im out in the mornin.

PETER : It'll soon blow over. We're just goin throu the motions.

EDDIE : I wisnae sure whether Lizars were Germans or no.

SANNY : Well, they're no frae Port Glasgow. I'll tell ye that for nothing.

PETER : They must be Germans.

JAKE : How dae ye make that out?

SANNY : Well, they wouldnae hav done the shop if they werenae, would they?

EDDIE : Good thinkin, Sanny. They're next door. Quiet as ye can, boys.

(*Sanny and Peter both go to the door of the Family Department. Sanny opens the door.*)

SANNY : Come on, Hughie. Nou dinnae gie us ony bother, lads.

(*Hughie comes back into the Public Bar, followed by all the others.*)

HUGHIE : What's the trouble, eh, constable?

SANNY : Where did ye get thae specs?

HUGHIE : Timothy White's.

SANNY : Aye, that'll be right.

HUGHIE : I sweir tae God.

SANNY : Dae ye always wear the two pair?

HUGHIE : Aye. The odd time. If I'm readin an' lookin a long distance ower the tap o the paper at the same time.

PETER : Ye're never stuck, are ye, Hughie?

HUGHIE : Where's the hauncuffs?

SANNY : We've ran out o hauncuffs. Hauf the toun's in the jyle.

HUGHIE : That's fine, then. We'll no be stuck for company. Can we hav a cairry-out, Eddie, tae drink in the jyle?

PETER : Na, ye cannae! Come on, youz!

(Sanny and Peter lead the criminals out. At the door Peter turns.)

PETER : Eddie . . .

EDDIE : What?

PETER : You should be shut.

EDDIE : Aye. I'm just going for the gates for the windaes nou. Somebody might get the idea that the MacCauslands are frae Munich!

PETER : Right. Good night, well.

EDDIE : 'Night, Sanny.

(Peter goes out.)

EDDIE *(to the three still at the table)*: Did ye no hear 'im? Time up, boys.

PAT *(to Willie)*: Come on. I've got tae get you hame.

WILLIE : I'll be aa-right.

JAKE : Come on, Pat. I'll get ye up the road.

PAT : I'm waitin for Willie.

WILLIE *(aggressively)*: I'm O.K., I tellt ye!

PAT : Aa-right. Don't bite my heid aff.

EDDIE : It's O.K., Pat. I'll get 'im up the road.

PAT : Fine. Thanks, Eddie. See ye in the mornin, Willie.

JAKE : On time, or ye're quartered.

(*Pat and Jake go out into the street.*)

EDDIE : I'll just pit the gates on, an' we'll be on our way.

(*Eddie goes out behind the counter to get the gate for the window. Willie rises, staggering slightly. One of the posters decorating the bar catches his eye. He goes nearer to it, stares at it.*)

WILLIE (*reciting*) : Your King and Country need ye,
        Ye hardy sons of toil :
        But will your King and Country
           need ye,
           When they're sharin out the
             spoil?

6. *Pat's House: October 1914*

(*Pat and Bernadette, his wife, are kneeling together near a child's coffin which has been placed on the kitchen table.*)

PAT : Our Father, Who art in Heaven, hallowed be Thy name. Thy Kingdom come. Thy will be done, on earth as it is in Heaven.

BOTH : Give us this day our daily bread, and forgive us our trespasses, as we forgive them that trespass against us. Lead us not into temptation, but deliver us from evil . . . Amen.

PAT : Hail Mary, full of grace, the Lord is with

thee. Blessed art thou among women, and blessed
is the fruit of thy womb, Jesus.

BOTH : Holy Mary, Mother of God, pray for us
sinners, now and at the hour of our death . . .
Amen. (*They go on until they have said the* Hail
Mary *ten times.*)

BOTH : Glory be to the Father

(*Willie comes in, dressed in his working clothes, but
wearing a black tie, and stands quietly, cap in hand,
until their prayer is over,*)

and to the Son, and to the Holy Ghost, as it was
in the beginning, is now, and ever shall be . . .
Amen.

(*Willie raises his head and waits. Pat rises. They
look at Bernadette. . . .*)

PAT : Bernadette. . . .

BERNADETTE : Thanks for comin, Willie.

WILLIE : Your mother wants tae see ye in the
room.

BERNADETTE : I don't want tae go ben there just
yet, I'll just start greetin again.

PAT : It's time ye went, hen. The men are here for
her.

WILLIE : Aye. Ye'd be best tae go.

BERNADETTE : I wish I could go tae the graveside.

PAT : No. It would only upset ye aa the mair. I'll
see the wee yin up the road.

WILLIE : Pat's right, Mrs Gatens. (*She goes out.
Pat's hand is on the coffin.*) Greet, if ye want tae,
Pat. There's naebody but me tae hear ye.

PAT : Greetin's for weemin an' weans.

(*Willie turns to go.*)

Don't go, Willie. As sure as God they'll never get me out o here if you go. I'll staun here thinkin o what she might hae grown tae. I never really thought o her as a wean. It's a fact. We had Anthony first, then Patrick an' Michael. Aa boys. I woulda done anything for thae boys, but Bernadette she wanted a wee lassie. When Teresa came it wis like a blessin, Willie. She wis a wee smasher. She's only two year auld, but I kept thinkin o her up. Ye know what I mean? Filled out an' 'at. Quite the young lady, ye know, breakin everybody's heart frae Kilmacolm tae Gourock. I kept wonderin if I'd be able tae talk tae her then. I wisnae carin if folk said I spoiled her. I woulda gien her the skin aff my back, Willie, so I would. Every faither's got a favourite. I'm sure ye have yoursel'. . . . When she was a wean, she had a wee convulsion or two just after Bernadette brought her back frae the Maternity. It was that bad we couldnae sleep for worry a couple o nights. I thought then she might no live, it was that bad. But we did what Nurse Lonie said, an' she came on fine. But what can ye dae about the scarlet fever, Willie? We're no even gien the chance. I'd chynge places wi her if I could, Willie. Honest. We're a good family. We go tae eight-o'clock Mass every Sunday. An' it's no just 'cause it's my duty tae go an' tae mak the weans go. I *believe* in going. Ye see some folk . . . they're in an' out of the jyle. We've met them oursel's, Willie. We see them marchin about the toun in khaki uniforms as if that made them intae saints. We're no saints, either, Willie, but you an' me, we've tried our best tae be decent folk. I've never sided wi a Catholic against you, Willie, an' you've never waved an Orange banner in my face, either. We're no Hibs or Masons, are we?

WILLIE : No.

PAT : Ye believe in God an' ye tell your weans tae believe in something as well an' then that scarlet fever comes . . . (*He almost breaks down.*) Can He no pick on somebody else? We'll remember this year aa-right, Willie.

WILLIE : There's a lot o families lost somebody.

PAT : Aye. Ye know I forgot aa about everythin'. The only thing I believed in was our Teresa, an' she was away. Ye cannae think o onybody else sufferin as much as you dae. Just think if I'd stayed at the drillin an' joined up. I wouldnae be here. Can ye imagine gettin a note in a week or a fortnight mebbie tellin ye ye havenae got a wee lassie ony mair?

WILLIE : Aye. Geordie MacLeod's wife got a note yesterday forenoon.

PAT : Aye. Ye tellt us : 'Missing, believed killed in action'.

WILLIE : Aye.

PAT : I never had much time for him. Ach, he wisnae a bad fella, Geordie. I cannae see ony end tae't.

WILLIE : They think they'll be hame for the New Year.

PAT : What year, but? . . .

WILLIE : Are ye ready nou, Pat?

PAT : Aye. Ready as I'll ever be. (*He lifts the coffin and carries it out.*)

7. *The Hills Above Greenock: December 1914*

(*Willie, Jake and Pat are walking together. Willie*

*is carrying a small leather case. Jake has a whippet
on a leash. They stop and look down from the hill-
side to the town and the river beyond.)*

WILLIE : Look at it! Spellbindin. Ye'd never think
Greenock could look sae fine.

JAKE : Aye. It's aa-right frae up here. It's no sae
fine when ye're stuck in the rain in the middle o't.

PAT : What the hell are yez talkin about? I'm
freezin. Who ever heard o goin a walk up the hill
in December?

JAKE : Willie wanted tae see me. Ye cannae keep
a whippet shut up in a kennel.

WILLIE : We'll no be a minute, Pat. I've got tae
explain tae Jake what's goin on.

PAT : I can go hame, then.

WILLIE : Och, haud your tongue an' sit doun, Pat.

PAT : Sit doun! I'll get a chill in my arse if I sit
doun.

*(Willie sits down. Jake and Pat crouch near him.
The whippet strains at the leash. Jake strokes its
long nose.)*

JAKE : What's on your mind, Willie?

WILLIE : It's the negotiatin committee, Jake. I
know your collar an' tie's kept ye out o the Union,
but your attitude's always been sympathetic . . .

JAKE : No always.

WILLIE : Ye know what I mean. I thought ye might
be able tae help us.

JAKE : Willie, I'm in a funny position. It's none o
my business. Neither the Union nor your negotiatin
committee. Christ, if any o the high heid-yins saw
me even talkin tae you two, I'd get the fuckin
bag!

WILLIE : I havenae slept for a week, Jake. That's honest. It's got tae be twopence an hour or nothin'. I know that. But I'm feart I'm gonna let the men doun.

PAT : Ther' mair nor you on that committee. Govan, Clydebank. Every yaird an' factory on the Clyde's represented. . . .

JAKE : Pat's right, Willie. Ye cannae blame yoursel' for the whole shootin-match.

WILLIE : Sure I can. The rest are like corn on the wind.

JAKE : Well, if they're aa sae glaikit, it should be nae bother tae get a haud o them by the scruff o the neck an' tell them tae sit on their arses till the employers up their offer tae twopence an hour. Ye don't need me tae tell ye that. I'm away tae run my dug. (*He rises and moves away with the dog.*)

WILLIE : I hoped you could gie me some information.

JAKE : How dae ye mean?

WILLIE : We went tae this meetin up in Glesga. Sit doun, Jake.

(*Jake crouches beside Pat.*)

We tellt the employers. Twopence an hour. Basic rate increase o twopence an hour. That's from thirty-six tae forty-five bob for the fifty-four-hour week. Clear. Right?

JAKE : Aye. Then *they* tellt ye they were skint.

WILLIE : That's right. They pleaded poverty an' offered us a hapenny.

JAKE : I hope ye told them where tae pit it.

WILLIE : They knew we would. They didnae come up the Clyde in a banana-boat. They came tae the

254

meetin tae go as far as three farthins, so they offered
us that. We said, 'Ye're not on,' an' they chucked
it.

JAKE : An' that's where ye are? Three farthins an
hour increase. It's nothin' tae dae wi me, but ye
musta spent mair than that on train-fares.

PAT : It's better than nothin'.

WILLIE : What would ye say tae a penny an hour,
Pat?

PAT : A penny would make a difference. I can see
the men settlin for that.

WILLIE : There ye are ! Oh, the big bugs know all
about you. They can read ye lik a book, Pat. That's
what they want. Can ye no see? Even at the committee meetin the other day . . . a committee
member, bi-Christ . . . chief o the 'Brassies' . . . 'A
penny, an we'll settle' . . . he kept sayin it over an'
over. 'A penny, an' we'll settle' . . . I thought he
might end up singin it . . . playin right intae their
haunds . . . as bad as you, Pat . . . tryin tae force
the Engineers tae settle for hauf.

JAKE : Haud on. Haud on, Willie. What have the
Engineers got tae dae wi this?

WILLIE : I'll start frae the beginnin.

JAKE : I wish ye would.

WILLIE : Two separate negotiatin committees, right?
The A.S.E., representin the Engineers. An' the
Allied Trades, that's us. Both aifter the same thing.
Twopence an hour. Right?

JAKE : With ye.

WILLIE : We, the Allied Trades, go in. They offer a
hapenny. We tell them tae stuff it. Three farthins.
Still stuff it. Then, in a roundabout way at the
negotiations, they let us know that they'll go tae
a penny, unofficially, like, knowin the bulk o our
members'll lap it up an' settle.

JAKE : But what's your point?

WILLIE : They're usin us, Jake. They're usin us tae get the Engineers tae settle. The smaller unions, like us, are bein used to betray their fellow workers. If somethin's no done fast, they'll offer the penny, official, our committee will accept it, and the Engineers'll have tae settle, tae. That's what I wanted tae see ye about, Jake.

JAKE : What dae ye want? Time aff?

WILLIE : No. You know folk, Jake. Find me an Engineer that's on the A.S.E. negotiatin committee. Let me talk tae'm, an' mebbie between us we can organise a united front tae tell the employers tae stick the penny up their arse before they've got the cheek tae offer it tae us.

JAKE : Ye'll get me hung, Willie. Christ, I wish they'd conscript ye, an' get ye tae hell away frae here.

WILLIE : They might, ye never know.

JAKE : I'm bloody sure they win't. They don't want a bloody mutiny on their hauns. (*They laugh.*) . . . I think I know a bloke. Works in Browns. Mebbie no. Might be Fairfields. Up the river.

PAT : Well, if 'at's the meetin over, I'm goin doun hame. I'm freezin. (*He moves away. Willie stands beside Jake.*)

WILLIE : What's this bloke frae Glesga like?

JAKE : You should get on well. He done time for throwin shite at some Councillor up there a coupla years back.

PAT : Oh, Christ, they'll baith hav bombs in their pockets at the next meetin.

JAKE : But what if Charlie agrees wi ye? His name's Charlie McGrath. He's only wan.

WILLIE : As long as he's the right wan. Thae meetins are beyond description. Wan o the managin

directors gie'in ye a wee talk about patriotism, an'
how we should grist tae the mill, an' shouther tae
the wheel, an' roll wir sleeves up, an' set a stout
heart tae a stey brae, an' tripe lik that. It's aa lies.
He wis near greetin when he described 'the plight
of our glorious brothers in foreign fields'. The tears
wis formin in his eyes. He made this speech . . .
well, it wis mair liker a hymn . . . real tears . . . I
couldnae believe it. The auld hypocrite. I tellt him
tae join up. He chynged his tune aifter that. Sat
like a dummy for the rest o the day.

JAKE: So it looks like ye'll be a wee while gettin
the twopence, Willie?

WILLIE: It's a rotten prospect, Jake, but I think
it'll take nothing short of strike action.

JAKE: Ever been out on strike, son?

WILLIE: No.

JAKE: Well, don't be in a hurry tae see what it's
like. It would be aa-right tae start wi, I suppose.
It's a kind o bravery for civilians. Aa thae folk 'at
havenae gone tae the Front . . . there's some 'at
think we're mebbie a wee bit feart . . . so ye down
tools an' show what ye're made o, a wee bit. Me
an' the ither hats'll go tae work . . . we'll drink tea
an' dae nothin' . . . no 'at that'll be much o a
chynge for us . . . but we'll look about us an' see
it . . . the deserted shipyard . . . like a graveyaird
full o bogie-men, an' the big cranns lookin doun
on us lik vultures. An' the boats'll no chynge that
wee bit week-bi-week, like they dae when ye're
workin . . . just stay the same . . . waitin for ye
tae come back tae finish them aff. An' aa you . . .
you'll be staunin on street corners . . . the money
ye've pit by'll soon be done, so you'll no be in the
pub. Ye'll be nae better 'an the man 'at cannae get
a job, or disnae want a job, or had wan an' got the

bag! You must look after the boys, Willie. Don't pit this toun intae that situation.

WILLIE : It would be mair than just this toun. It would be right up that river doun there.

JAKE : Christ!

WILLIE : Oh, I meant tae tell ye. Comin back frae the meetin I passed Greenlaw Goods Station. Know what I saw?

PAT : Na, What?

WILLIE : Two big guns ready tae be cairted aff tae the Front. Huge bloody things they were.

PAT : What's wrang wi that?

WILLIE : They've been sittin there for six weeks. The bosses are no gonna muve them till the Government pays higher transportation fees.

JAKE : 'S 'at a fact?

WILLIE : Them an' their 'boys in the trenches'! Ye know what else? They're sendin war materials tae neutral countries at ridiculous profits knowin full well that the stuff's eventually being sold to the Germans tae blaw the boys tae fuck *out* o the trenches!

JAKE : I wouldnae trust any o them as far as I could shite, so I wouldnae.

PAT : They're bastarts, so they are. Hey, I'm cauld.

JAKE : Aye. It's time we were movin. I cam up here tae run the dug, no tae listen tae propaganda aa night. (*Pat strokes the whippet.*) . . . Don't pet him, Pat. He'll never win a race if ye dae that.

PAT : Oh, I see. Dae ye chase hares, like?

JAKE : Aye.

PAT : Ever catch anythin'?

JAKE : Aye. Fuckin pneumonia.

(*He walks the whippet a few steps away from them. He talks to the dog, whistles, then shouts as he slips*

258

*it from the leash. The whippet runs off. Willie and
Pat have moved over, fascinated by Jake's handling
of the whippet.)*

Go, Teemo! (*He whistles.*) . . .

PAT : Seems fast enough tae me.

JAKE : I swear to Christ—some day I'll take that
dug out for a walk and run away frae it.

(They are still watching the dog's journey.)

WILLIE : Thanks, Jake.

JAKE : Aye. I'll pit ye in touch wi Charlie McGrath.
All right?

WILLIE : Sooner the better.

JAKE : He's your man, aa-right . . . Oh, that bloody
idiot dug. He's lost, bi-Christ! It's aa-right. Your
daddy's comin. . . .

*(He goes off after his dog. Willie goes down to look
at the view once again.)*

WILLIE : Would ye look at that view?

PAT : I've seen it afore. Come on. My teeth are
chitterin.

WILLIE : It musta been great here afore the cranns
came, and all this mechanisation. Can you imagine
haein a wee farm up here? Away from everybody.
Every time ye ploughed your field, an' that, ye
could come over here for a wee rest an' just look
doun at the river frae the Tail o the Bank tae the
Holy Loch. Great times. Mebbie. Mebbie no. Even
smells different up here. And it's quiet.

PAT : You're a romancer, Willie. Come on tae
fuck!

(They both go.)

259

8. *The James Watt Bar: February 1915*

(*Hughie and Eddie have the place all to them-selves. It's before lunch-time.*)

HUGHIE : Dae ye ken how mony that is?

EDDIE : Aye. Ye tellt us. It's twenty thousan.

HUGHIE : Sure it is. But, I mean, can ye *see* twenty thousan?

EDDIE : How dae ye mean?

HUGHIE : Well, ye dinnae get what it's like frae the report wance the War Office is finished wi't. Ye dinnae get the smell, for wan thing.

EDDIE : There's nae point upsettin folk ony mair than ye need, is there?

HUGHIE : Mebbie no. Gie's a Bell's, Eddie. On the slate.

EDDIE : I'm gonna get a clock in here. I'll tak the hauns aff an' I'll write on a bit o paper across its face : '*NO TICK*'.

HUGHIE : But, in the meantime, Eddie . . .

EDDIE : Ye said ye'd pey me at the New Year.

HUGHIE : I didnae say what wan, but. Come on, Eddie. Are ye?

(*Eddie pours out the drink, Hughie comes over to the bar to get it.*)

HUGHIE : Here's continuin prosperity tae ye, Eddie, in 1915. Aa-ra best!

EDDIE : Ye're a bit late.

HUGHIE : Flies in, din't it? It's Feb'ry aaready.

(*He drinks.*)

EDDIE : Did ye hear about wee Danny Blair frae East Crawford Street? Nice lad.

HUGHIE : Aye. I mean, ye cannae help likin a bloke wi a po-stumous decoration.

EDDIE : V.C.

HUGHIE : Aff 'is heid.

EDDIE : How?

HUGHIE : The two men he went tae save's aa-right. Wee Danny's deid, bi-fuck. Valour! Out o-ra question. Look at me. I've only got wan leg, an' I wis a coward. We had a hera in our squad an aa. He's deid, tae.

EDDIE : There are some things worth deein for, Hughie.

HUGHIE : What? You tell me.

EDDIE : Your country right or wrong.

HUGHIE : You're aff your heid, as well!

EDDIE : You werenae sayin that the night before they went away. I remember it well. Ye were staunin there talkin like wan o thae posters on the waa.

HUGHIE : I say mair nor my prayers, Eddie. Ye don't honestly think I believe any o it? I don't mean I'm a pro-German or anything, ye know? I mean, I'm on the right side, but I know. I've seen them. If ye gied hauf o them a gun in peace-time, they'd be locked up in the loony-bin for runnin amok, bi-Christ.

EDDIE : Where is everybody?

HUGHIE : Yaird gates. Big Union meetin.

EDDIE : Again?

HUGHIE : Aye. The Engineers have lowered themsel's tae talk tae the Allied Trades. Motion o solidadarity. Twopence an hour or nothing.

EDDIE : They'll settle for a penny. Bet ye anything.

HUGHIE: Of course they will. Willie Rough's dementit. He cannae win.

EDDIE: Nae chance.

HUGHIE: They'll be after him soon. Mark my words, Edward.

EDDIE: Who will?

HUGHIE: The Press Gang. Listen tae me. Twenty thousan men deid or missin. Have ye got that?

EDDIE: Eh?

HUGHIE: Morton's playin the Rangers at Cappie-low, right? Capacity crowd. Ye cannae breathe for Rangers supporters. Nou, imagine every single wan o thae men at that game. Twenty thousan. Imagine the whole fuckin lot o them blown right out o Sinclair Street intae the Clyde. Weans orphaned. Wives weidowed. Can ye imagine the size o the funeral? But there's nae big funeral. Wee Danny's mammy'll get the medal. The'll be naething left o him to have a funeral wi'. Bits. Even if 'is watch escaped unhurt, as it were, somebody's snaffled 'at!

EDDIE: Screw the bobbin, Hughie. Ye cannae take a man's glory away.

HUGHIE: Neither ye can, considering he only got it throu the post this mornin an' him deid.

EDDIE: They thought they'd be hame for the New Year.

HUGHIE: Propaganda. Pure an' simple. I'll gie ye the answer in one dreaded word. Conscription.

EDDIE: It's no as bad as that, is it?

HUGHIE: Dae ye think anither twenty thousan are itchin tae volunteer? Not at all. This time, it's you, you, an' you.

EDDIE: Mebbie ye're right. To tell ye the truth, Hughie, I havenae lost wan regular since yon night ye done Lizars.

HUGHIE : In this toun there's folk that's stupit, but there's mair folk that's no sae stupit. Am I right or am I wrong?

EDDIE : Ye're right.

HUGHIE : Ye want a message?

EDDIE : No. Ye want a drink?

HUGHIE : Aye. I've got money comin tae me.

EDDIE : How do you live, Hughie?

HUGHIE : I go messages for you.

EDDIE : Money, I'm talkin about.

HUGHIE : Anybody in by?

EDDIE : No.

HUGHIE : Ye'll no tell onybody?

EDDIE : What dae ye take me for, a clype?

HUGHIE : It's the *Telegraph*. Wan o the reporters is giein me a wee back-hander.

EDDIE : What for?

HUGHIE : I gie 'im the odd tip about the situation ower by.

EDDIE : Does Willie know?

HUGHIE : What dae you think?

EDDIE : I think he disnae.

HUGHIE : You'd be right. Listen tae me . . .

(*Charlie comes in. He's over thirty, dressed in quite a smart suit and a cap. He has just come down from Glasgow.*)

CHARLIE : Excuse me. Have ye seen Willie Rough?

HUGHIE : Yaird gates. Big meetin.

CHARLIE : He tellt me he'd be here.

HUGHIE : He'll no be long. I'm Hughie. This is Eddie.

CHARLIE : Charlie McGrath. I'm a frien o Willie's frae Glesga.

EDDIE (*serving*) : Yes?

263

CHARLIE : Have ye got lemonade?

EDDIE : Aye.

HUGHIE : He's got whisky an' aa.

CHARLIE : I don't drink.

HUGHIE : How? Was ye an alcoholic or something?

EDDIE : Lea' the fella alane, Hughie. (*He pours out some lemonade for Charlie.*)

CHARLIE (*to Hughie*) : You have another, Hughie?

HUGHIE : That's very kind o ye, Charlie. I'll hav a gless an' a pint.

(*Eddie pours out another drink.*)

CHARLIE : I don't know whether tae go over tae the yard or no.

HUGHIE : You look a bit agitaitit.

CHARLIE : I've got news for Willie. They've downed tools at Weirs o Cathcart. By the end o this week every man on the Clyde'll be out on strike.

EDDIE : Well, don't look sae cheery about it.

HUGHIE : If it's no a war, it's a strike. Is there naething cheery happenin at aa?

EDDIE : Disnae seem like it.

HUGHIE : There's nae point Weirs comin out about the rise. Negotiations havenae broken doun or onything, hav they?

CHARLIE : It's not the rise this time. Shortage of labour.

HUGHIE : Well?

CHARLIE : They've brought engineers over frae America.

HUGHIE : What's wrang wi that? They're no darkies or onything, are they?

CHARLIE : No, they're not, if ye must know. Anyway, they brought in thae Yanks. Skilled men all right, but what dae they do?

HUGHIE : What?

CHARLIE : Return tickets. Ten shillins a week more than our own men, an' a guaranteed ten-poun bonus at the end o six months. They've really done it this time. They're skilled men, but they don't know wan end o a discharge-pump frae the other. Willie Rough an' me. We knew they'd make their mistake. We waited. Here it is. Weirs o Cathcart —the bosses themsel's are gonna be instrumental in gettin twopence an hour frae Glesga tae the Tail o the Bank!

EDDIE : When, but?

HUGHIE : Aye. That's pit your gas in a peep!

CHARLIE : Not at all. Don't you believe it. I've lived for this morning. Can ye no see? War or nae war, this'll show that the unions'll survive. The working man's been the goods an' chattels of the employer class for far too long. We're in nae state tae think or feel or even live as human beings. A day like this is to exploit our hatred and kindle it intae rebellion. The day we tell them we're united. The-morra, we frighten them tae death. They can stick the Defence o the Realm Act. From now on they'll have to reckon wi us as a fighting organ of the working classes!

HUGHIE : The Band o Hope, bi-Christ!

(*Willie comes in with Pat and two other workers.*)

CHARLIE : Willie!

WILLIE : I thought it was you.

CHARLIE : Have ye heard about Weirs?

WILLIE : Aye, I heard.

CHARLIE : Well . . . are ye out? Are ye on strike?
WILLIE : Aye.

(*Willie and Pat move over to their table. Charlie follows.*)

CHARLIE : We knew wan o thae toffs would dae somethin' daft, didn't we? A Bell's, Willie?
WILLIE : Aye, thanks.
CHARLIE : Pat, you do the needful.

(*Charlie gives Pat some money. Pat goes over to the bar.*)

PAT : Glass o lemonade an' two Bell's, Eddie.
HUGHIE : Eh. Three Bell's. Fairly lashin out, that yin. Mair like a christenin nor a strike.
PAT : Wait tae I tell Bernadette.
HUGHIE : Nae alternative, tho.
PAT : Still, wait tae I tell Bernadette.
CHARLIE : It's good news, Willie.
WILLIE : Listen tae me, Charlie McGrath. I've just pit eight hunner men on the street, an' afore the day's out there'll be thousans, an' I don't think that's very good news, so I don't!
CHARLIE : But it's the mistake. The clowns have done it. They know where to stick their penny an hour. It's twopence or nothin'.
WILLIE : I wish I wis like you, Charlie. I dae sometimes. Honest! Ye're like that crann over there. Just like steel. Ye don't get that wee tightness in your stomach as if ye were gaunna spew your ring up. Aa mornin, when you've been thinkin about organisation, I've been thinkin about next week or the week aifter, when the excitement wears a bit thin, and they're dyin tae get back across that

street tae make the price o a hauf or a loaf or three eggs. Ye cannae live on the win'.

CHARLIE : I thought ye'd be glad, that's aa.

WILLIE : Glad? Ye've nae feelings at all, have ye?

(*Hughie lifts his crutch and moves to the door.*)

EDDIE : Ye goin tae *your* work nou, Hughie?

HUGHIE : You shut it. Cheerio, lads. Ye'll be back on Monday wi the increase aa sewn up.

PAT : I hope tae Christ we are!

(*Hughie goes out. Jake comes in and goes to the bar.*)

EDDIE : Hello, Jake. Ye'll be gey lonely over the road this aifternoon.

JAKE : Mebbie I'll be able tae teach that dug o mine how tae win a race.

EDDIE : Aye. Ye cannae be a gaffer if ye havenae got a squad.

PAT : I don't know what I'll dae. Bernadette'll soon want me out o the road. There's aye the picketin, I suppose.

(*Jake sees Charlie.*)

JAKE : Charlie. Long time.

CHARLIE : Dae ye want a drink, Jake?

JAKE : Dae ye no think we better buy wir ain?

ACT TWO

9. *A Street: February 1915*

(*Kate and Bernadette meet. Both are wearing scarves round their heads. Each carries a shopping-bag, but neither has made many purchases. Kate is visibly pregnant.*)

KATE : Hello.

BERNADETTE : Hello, Katie. It's that close.

KATE : We're due rain, I'm thinkin.

BERNADETTE : Aye. When are ye due?

KATE : April.

BERNADETTE : Oh. No be long now.

KATE : The men'll be back by then, surely.

BERNADETTE : Och, sure it's terrible. Pat comes hame an' says 'We're out. Solid!' Pleased wi 'imsel', like, and I says, 'Who's gonna feed us?' an' he says, 'There's mair important things than your belly', an' I says, 'What? What's mair important?' an' he goes on about infiltration an' agitation an' God knows what aa else, an' I says, 'Agitation'll no feed ye, nor four weans, neither,' an' he says, 'Be quiet,' an' I says, 'Na,' an' wan thing led tae anither, an' I got a skyelp on the face.

KATE : Oh.

BERNADETTE : We made it up again, tho. Your Willie must be worse. I mean, he's in charge, so 'e is, an' you expectin an' everything. How are you managin?

KATE : We manage.

BERNADETTE : Ye just hav tae.

KATE : Aye. That's about it. Willie says he'd live on tatty-peelins tae get 'is rights.

BERNADETTE : Pat's just as determined. An' there's nae sign o it endin?

KATE : Willie never talks tae me about it.

268

BERNADETTE : I thought he would. I mean . . . he must hav a lot on's mind.

KATE : Aye, but he's deep, my Willie. He keeps maist o't tae 'imsel'.

BERNADETTE : I wouldnae let Pat keep any secrets frae me.

KATE : I don't bother. The Union's the men's business. If they got the rise, it would be worth it.

BERNADETTE : Is your rent up?

KATE : Aye. I got a letter frae the factor this mornin.

BERNADETTE : So's ours. I went tae see wan o the Labour men on the Council. He tellt me no tae pay it.

KATE : Did 'e?

BERNADETTE : Aye. It seems there's a big protest goin on. It wis startit by a wumman up in Glesga. I've got a poster. Wait tae ye see. (*She takes the poster from her bag.*) . . . Haud that end.

(*Kate takes one end of the poster, and they spread it out between them. It reads 'DO NOT PAY INCREASED RENT'.*)

BERNADETTE : Do . . . not . . . pay . . . increased . . . rent. . . . *There ye are.*

KATE : Do ye think it's aa-right?

BERNADETTE : Aa-right or no, I'm no giein them ony mair. Two shillins! Where dae they think we get it, Katie? The men might as well be idle. The strike amounts tae the same thing. Nothin' a week!

KATE : We cannae afford it. If the men get the rise, mebbie. It'll be different then.

BERNADETTE : It's never ony different. Ye'll get a shillin a week extra on the mantelpiece on a Friday, an' by the weekend breid's gone up two-

269

pence, sugar's up a penny, an' there's anither penny
on a pot o jam an' cookin-fat. Afore ye can draw
breath, the car-fare's up a hapenny. Then you're
in the toun an' back, in an' back, that's a penny
a day, an' ye're right back where ye started. An'
you know what happens next?

KATE : The rent?

BERNADETTE : Na. The men's out again. Lockout.
Strike. Arbitration. Negotiations. Meetins, meetins,
an' mair meetins. They're no wise.

KATE : Ye don't think they like bein on strike, dae
ye?

BERNADETTE : I wouldnae pit it past them. My
Patrick got 'is photo in the *Telegraph* the other
day, an' in ablow't 'is name . . . He says, 'Look,
Bernadette!—Patrick Gatens!' He's still got it in
his wallet. He cut it out an' kept it.

KATE : I wis gonna keep some o the things they
said about Willie in a wee book, but he wouldnae
let us.

BERNADETTE : How no?

KATE : He says the papers is, what d'ye cry it? . . .
biased against the men.

BERNADETTE : Oh, I cannae mind what they said
about Pat. I just saw 'is name, like.

KATE (*suddenly looking ahead*) : Oh. Is 'at the time?
I've got tae go an' see Nurse Lonie.

BERNADETTE : She's 'at nice, isn't she?

KATE : Aye.

BERNADETTE : She's been in Greenock for years, ye
know. I'm sure she'll be the midwife when our
weans' weans is born.

KATE : So it's aa-right about the rent, ye think?

BERNADETTE : I'm no payin it. I cannae.

KATE : I just hope they don't get the polis on tae
us.

BERNADETTE : The men would wreck the factor's offices if that happened.

KATE : Aye. It disnae take much tae set them aff these days. I'll have tae go.

BERNADETTE : Oh. I hope I havenae kept ye back.

KATE : No.

BERNADETTE : I meant tae tell ye. Five fish. I bought five haddock. Know how much they wantit?

KATE : No.

BERNADETTE : Wan an' thruppence. Wan an' thruppence! Would ye credit it? Thruppence for wan fish. An' they're wee things. Tiddlers.

KATE : It's after four o'clock.

BERNADETTE : Oh, I'm terrible, so I am! What are we staunin here for? I'll walk ye doun. I forgot tae get a wee biscuit in.

(*They begin to go.*)

BERNADETTE : Aa we need's MacFarlane Langs tae pit a penny on digestives.

KATE : Is Pat on the picket?

BERNADETTE : Aye. I'd like tae see 'im tryin tae stop me if I wantit tae go in tae work.

KATE : They've got tae dae it.

BERNADETTE : You're as bad as the men.

KATE : Where can I get wan o thae banners about the rents?

BERNADETTE : They're aa over the toun.

KATE : Like the Coronation.

(*They both go off.*)

10. *The Temperance Institute: February 1915*

(*Pat and Charlie are sitting behind a long table.*

Willie stands between them addressing a Union meeting. He holds some papers in his hand.)

WILLIE : It's been a hard week. I've felt it. You've aa felt it. For wance the pubs are kinna empty, so the publicans have felt it. But, brothers, there's a few shipyards an' a torpeda factory no far from this hall, an' they're empty an' aa, so the bosses have felt it ! *(Cheers.)* I want to record some things on the minutes. First of all, as just wan o the organisers in this toun I want to say that I'm proud o every wan o yez. Your solidarity's a credit tae ye, an' I ask ye tae carry on till this great strike is over and *won* ! *(Cheers.)* I don't want to stand up here aa mornin, but I've got to acquaint ye wi a few facts. I've always tried tae tell ye the truth. An' the truth about the Unions during this strike stinks tae high heaven. Not with us. Not with the rank an' file, but the support given tae the Government by the national Trade Union leaders, including the Allied Trades . . . and the A.S.E . . . our ain high-ups, boys ! Their support o the Government is an act of the grossest treachery to the working man ! I've been told personally by a member of the National Executive that he was willing to agree with that wee Welsh . . . gentleman . . . Davie Lloyd George, to call off this strike an' to 'suspend' trade-union rights till the war's done. I'll tell ye exactly what he said. He said, 'It's aa-right for you blokes, but we've been called up by the Government. We could feel a threat behind what they told us.' I says, 'What threat?' 'The threat of imprisonment,' says he. 'Who for?' says I. 'For us,' he said. Best place for traitors, I thought. But the tragic fact remains that the people at the top o the tree . . . men who should be strong behind us . . . are, at the moment, daein it on their trewsers! They'll attempt to break us. But they'll never break us! (*Cheers.*) We're ready for them, aye, an' we'll be ready for Davie Lloyd George, tae, should he want to take us on! (*Cheers.*) Brothers, at this moment the very life of trade unionism is at stake. But remember, the committee behind this strike must always be known as the Labour-Withholding Committee. The very word 'strike' will send them panicking to the Defence of the Realm Act, or the Munitions Act, or some other instrument against the working people of this country, and as sure as there's a God in heaven they'll hae us aa breakin up stanes in Barlinnie. There's people in high places that hate and despise us, brothers. That means we're strong! Before we get back on the picket, I must make two things clear. This is not an unofficial strike. Not at all. This is a spontaneous strike—a swift and necessary action because of the introduction of privileged employees at Weirs. But up to a point we've ourselves to blame. Six months ago, in the same shop, Weirs o Cathcart, Chinese were employed. These Chinese workers were paid *less* for the same job, and no action was taken. When I learned this, my first words, in all confidence, were, it wouldnae have happened in a Greenock shop! (*Cheers.*) Brothers, we're in for more hard times in the week to come. I'm sorry tae say that nane o us are gonna get any richer. An' we're no gonna get fat, either. But we will be a credit to our movement, an' a credit tae oursel's. . . . One final an' very important item on the agenda. It proves we're no skint on Clydeside yet. The strike bulletin has made a profit of seven an' a tanner! (*Cheers.*)

11. *The James Watt Bar: February 1915*

(*The strike is still on, and so there are very few men in the Public Bar. Eddie stands behind the bar reading the evening paper. Hughie is sitting beside Sam at one of the tables. Sam is home on leave from the front. He is wearing uniform. His right arm has been amputated, and the sleeve of his tunic is pinned across his chest.*)

SAM : Aa packed in there like herrin in a box, so we were. Some hospital. I don't think the doctors knew what wis wrang wi ony o us.

HUGHIE : That's no the worst o't, believe you me.

SAM : What are ye talkin about?

EDDIE : Lea Sam alane, Hughie. He must have a lot on's mind.

HUGHIE : Never mind Eddie, Sam. This is the first drap o drink he's sellt aa week.

EDDIE : I'll pit you outside.

SAM : I wish I had steyed at hame. Honest.

HUGHIE : Not at all. Dinnae start sayin the likes o that, Sam. What would we have done 'ithout ye?

SAM : What about aa them bastarts across the road? Ye don't get blown tae bits runnin a strike.

HUGHIE : I understaun how ye feel.

SAM : Dae ye? You think, 'cause you were in that wee hauf-arsed rammy out there in Africa, you know what it's aa about, but ye don't. You havenae got the faintest idea what it's like in France. 'Over the top', bi-Christ! Five hunner men goin over the top at wan go, an' mebbie twenty-five gettin back alive, an' no aa in the wan bit, either. What dae ye think these boys think o thae bastarts across the road lyin in their ain beds every night

274

. . . out on bloody strike, bi-Christ? Dae ye think ye understaun that?

HUGHIE : Sure I dae, Sammy boy, sure I dae, but just you wait tae folk start tryin tae help ye. 'Can I get ye this, Sam, can I get ye that? Would ye like tae go for a wee walk? Dae ye fancy a game o puttin? Oh, sorry, I forgot. It wis your airm, wisnae't?' Treat ye worse nor a wean, so they dae.

SAM : Aye. It's like that in the house.

(*Jake comes from the street and walks over to the bar.*)

HUGHIE : How a' ye, Jake?

JAKE : No bad, Hughie, no bad. Sam. What are ye for, boys?

HUGHIE : Mine's a wee pint.

SAM : No, thanks.

(*Jake orders a half and a half-pint for himself and a pint for Hughie.*)

SAM : You win all round, don't ye, Jake?

JAKE : What ye sayin?

SAM : Well, you didnae go tae France, an' the haill toun seems tae be on strike, bar you!

JAKE (*paying for drinks.*) Aye. I'm past it, son.

HUGHIE : Ye've got your whole life in front o'ye, Sam.

SAM : What life? . . . What sort o life dae yez think I've got, eh? Twenty-wan. Twenty-wan year auld. Time just out, an' then this happens. A wan-airmed hauder-on! Where dae ye think I'll get a job?

JAKE : Ye'll get a start, Sam.

SAM : Much'll it cost us?

HUGHIE : Now, now, Sam.

SAM : How much, Jake?

JAKE : I might change my mind in a minute.

SAM : Aye, it's up tae you, Jake, in't it? I coulda won a fuckin battle, but when I come hame, it's still up tae you whether I can earn a copper or no.

JAKE : I understand why ye're bitter, son. Just forget it.

SAM : Forget it?

JAKE : Come on. Have a drink.

SAM : Would ye no rather buy a flag? It'll only cost ye a hapenny. I'll rattle my tin can, if ye like.

JAKE : I came in here for a drink, no an argument.

HUGHIE : Aye, cheer up, lads. It might never happen. Sam'll hae a glass o Bell's.

JAKE : Gie 'im what he wants, Eddie.

(*Eddie pours out a drink.*)

HUGHIE : Seen Willie the-night, Jake?

JAKE : No. He's speakin up the Temperance Institute.

(*Eddie gives Jake his drink.*)

JAKE : There's your whisky.

(*Sam rises and moves over to the bar to collect his drink.*)

SAM (*to Jake*) : Sorry I lost the place, Jake.

JAKE : That's aa-right. Come an' see me when it's settled.

SAM : When's 'at gonna be?

JAKE : Hard tae say. Willie's got them solid, an' that Charlie McGrath's never done agitatin. While yet.

276

HUGHIE : Thought Charlie wis a pal o yours, **Jake**.
JAKE : I know 'im. I cannae help that. He's no close or anything. Thank Christ. Too quick off the mark, if ye ask me.
SAM : Who is 'e?
JAKE : Frae Glesga. Engineer. Doun helpin Willie tae organise the strike.
SAM : Christ, they're better organised when they're out on the street than when they're at the tools.
HUGHIE : Aye. Nothing's simple ony mair. I thought bein on strike meant they sat in the house.
EDDIE : It looks like it the-night.

(*Willie and Charlie come in from the street.*)

HUGHIE (*sotto voce*) : It's the secret service.
SAM : Ye look pleased wi yoursel', Willie.
WILLIE : Hello, Sam. This is Charlie McGrath.
CHARLIE : Hello.
SAM (*to Charlie*) : Are you the commandin officer?
JAKE : You want somethin', Charlie?

(*Charlie sits down at one of the tables.*)

CHARLIE : No for me, Jake.
JAKE : I forgot. (*He goes over to the table where Charlie is sitting. Willie orders a drink.*)
WILLIE : A pint, Eddie.
JAKE : How's it goin?
WILLIE : Good meetin the-night. (*Willie and Jake sit down beside Charlie, Jake in the middle. Willie is looking at his notes.*)
JAKE : Sam's no feelin too good.
WILLIE : Oh.
JAKE : Understandable.

WILLIE : Sorry, Jake, I wisnae listenin. What were ye sayin?

JAKE : You've got mair important things on your mind.

CHARLIE (*to Willie*) : I'll try tae get aa that copy for the Strike Bulletin before the week-end. Went well the-night, I thought.

WILLIE : Champion.

CHARLIE (*taking bundles of paper out of his case*) : We'd better stack these voting forms.

(*They begin stacking the forms. Jake rises and goes over to the bar to join Sam and Hughie.*)

SAM (*to Hughie*) : I wisnae expectin a pipe band an' a hera's reception or anything, but, Christ, ye'd think folk might be pleased tae see ye. Willie Rough looked right throu us, so he did.

JAKE : A bit touchy, aren't ye?

SAM : Would ye look at them? Like a coupla stick-men for a squad o hures. . . .

JAKE : I don' know what tae dae wi mysel the-night.

SAM : Are they no talkin tae you, either? I don't know what's worse . . . bein wan-airmed like me, big men lik them, or sittin in the middle lik you.

JAKE : Aa-right, Sam, that's enough o your patter for wan night.

SAM : They don't need you ony mair, Jake. Look at them. They've got what they want. You're a back number.

JAKE : I don't know what the fuck I'm doin here! (*He leaves the pub.*)

(*Willie and Charlie go on piling up the ballot papers. They do not see Jake go.*)

12. *The Hills Above Greenock: February 1915*

(Willie stands staring straight ahead at the view below him. Charlie is sitting on the ground near him. He is scribbling on a jotter. He licks his pencil, then scribbles some more.)

WILLIE : It's great up here, so it is.

CHARLIE : Eh?

WILLIE : Aa this speakin's murderin me. My voice's goin. What ye writin?

CHARLIE : An article.

WILLIE : For a paper?

CHARLIE : There's nae paper would print what I want tae write, an' you know it.

WILLIE : Well, what is it?

CHARLIE : I'm gonna start wan.

WILLIE : A paper?

CHARLIE : Aye.

WILLIE : On your strike pay, like?

CHARLIE : Don't be funny. Ye've got tae think what comes after. What's the next demand? What's the next step? We cannae trust tired auld union men. We've got tae see a way ahead oursel's.

WILLIE : Aye, it's a rare gift tae be able tae see what's ahead o us. McLean's got it. He's a great man. I've never met anybody like him, an' you havenae, either, if ye were tae be honest about it.

CHARLIE : He's a dreamer. He's a wonderful dreamer, but he's still a dreamer. Sure, he tellt everybody what the war wis about, an' he did gie this river a bit o pride that it was badly in need o, but surely you can see 'at that's no enough.

WILLIE : Try as ye might, Charlie, ye'll no make me think any the less of him. If I hadnae heard him, how dae ye think I'd hav the gumption tae

279

run this strike? I'm tellin thae men what tae dae. That's a hell of a responsibility.

CHARLIE : Sure it is. But what's next? If Weirs send the Yanks packin, dae we go back, or dae we wait till Christmas for the twopence an hour?

WILLIE : We go back before we break our strenth.

CHARLIE : Then what?

WILLIE : You go back tae your patriots across the negotiatin table, an' I go back tae mine.

CHARLIE : That's gonna dae us a lot o good.

WILLIE : The Weirs situation is a different issue frae the tuppence an hour. When we've got some of our strenth back, we'll go for that.

CHARLIE : You're wrong : we must use our solidarity *now* for the overthrow o the whole system.

WILLIE : What ye gonna dae? Dae ye want tae string up Mr Cosgrave an' the whole jingbang o them in Cathcart Square an' sell tickets?

CHARLIE : Mr Cosgrave ! Can ye no see further than your ain midden, Willie?

WILLIE : I've got enough on my mind giein thae men the spunk tae stay out. If every shop wis as solid as mine we'd be laughin.

CHARLIE : What's that supposed tae mean?

WILLIE : Where's your shop? Glesga. That's where you should be. What ye daein here?

CHARLIE : You asked me down a while back. Remember?

WILLIE : Thanks for comin. Ye can skidaddle aff hame again as far as I'm concerned. Away hame an' write a book about it. This is the first half-hour's peace I've had in the last fortnight, an' I've come up here tae enjoy it. I want tae be up here lookin doun there. That's my wey o gettin free o't for a wee while. I can see my house, an' the school my laddie goes tae. There's the yard an' my church, an' the Municipal Buildings. Somehow I've always got mair go in me when I've been up here.

CHARLIE: You should get doun on yer hauns an' knees an' offer a prayer for our salvation.

WILLIE: There's some things ye don't joke about. Whit are ye, anyway?

CHARLIE: Ye mean am I a Catholic, Prod'sant, Wee Free, or Anabaptist, I suppose. I'm nothing. Nothing tae dae wi any o that nonsense, anyhow. How can ye staun there talkin about 'my church'? Ye seen the light, or something? Ye tryin tae convert me?

WILLIE: I'm no tryin tae convert anybody. A man has tae staun for somethin'. My religion's nothin' tae dae wi anybody else. I'm no explainin it. It's wan o the things that's mine.

CHARLIE: But ye tellt me the strike was condemned out o the pulpit in the Mid Kirk. Some o them think we're gettin a hand-out frae Berlin.

WILLIE: They're just feart. My minister wouldnae dare. We'd walk solid out o there an' aa, if he did.

CHARLIE: Dae ye walk under ladders?

(Willie reacts, but says nothing.)

Ye know when tae stop, dan't ye? That's hauf the trouble wi you.

WILLIE: There's somethin' tae you, Charlie. Sometimes I wish ye were at the bottom o the Clyde wi a hunnerweight o scrap roun your neck, but you've got a way wi ye, and I swear tae God I covet it sometimes.

CHARLIE: Ye're better away doun tae the kirk, then, ye've time for a psalm an' a lesson before the shop meetin.

WILLIE : Right. Right. Hauf time. We're like a couple o weans. Ye've got me as bad as yoursel'.
CHARLIE : I wish ye were.

(*He returns to his jotter, rereads what he has written, then licks his pencil, and scribbles some more.*)

WILLIE : I wish the gorse wis out. (*He lies flat looking at the sky. Silence . . . Then sitting up.*) Ye mean a whole paper?
CHARLIE : Aye. What dae ye think?
WILLIE : Well . . . I thought it wis like the Strike Bulletin.
CHARLIE : Na. A real radical paper that prints exactly what's happenin aa over the world, an' what should be happenin. No quarter. What about you writin somethin'? Ye write maist o the Bulletin.
WILLIE : That's different. That's my job.
CHARLIE : If I ever get it goin, I'll pay ye tae change your mind.
WILLIE : If I write anything for a socialist paper, I'll write it 'cause it needs written, I'll no be after any cash in hand!
CHARLIE : So ye will write something?
WILLIE : I might an' I might no.
CHARLIE : Nae hurry. . . .
WILLIE : What dae ye think?
CHARLIE : What?
WILLIE : The wife's out on a rent parade the-day.
CHARLIE : Is 'at a fact? They're aa over Glesga.
WILLIE : No wonder the sheriff's officers are feart, faced wi a pack o wild weemin armed wi brushes, clathes-poles, an' God knows what else. I wouldnae like tae face them. There'll be hunners o prosecutions, I tellt Katie.

282

CHARLIE : Mebbie I should be askin her tae write a wee bit for my paper.

WILLIE : I'll write it. I'll dae the article for ye. Satisfied?

CHARLIE : Satisfied.

WILLIE : Hey! That's twenty-five past three on the Mid Kirk clock. Ye comin?

CHARLIE : Aye. I've got tae get up tae Glesga an' sort out a few waverers.

PAT (*off*) : Willie!

WILLIE : I tellt ye ye should be at hame.

PAT (*nearer*) : Willie!

WILLIE (*to Charlie*) : Who's 'at?

CHARLIE : Dae they want you?

PAT (*nearer still*) : Willie! Willie!

(*Pat arrives, breathless, holding his shoulder in pain. His head is bleeding. Hughie follows close behind him. Pat collapses exhausted. Willie and Charlie go over to him, followed by Hughie.*)

Willie, ye've got tae get doun by. They cam aff the three-o'clock train . . . strike-breakers . . . I don't know who's payin 'em. There's broken heids everywhere.

HUGHIE : Right throu the picket they went.

CHARLIE : Where are they?

HUGHIE : In the yard. Where dae ye think? (*Charlie runs off very quickly.*) No, Charlie. It's no you that's wantit. Charlie!

WILLIE : Nou, caa canny. Canny, boys. Are the polis there?

HUGHIE : No many.

PAT : It wis sudden, like. I've never seen any o them afore.

HUGHIE : Hard men. Bastarts. Listen tae me,

Willie Rough, you get doun that yard at wance, afore Charlie starts an even bigger rammy an' pits the ba on the slates aathegither.

WILLIE : He'll no dae anythin' till I get there.

HUGHIE : I'm lame, but you're fuckin blind!

WILLIE : Can ye get up, Pat? (*He lifts Pat to his feet.*)

PAT : I had tae come an' get ye, Willie. I didnae ken what tae dae. I wis feart tae dae the wrang thing.

HUGHIE : Come on! Are you waitin tae it gets dark?

WILLIE : I'm comin. I've just got tae think what I'm gonna dae.

HUGHIE : Think on the road doun. Are ye fit, Pat?

PAT : Don't worry about me.

WILLIE : Gie'm a haun, Hughie.

HUGHIE : Who's gonna gie *me* a haun?

PAT : I'm aa-right, I tellt yez! (*He goes off.*)

WILLIE : Nou, you bloody well stay out o it, Hughie.

HUGHIE : Aye. We'll see. We'll see. We'll see.

(*Willie runs off. Hughie follows.*)

13. *A Ward In Greenock Royal Infirmary: February 1915*

(*Hughie is lying on a simple, iron hospital bed. His eyes are shut. Willie comes in quietly and moves over to him. Hughie opens his eyes.*)

HUGHIE : What?

WILLIE : Hello, Hughie.

HUGHIE : Is 'at you, Willie? Aye. I'm glad it's you.

WILLIE : Is the pain bad?

HUGHIE : I don't know. It's that dope. I cannae feel a thing, so there's nae wey o tellin how bad I am. The doctor musta decided I wouldnae be able tae thole it. If he's right, I'm finished.

WILLIE : Don't talk daft, Hughie. You'll be on your feet in nae time.

HUGHIE (*smiling*) : Hav I got any feet?

WILLIE : Och, Hughie!

HUGHIE : Figure o speech. Dinnae be saft, Willie. I've got used tae only haein the wan. What's the difference? Sure, I hope ye're right. I don't care if I hav tae wheel mysel' about on a wee bogie like a damaged wean as lang as I get out o here. Skatarry's no in it.

WILLIE : But it wisnae your fight, Hughie. I tellt ye to stay out o it.

HUGHIE : I wis tryin tae help ye, Willie. When I saw our boys gettin stuck intae thae dirty bastards, I just had tae try an' blooter wan or two wi the auld crutch. I couldnae help mysel'. I'm leanin against this waa layin about me, when this big red-heidit fella starts runnin for the gates. He had somethin in his haun, ye see? I shouted : 'Where the fuck did that come frae?' It looked lik a gun, but I thought it was a wee toy. It didnae look lik a real wan. I didnae think it was gonna blow ma fuckin leg aff.

WILLIE : I don't know what tae say, Hughie. I swear tae God, I wish I wis lyin there in your place.

HUGHIE : What did the band play?

WILLIE : Ye're the only man who rushed in the gates wi us that had nothin' tae gain.

HUGHIE : Are ye daft aathegither? Everybody in this toun shoulda been behind ye. We aa shoulda rushed past the polis tae get our hauns on thae bastarts. If you an' the men had no been so resolute. If ye hadda been in two minds about goin back, they wouldnae had tae send anybody doun frae wherever it was they cam frae. You an' folk like ye are costin some o the big bugs a fortune, so yez are. They dinnae like that too much. They'll hav tae invite ye back e'nou. Wait tae ye see. Ye havenae got a wee dram about ye?

WILLIE: Eddie gied me a gill o Lang's for ye. The Bell's is aa done.

HUGHIE: Oh, Lang's is just champion. Gie's it.

(*Willie looks round to see if there are any doctors or nurses about, then quickly hands the bottle to Hughie. Hughie opens it and takes a long slug.*)

I can really taste it. Down. Down. Down she goes. That's hell of a good o ye, Willie. To the last drop.

WILLIE: Keep some o it.

HUGHIE: Just a wee tait mair.

WILLIE: You're a hell of a man.

HUGHIE (*finishing the whisky*): The last drop. I used tae hav a set o whisky glesses, ken? Afore the wife deed. They were engraved. Ye saw a man on the gallows bein hung, like. Below 'im it said, 'The last drop' . . . on the bottom o the gless, like. . . . Dae ye no see it?

WILLIE: I'll come back in the mornin.

HUGHIE: I might no be here. Onywey, we drove them out. I suppose that means we wun?

WILLIE: The doctor said I should only stay a wee while.

HUGHIE: Willie, would ye tak a wee bit o advice, if I gied it ye?

WILLIE: What's 'at?

286

HUGHIE : Gie's your haun. Listen. Try tae keep the company o our ain lads. Pat an' Jake an' 'at. Stay awa frae Charlie McGrath. He's . . . Ye know what I think o him. Just dae what I tell ye. How's Pat?

WILLIE : It's just a sprain.

HUGHIE : That's good. (*Groaning in pain.*) Mebbie this auld heart couldnae staun them takkin the leg aff, or mebbie I'm just no as young as I wis, but that pain's gay bad, dope or nae dope. It's funny. Ye ken, in Africa, I kent I'd come hame. This is a different thing aathegither. Willie, I think ye'd better get the priest.

WILLIE : I never knew ye were a Catholic, Hughie.

HUGHIE : Waddins an' funerals.

WILLIE : I'll get wan.

HUGHIE : I'll pit in a good word for ye up the stair. Here! Mebbie it's doun by I'm goin.

WILLIE : I'll come back wi the priest.

HUGHIE : I wish ye didnae have tae. (*Willie moves a step away.*) Try an' get, eh . . . what d'ye cry him? Flynn. Aye. Canon Flynn, an' hope tae Christ he remembers me.

WILLIE : Eh . . . Hughie . . . what's your ither name, again?

HUGHIE (*smiling*) : Naebody knows it. Fri*zell*. Stupit name, in't it? Hughie Fri*zell*.

WILLIE : Anythin' ye want?

HUGHIE : I don't think the priest would approve o my last request.

WILLIE : Eh?

HUGHIE : It's that long since I've had my hole, so it is. I wouldnae mind a wee bit o stuff.

WILLIE (*laughs*) . . . The pain bad?

HUGHIE : It's muvin about inside me. I doubt the haill engine's giein it up as a bad job.

WILLIE : I'll no be long. (*He goes out.*)

HUGHIE : Nurse? . . .

(*Hughie is in pain. The Nurse seems a long time coming. Eventually she comes in, a plain, scrubbed girl with dark hair.*)

Nurse, could ye oblige me wi a cigarette?

NURSE : You know you're not supposed to be smoking.

HUGHIE : But ye'll gie me wan, win't ye? (*She gives him a cigarette, then lights it for him. He takes a long draw.*) . . . Ye got (*weakly*) a heavy date the-night?

NURSE : No.

HUGHIE (*growing weaker and weaker*) : Ye a local lassie?

NURSE : Kilmarnock.

HUGHIE : I like it doun there.

NURSE : It's nice enough, I suppose.

HUGHIE (*weaker*) : Ye've got a nice face.

NURSE (*serious, but humouring him*) : You're terrible!

HUGHIE (*now very faintly*) : Honest. . . .

(*The Nurse takes the cigarette from his mouth. He closes his eyes. She leaves, carrying the cigarette awkwardly to save the ash from falling on the polished floor. Hughie reopens his eyes. He stares in front of him.*)

14. *The Shipyard: April 1915*

(*There are a few tin drums and a couple of wooden boxes to sit on. The Apprentice comes in carrying some metal tea-cans with handles. He is just going off to make the tea. The horn blows loud and long for lunch-time. Pat comes in, carrying his own tea-can.)*

PAT : Hey, you!

APPRENTICE : What?

PAT : Will ye boil my can?

APPRENTICE : Much ye gie us?

PAT : I'll gie ye a kick up the arse if ye don't.

APPRENTICE : Where's you ain can-boy?

PAT : Yeeprez.

APPRENTICE : Oh. My gaffer says I'll hav tae go if conscription comes in. Will I?

PAT : What age are ye, son?

APPRENTICE : Fifteen past. I'm nearly sixteen, so I am.

PAT : Christ!

APPRENTICE : Here's Jake comin. It's time I wasnae here.

(The Apprentice runs off taking Pat's can. Pat sits down on one of the boxes. Jake comes in. The others are in their working-clothes, and all wear caps. They are dirty, and speak louder than before.)

JAKE : Patrick.

PAT : Hello-rerr, Jake.

(Jake sits down on a drum. Pat begins to unwrap his 'piece', which consists of thick sandwiches wrapped in newspaper.)

JAKE : Did ye see that boy?

PAT : Aye. He's away tae boil the cans.

JAKE : Dead slow an' stop, that yin.

(*Willie comes in. He sits down on a drum and takes out his 'piece'.*)

WILLIE : Workin hard, Pat?
PAT : Aye, kept goin. What about you?
WILLIE : Rush job.
JAKE : Aye. Cosgrave's been at me about it. It was supposed tae be finished in the month o Feb'ry, but the strike put the kybosh on that. He'll be lucky tae deliver by the Fair, so 'e will, an' that's three months away.

(*The Apprentice comes on carrying the steaming cans of tea. He gives one to each of the men.*)

JAKE : Did ye hav tae plant it first?
APPRENTICE : I've only got wan pair o hauns.
JAKE : Changed days since I wis a boy.
APPRENTICE : Wis 'at in the good old days?
JAKE : Nane o your lip. Scram!
APPRENTICE : Can I no hav my piece wi youz?
JAKE : No, ye cannae. We're talkin. Get tae fuck.

(*The Apprentice goes. Each man has a little tin of sugar in the breast-pocket of his dungarees, and a medicine-bottle full of milk in his jacket-pocket. They stir their tea with pencils.*)

PAT : What ye got the-day, Willie?
WILLIE : Cheese.
PAT : Gie ye a corn' mutton for a cheese wan.
WILLIE : Right y'are.

(*They exchange sandwiches. The men eat their lunch and drink the tea from their cans, blowing on it first. Pat is still reading the paper.*)

PAT : Listen tae this. (*Reading paper*.) Churchill . . . 'We will sacrifice our last shilling and our last man.' Our last man! Hey, I don't like the way he's talkin about me.

WILLIE : He's no talkin about you, Pat. He's talkin about himsel'.

JAKE : Nae flies on him. He's got a good job.

PAT : He's dead jammy, so 'e is.

(*They go on eating and drinking.*)

JAKE : Oh, Willie, I meant tae tell ye.

WILLIE : What's 'at, Jake?

JAKE : The wife got a wee present for your new wean.

WILLIE : Oh, ye shouldnae hav bothered, Jake.

JAKE : It's just a wee mindin.

WILLIE : That's hell of a good o ye.

JAKE : A wee rattle.

PAT : Three nou?

WILLIE : Aye.

JAKE : Are you two havin a race, or something?

WILLIE : I don't know what tae call her. Katie thought it was gonna be a wee boy.

JAKE : We've been talkin about adoptin wan.

WILLIE : Ye should, Jake.

PAT : Hey, listen tae this, lads. It's about us. Christ Almighty! Wait tae ye hear this.

WILLIE : Out wi't, then.

PAT : 'If one asks what event disillusioned the Liberal Government—the answer is the Clyde dispute, and nothing else.'

JAKE : Mebbie it was worth it, then.

WILLIE : I wis never sae sure o anythin' in my life.

PAT : What exactly is this Clyde Workers Committee?

WILLIE : I'm stayin away frae that.

PAT : But they asked ye on tae it, din't they?

WILLIE : Aye, sure. But ye'd never be at your ain fire-side. Too much. It's aa-right for the likes o Charlie. He's no mairried or anything. He can shoot 'is mouth aff three nights on a Sunday, an' naebody'll complain.

PAT : I'd sooner hav you tae represent us than the likes o him.

WILLIE : Charlie McGrath's tryin as hard as anybody else I know tae get better conditions o work on this river. Him an' the whole Workers Committee'll no staun any shite frae anybody. Aye, an' that's includin Lloyd George himsel', so it is.

JAKE : I think ye'd quite like tae be on it, aa the same, Willie.

WILLIE : What if I would?

JAKE : They need somebody a wee bit level-headit.

WILLIE : Oh, I keep in touch wi them, like, tae keep our branch informed. I'm writin a wee article for their magazine.

(*Pat takes the magazine from his pocket.*)

PAT : Is it in this wan?

WILLIE : No. It'll be in the next wan.

(*Jake looks over Pat's shoulder.*)

JAKE : *The Worker*, 'Organ of the Clyde Workers Committee'. It looks quite interestin. Gie's the wire when your name's in it.

PAT : Keep that, if ye like, Jake. I've read everythin' I wantit tae read in it.

JAKE : I cannae be seen wi the likes o this!

WILLIE: What's wrang wi't?

JAKE: Are you forgettin I'm a foreman? Can ye imagine me at a meetin up the stairs, an' that faain out o ma pocket, an' Cosgrave pickin it up an' readin about what's gonna happen tae the likes o him when the Revolution comes? I'd be out o here faster than my dug gets aff 'is mark.

(*They all laugh.*)

By Jeeze, that's no very fast, maist o the time.

WILLIE: It's no like you tae be feart, Jake.

JAKE: I'm keepin my nose clean.

WILLIE: Ye chynge wi the win', Jake.

JAKE: What about you? You're savin a lot on train fares these days.

WILLIE: I tellt ye. This branch an' this yaird an' this toun's aa that concerns me at present. 'S 'at no enough for wan man?

PAT: Dis this new Rent Act mean 'at our rents'll no go up at aa, even if the war goes on anither year?

WILLIE: Ten years! Till the end o the war, an' six months beyond, rents are restricted. It's in black an' white.

PAT: Bi-Christ, thae weemin did what the men couldnae dae. We're still waitin on that rise.

WILLIE: Formality nou, Pat. Keep the workers happy. That's the new plan.

JAKE: What's the catch?

WILLIE: Conscription. They'll be losin men aa over the place. Potential tradesmen, anyway.

PAT: Aye. That boy there. He's only fifteen, bi-Christ. He'll hav tae go, tae. Ye're aa-right if your time's out. We're aa-right.

JAKE: Who's gonna boil the can?

293

WILLIE : Dilution. Weemin'll be platin an' caulkin an' hole-borin an'. . . .

JAKE : An' a few things mair, if I know some o the dirty buggers in here.

(*They laugh.*)

Can you imagine this yaird wi nae swearin?

PAT : Is this dilution serious, Willie?

WILLIE : Mebbie no here, but the torpeda factory'll definitely get its quota.

PAT : How much are they gonna pey them?

JAKE : How? Ye thinkin o gettin the wife out heatin rivets?

PAT : No, just curious. What's the rate, Willie?

WILLIE : Washers. They'll pay them in washers. Plenty there for the Clyde Workers' Committee tae get their teeth intae. By Jeeze, I'm glad I turned doun that big Committee job.

JAKE : Are ye sure o that, Willie?

WILLIE : Aye. When ye get on that train tae Glesga it's aa politics.

PAT : I'm glad ye're daein a wee bit for the *Worker*, tho. We're quite a famous shop because o you.

WILLIE : I don't know if they'll pit the article in or no. I wrote it in the heat o the moment, like.

PAT : When?

WILLIE : When I cam hame frae Hughie's funeral.

JAKE : It's taken ye a hell of a long time tae get it in.

WILLIE : I wis gonna send it, then I wisnae, ye know? It's in my pocket. If Charlie comes doun, I'll gie'm it. If he disnae, I willnae.

JAKE : Ye feart they'll tell ye it's rotten?

WILLIE : Mebbie that's it.

JAKE (*rising*) : I'll away an' see that job lined aff.

PAT: Stick in, Jake. Ye'll be up the stair yet.

JAKE: I'm savin up for a bowler hat. (*He goes off.*)

WILLIE (*taking a last sip of tea*): I meant tae tell ye, Pat.

PAT: What?

WILLIE: Somebody threw a brick at us last night.

PAT: When?

WILLIE: On the road hame. It just missed us.

PAT: Mebbie it wis a wee boy playin.

WILLIE: No. It wisnae.

PAT: How dae ye know?

WILLIE: It was too near the bloody mark.

15. *Princes Pier, Greenock: May 1915*

(*Charlie sits on a bollard reading Willie's article. Willie stands looking out to sea. Foghorns alternate with an occasional snatch of military music—a brass band one time, pipes and drums another.*)

WILLIE: Would ye credit it? 'More men. . . . More men.'

CHARLIE: This is good, Willie.

WILLIE: Ye can read it when ye get hame. Just look at them boats. Filled tae the brim, so they are. A lot o them's just boys.

CHARLIE: We cannae win that fight nou, Willie. Worry about what's goin on at hame. Dilution.

WILLIE: What dae I care about a few weemin goin take make torpedas when the Clyde's full of troopships in front o me?

CHARLIE: There's folk that want the war tae carry on a bit longer.

WILLIE: Aye. They'll be retirin on their winnins when it's done.

CHARLIE : No only them, but. There's friens o mine that think we could take advantage o the war.

WILLIE : Ye're way ower my heid again, Charlie.

CHARLIE : What are ye talkin about? It's aa in your ain article here. 'Should the workers arm?' I thought it wis a bit strong for the likes o you.

WILLIE : I wrote that a long time ago.

CHARLIE : Did ye mean it?

WILLIE : Aye, sure I meant it . . . (*Realising he's caught.*) You're a fly man, Charlie. Don't try to make me intae some kind o a revolutionist. I'm no John McLean. Aye, an' I'm glad I'm no. Ye cannae dae much for your shop breakin up stanes in Peterheid. But I'll tell ye wan thing. If you an your cronies are gonna pit the Red Flag on top o the City Chambers in George's Square, that'll be because it wis in your ain heids tae dae it. Don't pit the blame on some scribbles o mine.

CHARLIE : Ye're a changed man, Willie. What's the maitter?

WILLIE : Nothin'.

CHARLIE : It's done a lot o damage tae be nothing.

WILLIE : Folk hav been gey suspicious o me since the strike.

CHARLIE : But ye knew that would happen.

WILLIE : Aye, but knowin's wan thing, an' havin it happen tae ye's anither. Somebody chucked a hauf-brick at us. If I'd got in the road, I'd be deid. An' last Sunday, last Sunday in the pulpit o my ain church, fire an' brimstone aa about us! I could tell the Minister wis talkin about me. There wisnae wan that said 'Cheerio' tae either Katie nor mysel' aifter the service, so there wisnae. That's the faithful for ye.

CHARLIE : You don't have to stay here, ye know. Ye could muve up tae Glesga. Take your place on the Committee.

WILLIE : I've moved enough. I like Greenock. I'm stayin. It's too big. The whole thing's got too big for a man tae understaun. Too much has happened since I cam tae this toun. Look at thae boats. Rule Britannia! Us an' folk afore us built some o thae boats, an' look what they're carryin nou. An' it's no only the wans that'll no come back that worry me, it's the woundit an' aa. What the fuck are we gonna dae wi' them? Folk don't need that many baskets. An' you, Charlie, wi' your revolt. That's war an' aa. I want the quiet back again. That's aa I want. The quiet.

CHARLIE : Ye're no the man ye were, Willie. I sometimes wish we really were 'in league wi the dreaded Hun'.

WILLIE : Ye aff your heid?

CHARLIE : They'd gie us guns like a shot, so they would.

WILLIE : Guns! Dae you know what ye're talkin about?

CHARLIE : We know aa-right.

WILLIE : Is 'at aa ye dae on that Committee? Ye havenae forgotten about the rise, I hope.

CHARLIE : That'll be throu in nae time at all. We're busy just nou settin up a welcomin party when the wee man comes tae see us.

WILLIE : He's braver'n he looks, comin up here.

CHARLIE : He's refused tae talk tae the Committee. Don't you worry yoursel'. He'll see us.

WILLIE : Lloyd George. I wouldnae mind five minutes wi him.

CHARLIE : Ye've missed your chance, Willie. (*The pipes and drums which have been coming and*

297

going now sound much nearer. Tune : Happy we've been aathegither.)

WILLIE : Would ye listen tae that !

CHARLIE : I'll miss my train. Nou, dae ye want me tae take this for the paper or no ?

WILLIE : I gied ye't, didn't I ?

CHARLIE : Ye want it printed ?

WILLIE : I want it printed.

(*Charlie puts the article away in his pocket. The pipes sound louder and louder.*)

The bands don't get any quieter, an' the songs are still hell of a cheery. It's aa lies. Frae Lloyd George right doun tae some big fat polis playin the pipes !

CHARLIE : They make a hell of a noise at the best o times.

(*On the other side, very near, a brass band strikes up* See the Conquering Hero Comes, *very loudly.*)

Jesus Christ !

WILLIE : Surrounded !

(*They both go off.*)

16. *The Hills Above Greenock: December 1915*

(*Willie and Kate, both wearing overcoats, walk past the stump of a dead tree. Willie is pushing the pram. He brings it to a halt and looks down at the town.*)

KATE : We'll catch our death up here.

WILLIE : It's great, the snow.

KATE : Ye're as bad as William wi's sledge.

WILLIE: It's as well I got Pat tae make 'im that. He'll no be gettin much else this Christmas.

KATE: But they'll no jyle ye, Willie. Surely. They cannae. How am I supposed tae feed three weans wi my man in the jyle?

WILLIE: I don't know what's gonna happen.

KATE: Are ye feart, Willie?

WILLIE: Aye.

KATE: They might let ye aff.

WILLIE: No chance. How dae ye think they're havin the trial in Edinburgh?

KATE: But it wis only words, Willie. A wee article in a paper. Very few read it. Oh, Willie, I wish ye'd never written it!

WILLIE: What's done's done.

KATE: I've never been tae Edinburgh.

WILLIE: You're no comin.

KATE: I want tae be wi ye, Willie.

WILLIE: As sure as God's in heaven, I'll get a year, or at the very least six months, an' I don't want tae see your face when they haul me out o that court.

KATE: I'll bring the weans tae see ye.

WILLIE: No. Tell them I'm away tae England tae work.

KATE: We've never tellt them lies, Willie, an' I'm no about tae start, so I'm no. They'll find out anyway.

WILLIE: How?

KATE: Folk'll tell their weans, an' their weans'll soon tell William in the school playground. There's no many secrets in this toun.

WILLIE: No. Ye're right. Oh, I'm stupit! I wis in two minds whether tae gie it tae Charlie or no.

KATE: I wish ye'd never clapped een on him, so I dae.

WILLIE : It's past, Katie. At least it soon will be. The day aifter the-morra they'll at last hav me in some kind o uniform. I wonder if they've really got wee arrows on the jaicket.

KATE : What are we gonna dae, Willie?

WILLIE : There's nae point greetin about somethin' we don't know. I might be lucky an' only get the six months, but wi that Zeppelin raid over Edinburgh last night the jury'll be sharpenin the knife, I'm thinkin. Six months isnae long. It's mair'n six months since wee Sarah was born.

KATE : I knew somethin wis gonna happen, Willie. I knew it. Just as we were beginnin tae get over the strike, an' people starin at us a wee bit less, this has tae happen. We were just back tae normal. We were gettin on our feet, so we were. We mighta saved a shillin or two nou that the rent's no chynged. We need a bigger house, Willie, wi three weans.

WILLIE : Dae ye think I want tae go tae the jyle? What's gonna happen tae the Union when I'm in Peterheid? Christ only knows.

KATE : If ye'd worry a bit mair about yoursel' insteid o other folk, we might no be in this mess nou. What possessed ye tae write that stuff? If Charlie McGrath wants tae run the country, he can staun as an M.P. lik onybody else. The people would soon show who they wantit, an' it might no be him.

WILLIE : It wis my ain doin. I wisnae thinkin about anybody else. I wisnae even thinkin about you.

KATE : I don't understand ye Willie. What did ye dae it *for*?

WILLIE : I wis angry.

KATE : Ye'll hav time tae regret it nou, aa-right.

WILLIE : But I don't regret it. . . .

KATE : It's freezin, Willie. Come on doun. The best way tae look at a white Christmas is through the room windae, when the fire's on.

WILLIE : I'm comin, Katie. When I get out, I think we'll pack up an' get away frae this place aathegither.

KATE : Australia or someplace lik that?

WILLIE : Canada, America mebbie.

KATE : But we don't know anybody, Willie.

WILLIE : We didnae know anybody here when we came. We're still strangers tae maist folk.

KATE : I don't think ye want tae, Willie. Ye're thinkin ye might hav tae, in't ye?

WILLIE : I'll no be short o time tae make my mind up, will I?

KATE : Come on doun intae the warm. I don't want her tae get a chill.

WILLIE : Right. It's nae life for you, Kate. Where hav ye been? Naewhere.

KATE : I'm no complainin.

WILLIE : That's true, Kate. Ye've never done much o that. (*He begins to walk away. Kate turns the pram towards home.*) Well, we'll no be up here for a while. (*Kate walks over to him. She takes his arm. Together they walk off down the hill with the pram.*)

17. *Edinburgh: A Cell: December 1915*

(*Willie and Charlie sit waiting to be taken to prison. Charlie has some books beside him on the bench.*)

CHARLIE : You in the huff? . . . Do I detect a wee wave o huffiness?

WILLIE : You might have said *somethin'*.

301

CHARLIE : No point.

WILLIE : Six months in prison's worth complainin about, is it no?

CHARLIE : Sure, it wis a fine wee speech ye made, Willie, but naebody wis listenin tae ye. This is Edinburgh . . .

WILLIE : Ye let me down, Charlie. (*He takes a fag from his packet of Gold Flake, lights it, and inhales deeply.*) I'll miss the New Year.

CHARLIE : Aye, an' I'll miss it next year as well. Still . . . what's the odds? Cannae be bothered wi't anyway.

WILLIE : I cannae fathom you, Charlie. . . . Ye don't smoke, don't drink . . . nae wife . . . nae weans. . . .

CHARLIE : No problems.

WILLIE : Apart frae eighteen months in the clink.

CHARLIE : What d'ye expect me tae dae about that, Willie? Burst out greetin? No point. I've been inside before, but I'm no gonna waste my energy fightin wi' the warders this time.

WILLIE : Didnae take ye for a hard man, Charlie.

CHARLIE : Oh, not at all, reformed character. It's ages ago. Now I'm quite prepared to sit an' read Marx, Engels, an' *Moby Dick* over an' over again until they open the gates. It's not all tottie-howkin and breaking stones, you know.

WILLIE : It's a bloody holiday for you, in't it?

CHARLIE : You've got to face facts, Willie. What else can ye dae? Mebbie ye think ye can jump ower the waa, or something? Well, I've got news for ye—they're kinna high, an' ther' a hell of a lot o big teuchtar warders tryin tae keep ye in, for that's what they've been tellt tae dae. If ye think about the outside aa the time, ye'll go mad. It happens tae some. You've got tae use the heid.

There's ways of makin a wee stretch like yours count. Look at the history of the Revolution. Many a reputation was made behind bars.

WILLIE : I'll say this for ye, Charlie : ye're the first man I ever met 'at *wanted* tae be in the jyle.

CHARLIE : There's worse places.

WILLIE : But we didnae commit a crime, Charlie. For the first time in my life I wrote doun something I believed in. Sure, I wis willin tae go tae jyle for my convictions, because I kent that wis the law. But the law's wrang. A man should be free tae criticise. If there's nae criticism, there'll be nae chynge, an' the same fools'll be runnin the country election aifter election, and the voice o the workin people will never be heard ! That's what that sentence this mornin wis about, an' that's why I wis ashamed o your silence.

CHARLIE : But I'm tellin ye how tae win. If you stick wi' me, 'Willie Rough' could amount tae something. You're no exactly a household word, are ye? You wait. In eighteen months' time, when I come out o the gates, folk'll know all about it. The newspapers'll even be there waitin for me.

WILLIE : Big man.

CHARLIE : Sure. See you. You cannae see further than your ain nose. When you were knockin your pan out doun there in Greenock, I wis gettin mysel' known, makin contacts, gettin some kinna future aa sewn up for mysel'. Engineerin ! It's a mug's game. You think I'm daft?

WILLIE : Ye're a lot o things, Charlie, but ye're no daft.

CHARLIE : These friens o mine, Willie. They've got influence. They decide what goes . . . in the Unions . . . in the Party . . . they're in charge o our bit o the world, son, an' I've made damn well sure they'll look after me all right. As for you . . . you don't know the difference between Winston Churchill an' Tommy Hinshelwood.

WILLIE: Who's Tommy Hinshelwood?

CHARLIE: Big fella wis in my class at school. Havenae heard o'm since. A nobody, Willie. A number. A private o the line, or a stupid shipbuilder who's content tae turn 'is ticket aa 'is life. I've made damn sure that's no how I'm gonna end up. The other day . . . Thursday, it wis . . . I wis walkin by the tenement I wis born in. The windaes wis aa smashed tae bits. Broken glass everywhere. Condemned. An' you know what? I wis ashamed tae tell the person 'at wis wi me 'at that wis the house I wis reared in. That attic, up that close, in that condemned tenement, wi'ts windaes aa broken. An' that disnae mean I'm ashamed o what I cam up frae, or o onything my faither or mither did by me. It just means 'at I want a hell of a lot mair out of life than ony o them got. I've found out how it's done, so I'm daein it. That's all.

WILLIE: Weill, ye'll no be daein it for a year an' a hauf, onywey. (*Smiling.*) We're safe till then.

CHARLIE: It's no funny, Willie. We're no aa as saft as you, thank Christ! When you get out, ye'll be back tae the yaird hopin everything's quietened doun a wee bit. Then it's back tae the bulk-heid bangin your hammer frae six o'clock till midnight, if they'll pay ye the overtime. I'm no goin back tae the tools for anybody.

WILLIE: Rivetin's my trade, Charlie. I'm good at it. I'll ey get a start at it. You cannae be up tae much as an engineer when ye're chuckin it.

CHARLIE: Ye're no gonna gie's a wee lecture on the glorious tradition of British craftsmanship, are ye?

304

Ye've got tae go after the main-chance. There's nae future in bangin in rivets. A man like you could do very well workin wi the Union. Organisin ... gettin better conditions for the boys, and the best part is that while ye're daein it, ye'll have a hell of a lot better conditions for yourself! Collar an' tie. Travellin expenses. No sweat. Nothing like it.

WILLIE : I'm happy enough in Greenock.

CHARLIE : Tae hell wi Greenock! I'm fed up hearin about Greenock. Come up tae the City. Get workin at headquarters. It would take ye about a week tae replace that balloon ye've got for a Secretary in the Allied Trades.

WILLIE : I've got a job, Charlie. I'm no aifter onybody else's.

CHARLIE : Know something, Willie?

WILLIE : What?

CHARLIE : You're a mug! (*He picks up a book.*)

WILLIE : They'll be comin for us soon. Six months'll no be lang goin in.

CHARLIE : Ye cannae wait tae get back hame, can ye? Just wan thing, Willie ... take a note o the day I'm due out.

WILLIE : How? What are ye gonna dae?

CHARLIE : Treat mysel' tae a new suit.

18. *The Shipyard: June 1916*

(*Pat sits on a drum, sipping his can of tea and reading his paper. Willie comes in, dressed in a suit. He stops. Pat turns round.*)

PAT : Willie Rough ... hey! (*He gets up, walks over, and shakes Willie's hand.*) Christ! How are ye, pal?

WILLIE : Fine, Pat.

PAT : When did ye get out?

WILLIE : Yesterday mornin.

PAT : In for a start, like?

WILLIE : Aye. Where's Jake?

PAT : He's doun the yaird. I'll get 'im.

WILLIE : There's nae hurry.

PAT : Christ, it's great tae see ye, Willie. I've missed ye, so I hav.

WILLIE : How's Bernadette?

PAT : She's fine. You?

WILLIE : I'm no bad.

PAT : How wis it?

WILLIE : Well, I'm in nae hurry tae go back, if that's what ye mean.

PAT : Na. I'm sure an' ye're no.

WILLIE : Busy?

PAT : Kept goin. There's a launch the-morra.

WILLIE : Aye. I passed the boat. Is 'at where Jake's workin?

PAT : Aye. I'll get 'im. Look, Willie, come doun the-morra. It's no every day Cosgrave's haunin out the free drink.

WILLIE : No. Aye, I'll take a race doun.

PAT : I cannae tell ye how good it is tae see ye back. Things've been quiet 'ithout ye.

WILLIE : It's a long time.

PAT : I want tae know aa about it. Just curious, like. But it's time I wisnae here. I've had my break. They'll bag me if I don't get back tae the job. I'll run over an' get Jake for ye. Ther' a wee drap tea there. (*Giving Willie his can.*)

WILLIE : Thanks, Pat. (*Drinking.*) I forgot what yaird tea tastes like.

PAT : Aye. Parish Priest's tea, the wife caas it.

WILLIE : It's good.

PAT : I'll away an' get ye Jake. Be seein ye.
WILLIE : Aye. Thanks, Pat.

(*Pat goes off. Willie sits down on a box. He drinks his tea. After some time Jake comes on.*)

JAKE : Hello, Willie.
WILLIE : Jake!
JAKE : Long time, eh? How was it?
WILLIE : It wisnae exactly a wee holiday.
JAKE : Six months.
WILLIE : A hunner an' eighty-nine days.
JAKE : I bet ye're sorry ye spoke.
WILLIE : I am not.
JAKE : Oh. . . . I had my dug out at a meetin last night.
WILLIE : Did ye? How did ye do?
JAKE : Outclassed.
WILLIE : Hard lines.
JAKE : Honest tae Christ, ye work your drawers aff trainin thae dugs, so ye dae. But ye can only take them so far.
WILLIE : I wis wonderin about a start, like.
JAKE : Aye. I wis thinkin that. Look . . . eh. It's hard the-nou . . . eh, Willie, ye know. I mean, I tried my hardest tae haud on tae your job, like, but ye know how it is. It's nothin' tae dae wi me, ye understaun. It's upstairs. Ye know what they're like. I got tellt by Cosgrave 'imsel' personally, like. If I wis the manager, it'd be different. It would be up tae me then, but I've got my boss, tae. You know how it is, Willie . . .
WILLIE : Barred, is it?
JAKE : I wouldnae go as far as tae say that.
WILLIE : What would ye say, Jake?
JAKE : It's no my fault!

WILLIE : Is it no? Whose fault is it, then? If that's no victimisation, what is? I've had men threaten strike action for less.

JAKE : Aye. That's what you would dae! But it's changed days nou, so it is. It's a different yaird aathegither frae the way you left it. There's nae mair o your cairry-on. Nae mair strikes. Nae mair weeks 'ithout a pay-packet. Nae mair debts docked aff the first pay. Aa that's over an' done. Paid on a Saturday, an' there's a wee bit o piecework, an' the rise is throu an' aa. There's nae need for any mair trouble.

WILLIE : An' how dae ye think ye got the rise? Tell me that, Jake.

JAKE : Don't start, Willie, for Jesus' sake. Ye're only out o the jail five minutes. I'm sorry. I mean that. But there's nothin' I can dae about it. Another yaird that disnae know ye might start ye. It's no the end o the world.

WILLIE : It's the end o somethin' tho, Jake, in't it? It's the end of staunin up tae Cosgrave an' everybody like 'im. An' when strong men, like you who were on our side, chynge your tune, it's the end o any chance o winnin. Oh, I wis feart o't, Jake. Somethin' tellt me it would happen, but nou that it's happenin tae me, I cannae believe it. I changed you. I did. I know I did. I changed you, Jake Adams. Who changed ye back? Is it too much tae trust a man? Is that too much? Dae ye believe in anythin at aa, Jake? Tell me that.

JAKE : I don't know what ye expect frae me. You trusted people far too much. That's the trouble wi you.

WILLIE : I'm sure o wan thing. I trusted you, Jake. Honest tae Christ, I trusted you. I musta been aff my nut.

JAKE : It was different then, Willie. I wisnae actually involved in it, but I wis caught up in it. It wis like a fever up an' doun this river. McLean wis speakin wan night, Gallacher the next. You were tellin us what it meant. An' you were right *then*, Willie. But the war's a bit mair serious nou. Folk are dyin. They're no comin back. An' they're no folk we've never heard o. It's the man in the next close an' the boy next door that went tae the Sunday School. It's Greenock folk. Relatives an' friens, bi-Christ. We just stopped fightin the bosses an' got on wi the job. The likes o me find out ye cannae win. Ye can only make the best o what ye've got. An' aa that other stuff. Where did it get you? You an' your pamphlets an' your speeches. Six months in Peterheid, an' if ye cannae get a start, ye'll be at the Front wi a gun in yer haun.

WILLIE : I bet ye'd like tae see me marchin doun Princes Pier aa in khaki wi the band playin.

JAKE : I wouldnae mind. Folk as good as you hav had tae go. It's no near done yet. I'd go mysel' if I wis young enough.

WILLIE : The whole machine's been at ye, hasn't it, Jake? My wee bit o sense hasnae been aroun for a wee while.

JAKE : You think a hell of a lot o yoursel', don't ye?

WILLIE : Mebbie I dae. Mair than I think o the likes o you, Jake. That's a fact.

JAKE : Ye're sayin things ye'll be sorry for. There was a time when I thought the sun shone out o ye. It's true, that, an' ye winnae believe me, but I'm sorry I cannae start ye.

WILLIE : In some roun-about wey, I suppose ye are. Oh, God help ye, Jake, an' God help the country. When the likes o you stop botherin, the country's finished. Ye'll be forgettin tae go out an' vote next, an' that'll be the end. Ye deserve what's comin.

JAKE : Mebbie ye'll get a start in Lithgows or up there in Siberia.

WILLIE : If they've got you feart, Jake, the foremen up there must be really crappin it.

JAKE : Aye. Well . . . there's plenty o work in Glesga.

WILLIE : I've only been in Greenock a coupla years, Jake, but don't try throwin me out o my ain toun.

JAKE : What's sae great about Greenock?

WILLIE : There's bugger-aa great about it, but it's where I live, till I decide tae move.

JAKE : Look, Willie, I'm tryin tae help ye.

WILLIE : Oh, stop it, for Christ's sake! Would ye stop tryin tae be nice? I cannae forgive ye. How can I? Ye've let me down. I wis sure about you, an' by Christ I wis wrang. I wish ye would go, Jake. If ye don't, I might hit ye. An' if I did, I might no stop. Ye know why? 'Cause you knew I trusted ye. Ye must have. You knew ye had that trust, an' knowin that ye broke it, like ye break a stick every night tae kindle the fire. As easy as that. Away ye go, Jake. If ye see me comin toward ye, on West Blackhall Street, cross over. Don't say Hello as if nothin's happened. Forget ye were ever a brother o mine.

(*Pat comes back along the yard towards Jake and Willie. He stops near them.*)

JAKE : Cheerybye, Willie. There's a lot o folk in this yaird sorry ye ever walked in thae gates, an' I'm no wan o them, but I'll be as glad as them tae see the back o ye. I don't suppose I can shake your hand, so, as you say, I'll just go. (*To Pat.*)

Ye've got wan minute tae get back on the job,
Gatens! (*He goes off.*)

PAT : What's the maitter wi' him?

WILLIE : The bastart'll no start me.

PAT : How no?

WILLIE : Orders. For wan man I've got a lot o folk
hell of a feart.

PAT : Ye'll get a start somewhere.

WILLIE : Where?

PAT : They don't know ye everywhere, Willie.

WILLIE : But I want tae be known. I'm ashamed
o nothin' I've done.

PAT : But ye've got to pay the rent an' 'at. How's
Kate been managin?

WILLIE : She's been out washin stair-heids. How
dae ye think I feel about that? Aa I want's a day's
work, an' that's honest.

PAT : There's other jobs forbye rivetin.

WILLIE : Aye. The Army.

PAT : Don't be daft. There's the farmin. They need
farmers the-nou. Get out o the grime. I wish I
could go tae the country.

WILLIE : I like the grime. I've got tae stay, Pat.
I've got tae show folk what it's like tae live by
somethin' ye believe in. Mebbie I can change them
by showin them that. Mebbie I cannae. But I've
got tae haud my heid up, so that they can stick up
for themselves an' no be feart tae demand what's
theirs by rights. They can call me any name they
like. They can brand me wi any slogan, any party,
an' I'll answer tae them aa. They can jyle me
again if they want tae, an' if they throw anither
brick at my heid, it had better kill me! 'Cause I'm
here, an' I'm gonna haunt Jake Adams an' every
worker in this river an' Cosgrave an' aa. I'll haunt
them till they see sense or tae my time's spent. I'll

311

turn everything upside doun an' backside foremost or die tryin. There's worse tae come.

PAT : But ye havenae got a start yet, Willie.

WILLIE : But I will, Pat. I've got tae.

The horn blasts long and loud. Pat slowly walks away. Willie is on his own.

PLAYS OF THE YEAR

Plays of the Year was launched in 1949. So far forty-one volumes (and two Specials, *The Six Wives of Henry VIII* and *Elizabeth R*) have appeared, chosen and edited by J. C. Trewin. It is regretted that volumes 1, 2, 3, 4, 5, 7, 8, 9, 10, 12, 13, 14, 15, 16, 17, 19, 21, and 22 are now out of print.

VOLUME 1 1948-49

COCKPIT by BRIDGET BOLAND

FAMILY PORTRAIT by LENORE COFFEE and W. JOYCE COWAN

THE HAPPIEST DAYS OF YOUR LIFE by JOHN DIGHTON

THE MISER by MOLIERE, adapted by MILES MALLESON

THE PARAGON by ROLAND and MICHAEL PERTWEE

DON'T LISTEN LADIES! by SACHA GUITRY, adapted by STEPHEN POWYS and GUY BOLTON

VOLUME 2 1949

ANN VERONICA by RONALD GOW, based on the novel by H. G. WELLS

DARK OF THE MOON by HOWARD RICHARDSON and WILLIAM BERNEY

BLACK CHIFFON by LESLEY STORM

THE LATE EDWINA BLACK by WILLIAM DINNER and WILLIAM MORUM

THE KING OF FRIDAY'S MEN by MICHAEL MOLLOY

BEFORE THE PARTY by RODNEY ACLAND, from a story by W. SOMERSET MAUGHAM

VOLUME 3 1949-50

THE HOLLY AND THE IVY by WYNYARD BROWNE

YOUNG WIVES' TALE by RONALD JEANS

BONAVENTURE by CHARLOTTE HASTINGS

CASTLE IN THE AIR by ALAN MELVILLE

*TARTUFFE by MOLIERE, adapted by MILES MALLESON

TOP OF THE LADDER by TYRONE GUTHRIE

VOLUME 4 1950

SEAGULLS OVER SORRENTO by HUGH HASTINGS

HIS EXCELLENCY by DOROTHY and CAMPBELL CHRISTIE

BACKGROUND by W. CHETHAM-STRODE

TO DOROTHY, A SON by ROGER MACDOUGALL

THE THISTLE AND THE ROSE by WILLIAM DOUGLAS HOME

VOLUME 5 1950-51

LACE ON HER PETTICOAT by AIMEE STUART

COUNT YOUR BLESSINGS by RONALD JEANS

DOCTOR'S DELIGHT by MOLIERE, adapted by SIR BARRY JACKSON

THE GENTLE GUNMAN by ROGER MACDOUGALL

THE CHILDREN'S HOUR by LILLIAN HELLMAN

VOLUME 6 1951

SAINT'S DAY by JOHN WHITING

THE PRODIGIOUS SNOB ("Le Bourgeois Gentilhomme") by MOLIERE, adapted by MILES MALLESON

THE SAME SKY by YVONNE MITCHELL

WHO GOES THERE! by JOHN DIGHTON

GUNPOWDER, TREASON AND PLOT by HUGH ROSS WILLIAMSON

VOLUME 7 1951-52

*THE YOUNG ELIZABETH by J. DOWLING and F. LETTON

NIGHTMARE ABBEY by ANTHONY SHARP, from THOMAS LOVE PEACOCK'S novel

UNDER THE SYCAMORE TREE by SAMUEL SPEWACK

THIRD PERSON by ANDREW ROSENTHAL

DIAMOND CUT DIAMOND by HUGH ROSS WILLIAMSON

VOLUME 8 1952-53

DEAR CHARLES (Les Enfants D'Edouard) by MARC-GILBERT SAUVAJON and FREDERICK JACKSON, adapted by ALAN MELVILLE

AFFAIRS OF STATE by LOUIS VERNEUIL

MURDER MISTAKEN by JANET GREEN

FOR BETTER, FOR WORSE by ARTHUR WATKYN

*****WALTZ OF THE TOREADORS** (La Valse des Toréadors) by JEAN ANOUILH, adapted by LUCIENNE HILL

VOLUME 9 1953

TRIAL AND ERROR by KENNETH HORNE

ANASTASIA by MARCELLE MAURETTE, adapted by GUY BOLTON

THE RETURN by BRIDGET BOLAND

AS LONG AS THEY'RE HAPPY by VERNON SYLVAINE

BIRTHDAY HONOURS by PAUL JONES

VOLUME 10 1953-54

THE PRISONER by BRIDGET BOLAND

*****THE SCHOOL FOR WIVES** by MOLIERE, adapted by MILES MALLESON

MEET A BODY by FRANK LAUNDER and SIDNEY GILLIAT

WAITING FOR GILLIAN by RONALD MILLAR

BOTH ENDS MEET by ARTHUR MACRAE

VOLUME 11 1954

SIMON AND LAURA by ALAN MELVILLE

THE PARTY SPIRIT by PETER JONES and JOHN JOWETT

THE MISANTHROPE by MOLIERE, adapted by MILES MALLESON

SGANARELLE by MOLIERE, adapted by MILES MALLESON

THE LITTLE GLASS CLOCK by HUGH MILLS

SERIOUS CHARGE by PHILIP KING

VOLUME 12 1954-55

THE LONG SUNSET by R. C. SHERRIFF

SOUTH by JULIEN GREEN

UNCERTAIN JOY by CHARLOTTE HASTINGS

SAILOR BEWARE! by PHILIP KING and FALKLAND CARY

THE SHADOW OF DOUBT by NORMAN KING

VOLUME 13 1955

THE WHOLE TRUTH by PHILIP MACKIE

SMALL HOTEL by REX FROST

THE ERMINE by JEAN ANOUILH, translated by MIRIAM JOHN

DEAD ON NINE by JACK POPPLEWELL

VOLUME 14 1955-56

THE STRONG ARE LONELY by FRITZ HOCHWALDER, translated by EVA LE GALLIENNE

THE HOUSE BY THE LAKE by HUGH MILLS

ONE BRIGHT DAY by SIGMUND MILLER

ANNE BOLEYN by PETER ALBERY

VOLUME 15 1956

*****THE TELESCOPE** R. C. SHERRIFF

MEDEA by JEAN ANOUILH, translated by LOTHIAN SMALL

PLAINTIFF IN A PRETTY HAT by HUGH and MARGARET WILLIAMS

THE STRANGE CASE OF DR. JEKYLL AND MR. HYDE by LANCE SIEVEKING, adapted from R. L. STEVENSON'S novel

BE GOOD, SWEET MAID by C. E. WEBBER

VOLUME 16 1956-57

A DEAD SECRET by RODNEY ACLAND

THE IRON HARP by JOSEPH O'CONOR

DEAR DELINQUENT by JACK POPPLEWELL

THE PUBLIC PROSECUTOR by FRITZ HOCHWALDER, translated by KITTY BLACK

VOLUME 17 1957-58

NOT IN THE BOOK by ARTHUR WATKYN

THE DOCK BRIEF by JOHN MORTIMER

WHAT SHALL WE TELL CAROLINE? by JOHN MORTIMER

PADDLE YOUR OWN CANOE by MAX REGNIER, adapted by LUCIENNE HILL

THE HAPPY MAN by HUGH and MARGARET WILLIAMS

VOLUME 18 1958

ANY OTHER BUSINESS by GEORGE ROSS and CAMPBELL SINGER

THE QUEEN AND THE WELSHMAN by ROSEMARY ANNE SISSON

THE PARTY by JANE ARDEN

TOUCH IT LIGHT by ROBERT STOREY

VOLUME 19 1958-59

THE GRASS IS GREENER by HUGH and MARGARET WILLIAMS

THE IMAGINARY INVALID by MOLIERE, adapted by MILES MALLESON

THE SPLENDID OUTCASTS by ROSEMARY ANNE SISSON

LET THEM EAT CAKE by FREDERICK LONSDALE

VOLUME 20 1959

THE EDWARDIANS by RONALD GOW, from V. SACKVILLE-WEST'S novel

ROLLO by MARCEL ACHARD, adapted by FELICITY DOUGLAS

HEART OF BRUCE by HUGH ROSS WILLIAMSON

THE SOUND OF MURDER by WILLIAM FAIRCHILD

VOLUME 21 1959-60

DOUBLE YOLK by HUGH and MARGARET WILLIAMS

SIWAN by SAUNDERS LEWIS, translated by EMYR HUMPHREYS

A CLEAN KILL by MICHAEL GILBERT

THE AMOROUS PRAWN by ANTHONY KIMMINS

CREDITORS by AUGUST STRINDBERG, translated by ELIZABETH SPRIGGE

VOLUME 22 1960

A SHRED OF EVIDENCE by R. C. SHERRIFF

NAKED ISLAND by RUSSELL BRADDON

THIS YEAR, NEXT YEAR by JACK RONDER

WATCH IT, SAILOR! by PHILIP KING and FALKLAND CARY

VOLUME 23 1960-61

THE IRREGULAR VERB TO LOVE by HUGH and MARGARET WILLIAMS

HOUSE OF COWARDS by DANNIE ABSE

THE BARGAIN by MICHAEL GILBERT

JOHN GABRIEL BORKMAN by HENRIK IBSEN, adapted by NORMAN GINSBURY

VOLUME 24 1961

GUILTY PARTY by GEORGE ROSS and CAMPBELL SINGER

*THE KEEP by GWYN THOMAS

THE TINKER by LAURENCE DOBIE and ROBERT SLOMAN

TERESA OF AVILA by HUGH ROSS WILLIAMSON

VOLUME 25 1961-62

THE CHANCES by BEAUMONT and FLETCHER; adapted by the DUKE OF BUCKINGHAM; Laurence Olivier's version

THE EMPIRE BUILDERS by BORIS VIAN, translated by SIMON WATSON TAYLOR

GORDON by BRIDGET BOLAND

THE BIG KILLING by PHILIP MACKIE

VOLUME 26 1962-63

RATTLE OF A SIMPLE MAN by CHARLES DYER

THE DOUBLE DECEIT; OR, A CURE FOR JEALOUSY by WILLIAM POPPLE

JACKIE THE JUMPER by GWYN THOMAS

A CHEAP BUNCH OF NICE FLOWERS by EDNA O'BRIEN

VOLUME 27   1962-63

OUT OF THE CROCODILE by GILES COOPER

THE SKY IS GREEN by BRIAN GEAR

DIFFERENCE OF OPINION by GEORGE ROSS and CAMPBELL SINGER

SAY NOTHING by JAMES HANLEY

VOLUME 28   1963-64

THE WINGS OF THE DOVE by CHRISTOPHER TAYLOR from HENRY JAMES' novel

THE POKER SESSION by HUGH LEONARD

THE FORMATION DANCERS by FRANK MARCUS

THE CITY MADAM by PHILIP MASSINGER

VOLUME 29   1964-65

THE LITTLE CLAY CART attributed to KING SUDRAKA; translated by REVILO PENDLETON OLIVER; adapted by JAMES ROOSE-EVANS

A MEASURE OF CRUELTY by STEVE PASSEUR; adapted by YVONNE MITCHELL

THE CREEPER by PAULINE MACAULAY

DON'T LET SUMMER COME by TERENCE FEELY

VOLUME 30   1965

A HERITAGE—AND ITS HISTORY by JULIAN MITCHELL, from the novel by IVY COMPTON-BURNETT

HOW'S THE WORLD TREATING YOU? by ROGER MILNER

THE MINES OF SULPHUR by BEVERLEY CROSS

PORTRAIT OF A QUEEN by WILLIAM FRANCIS

VOLUME 31   1965-66

THE KILLING OF SISTER GEORGE by FRANK MARCUS

THE ANNIVERSARY by BILL MacILWRAITH

LET'S GET A DIVORCE! by VICTORIEN SARDOU and EMILE DE NAJAC; trans. by ANGELA and ROBERT GOLDSBY

SIXTY THOUSAND NIGHTS; devised by VAL MAY; script by GEORGE ROWELL

VOLUME 32   1966

THE DANCE OF DEATH by AUGUST STRINDBERG, adapted by NORMAN GINSBURY

THERE'S A GIRL IN MY SOUP by TERENCE FRISBY

THE MEMBER FOR GAZA by BENN LEVY

THE PORTSMOUTH DEFENCE by NEMONE LETHBRIDGE

VOLUME 33   1967

HADRIAN THE SEVENTH by PETER LUKE

BEWARE OF THE DOG by GABRIEL AROUT, adapted from the short stories of Chekhov; translated by YVONNE MITCHELL

COUNTRY DANCE by JAMES KENNAWAY

RAFFERTY'S CHANT by KEITH DEWHURST

VOLUME 34   1967-68

CALL ME JACKY by ENID BAGNOLD

THE MAN IN THE GLASS BOOTH by ROBERT SHAW

THE HAPPY APPLE by JACK PULMAN

TINKER'S CURSE by WILLIAM CORLETT

VOLUME 35   1967-68

THE RESTORATION OF ARNOLD MIDDLETON by DAVID STOREY

MRS MOUSE, ARE YOU WITHIN? by FRANK MARCUS

THE QUEEN'S HIGHLAND SERVANT by WILLIAM DOUGLAS HOME

MARYA by ISAAC BABEL; adapted by CHRISTOPHER HAMPTON

VOLUME 36   1968-9

THE PRINCE OF HOMBURG by HEINRICH von KLEIST, translated by JONATHAN GRIFFIN

THE UNKNOWN SOLDIER AND HIS WIFE by PETER USTINOV

THE SECRETARY BIRD by WILLIAM DOUGLAS HOME

THE SERVANT OF TWO MASTERS by CARLO GOLDONI; adapted by DAVID TURNER

VOLUME 37   1969

THE CARDINAL OF SPAIN by HENRY DE MONTHERLANT, translated by JONATHAN GRIFFIN

HAVE YOU ANY DIRTY WASHING, MOTHER DEAR? by CLIVE EXTON

THE BLACK SWAN WINTER by JOHN HALE

THE SACKING OF NORMAN BANKS by GEORGE ROSS and CAMPBELL SINGER

VOLUME 38   1969

SPITHEAD by JOHN HALE

IN CELEBRATION by DAVID STOREY

THE MAGISTRATE by ARTHUR WING PINERO

KNIGHT IN FOUR ACTS by JOHN HARRISON

VOLUME 39   1969-70

UNCLE VANYA by ANTON CHEKHOV; new version by CHRISTOPHER HAMPTON

THREE MONTHS GONE by DONALD HOWARTH

ABELARD AND HELOISE by RONALD MILLAR

ENEMY! by ROBIN MAUGHAM

VOLUME 40   1970-71

THE CONTRACTOR by DAVID STOREY

THE JOCKEY CLUB STAKES by WILLIAM DOUGLAS HOME

CHILDREN OF THE WOLF by JOHN PEACOCK

UNACCOMPANIED CELLO by JOHN HARRISON

VOLUME 41   1971-2

HOME by DAVID STOREY

THE PATRICK PEARSE MOTEL by HUGH LEONARD

TRELAWNY by AUBREY WOODS, JULIAN SLADE, and GEORGE ROWELL (from PINERO'S TRELAWNY OF THE 'WELLS')

VOLUME 42   1972

NOTES ON A LOVE AFFAIR by FRANK MARCUS

LLOYD GEORGE KNEW MY FATHER by WILLIAM DOUGLAS HOME

MR SYDNEY SMITH COMING UPSTAIRS by BRIAN OULTON

THE DRUMS OF SNOW by DAVID PINNER

SPECIAL   (1972)

THE SIX WIVES OF HENRY VIII: Plays by ROSEMARY ANNE SISSON, NICK McCARTY, IAN THORNE, JEAN MORRIS, BEVERLEY CROSS, JOHN PREBBLE

SPECIAL   (1972)

ELIZABETH R: Plays by JOHN HALE, ROSEMARY ANNE SISSON, JULIAN MITCHELL, HUGH WHITEMORE, JOHN PREBBLE, IAN RODGER

* Plays marked thus are also available in **single editions**, cloth-bound and paper-bound.

Also available

A SWORD FOR A PRINCE and Other Plays for a Young Company, by J. C. Trewin   8s 6d